FROM CRAFT TO PROFESSION

*The publisher gratefully acknowledges
the generous contributions
provided by the following organizations:*

THE ARCHITECTURAL HISTORY FOUNDATION

THE COLLEGE OF FELLOWS OF THE AMERICAN INSTITUTE OF ARCHITECTS

THE ART BOOK ENDOWMENT FUND
OF THE ASSOCIATES OF THE UNIVERSITY OF CALIFORNIA PRESS

*which is supported
by a major gift from
the Ahmanson Foundation*

FROM CRAFT TO PROFESSION

The Practice of Architecture in Nineteenth-Century America

MARY N. WOODS

UNIVERSITY OF CALIFORNIA PRESS

BERKELEY   LOS ANGELES   LONDON

University of California Press
Berkeley and Los Angeles, California

University of California Press, Ltd.
London, England

**Library of Congress
Cataloging-in-Publication Data**

Woods, Mary N., 1950–
    From craft to profession : the practice of
architecture in nineteenth-century America /
Mary N. Woods.
        p.   cm.
    Includes bibliographical references and
index.
        ISBN 0-520-21494-3 (alk. paper)
        1. Architectural practice—United States—
History—19th century.   I. Title.
    NA1996.W64   1999
    720′.23′73—dc21   98-41510

Printed in the United States of America
9   8   7   6   5   4   3   2   1

The paper used in this publication meets the
minimum requirements of American National
Standard for Information Sciences—Perma-
nence of Paper for Printed Library Materials,
ANSI Z39.48-1984.

To the memory of my mother,
Mabel Virginia Jones Woods,
and for
Michael Radow

CONTENTS

ILLUSTRATIONS

ACKNOWLEDGMENTS

It is a pleasure and, quite frankly, a relief to finally write the acknowledgments for this book. I have accumulated many debts—intellectual, professional, and personal—during the years that it took to research, write, revise, and edit this manuscript.

First, I am grateful to Adolf K. Placzek, Joseph Connors, David De Long, Kenneth Jackson, Rosemaric Bletter, William Foulks, and finally the late George R. Collins. They were my professors, advisers, and mentors at Columbia University, and they have supported me in countless ways after graduate school. Former graduate students never fade away; they continue to hound their advisers with requests for help and letters of recommendation. I only hope that I can be as gracious, generous, and encouraging with my students as my Columbia professors have always been with me.

The late William Jordy, Thomas S. Hines, Richard Guy Wilson, David Van Zanten, Leland Roth, Robert Bruegmann, Jane B. Davies, Barry G. Bergdoll, Mosette Broderick, Edward Kaufman, Daniel Bluestone, Zeynep Celik, Sarah Landau, Dell Upton, Michael Lewis, Jeffrey Cohen, Ellen Weiss, J. A. Chewning, Patrick Snadon, Robert Gutman, Magali Larson, and Dana Cuff have inspired me with their insights into American architecture and building, architectural practice, and the professions. Some may be surprised to find themselves mentioned here, but their work led me to new sources and challenged me to puzzle out larger issues. I also want to thank Professors Hines, Roth, Wilson, and Van Zanten for support at critical stages in my career as well as this book. I am especially grateful to Professor Dana Cuff for readings of my manuscript that were always incisive and constructive. While I acknowledge these scholars' help, they are not responsible in any way for the shortcomings of this book.

Equally important were the curators, archivists, and librarians who helped me. Tony P. Wrenn, archivist at The American Institute of Architects Archives, has been a mainstay, intellectually and personally, for me since my days as a graduate student. I am fortunate to be one of his many academic offspring. Mary Beth Betts, curator of architectural collections at the New-York Historical Society, and Janet S. Parks, curator of architectural drawings at the Avery Fine Arts and Architectural Library at Columbia University, were invaluable colleagues and advisers for this project as well as good friends. Other contributors to my research were Sherry Birk, curator of prints and drawings at The American Architectural Foundation; C. Ford Peatross, curator of architectural and engineering drawings at the Library of Congress; Mary Ison, Prints and Photographs Division, Library of Congress; Wendy Shadwell, curator of prints at the New-York Historical Society; Dale Neighbors, curator of photographs at the New-York Historical Society; Herbert Mitchell, former rare book librarian at Avery Library; Neville Thompson, director of the Winterthur Library; Mary Woolever, archivist at the Ryerson and Burnham Libraries, Art Institute of Chicago; and Wim de Wit, former curator of architecture at the Chicago Historical Society. Scholarship and collegiality are alive and well at these institutions because of them.

Research and writing, to be blunt, require money and time. I am deeply appreciative of that support from the following institutions: the College of Fellows of the American Institute of Architects; the National Endowment for the Humanities; the American Philosophical Society; the Institute for the Arts and Humanistic Studies, Pennsylvania State University; the Dean's Fund for Excellence, College of Architecture, Art, and Planning, Cornell University; and the Humanities Faculty Grant, College of Arts and Sciences, Cornell University. I am grateful to Mark Cruvellier, chair of my department, for underwriting the indexing costs. I was fortunate to receive a fellowship from the Buell Center for the Study of American Architecture at Columbia University's Graduate School of Architecture, Planning, and Preservation. I am grateful to Professor Gwendolyn Wright, former Buell director, for her friendship and her support of my work. She challenged me with her incisive comments and the provocative colloquia she arranged while I was at the Buell Center. Finally, I am grateful to the Architectural History Foundation and the College of Fellows of the American Institute of Architects for their subventions to my publisher and to the Associates of the University of California Press for supporting this book.

The Architectural History Foundation had originally arranged to publish this book. I am grateful to Victoria Newhouse, her editorial board, and her reviewers for their early support of my work. I regret that I was unable to complete the manuscript before the foundation publishing program ceased operations. However, it was my good fortune that the University of California Press then accepted my orphaned manuscript. Stephanie Fay, fine arts acquisitions editor, has been a godsend. She and the press embody the finest traditions of academic publishing, sadly all too rare in today's publishing world. She, her reviewers, and the editorial board have nurtured me and my project, provided substantive and constructive criticism, and given me careful and inspired editing. Susan Ecklund was a crack copy editor, and Carol Roberts was an expert indexer. I also want to thank Jeanne Park at the press for her help. I am deeply appreciative and can only hope, as Rick said in *Casablanca,* that this is the beginning of a beautiful friendship.

I want to acknowledge the help and support of my first academic colleagues at the Pennsylvania State University: Hellmut Hager, Elizabeth B. Smith, George Mauner, Anthony Cutler, Heinz Henisch, Susan Munshower, and Roland Fleischer. At Cornell I am lucky to have the following as colleagues and friends: Andrea Simitch, Val K. Warke, John C. Miller, Vincent Mulcahy, Jerry Wells, John Shaw, Mark Cruvellier, Jonathan Ochshorn, Leonard Mirin, Mario Schack, John Reps, Susan Christopherson, Claudia Lazzaro, Lourdes Beneria, Jan Jennings, DeDe Ruggles, Elisabeth Meyer, Margaret Webster, and William Staffeld. I thank Mark Jarzombek, William G. McMinn, and Martin Kubelik, now sadly former Cornellians, for their support and friendship in good and bad times.

I have learned much from my Cornell students. I am especially grateful for the work and insights of Cecelia Manning, Christian Nielsen-Palacios, David Breiner, Lee Gray, Kristen Schaffer, Irene Ayad, Wendy Allison Hart, Susanne Warren, John Lauber, Diana Prideaux-Brune, Petur Armannsson, David Bergstone, Sarah Pelone, Jennifer O'Shea, Hansy Luz Better, Todd Thiel, Nathaniel Guest, and Angel David Nieves. They and Michael Adams and Matthew Jarocsz, my students in a Buell Center seminar, were as much colleagues as students.

I would not have made it through the long process of research and writing without family and friends. My sister, Michaele Woods, and my friends Laurel Radow, Roberta and Doug Colton, Marjorie Rosenberg, Carol Mandel, and Sheryl Dicker provided friendship and hospitality during my long research trips to Washington, D.C., Chicago, and New York. I also thank I. Fred Koenigsberg for his legal counsel. I would not have lived to finish this book without the medical care and emotional support of Drs. Joseph Ruggiero, Robert Sassoon, Eugene Nowak, Timothy Cardina, and Florence Chu. They truly taught me the meaning of professionalism.

Finally, this book is as much the work of my mother, Mabel Virginia Jones Woods, and my partner and friend, Michael Radow, as my own. My mother did not live to see the publication of this book. She first taught me about the joys of art and architecture, and she was my first and best role model. I will always be grateful for her unstinting emotional and financial support. Michael Radow has been and still is my mentor, adviser, curator, and comic relief in the best and worst of times. I will never be able to thank him enough for sharing his life and his Upper West Side apartment with me.

INTRODUCTION

I never finished *The Fountainhead*, Ayn Rand's novel about art, freedom, and architecture. I never got through the film, adapted from the novel, without squirming, yawning, and giggling. I found Howard Roark, Rand's architect-protagonist, neither sympathetic nor charismatic. I remember his monologues, whether in print or in Gary Cooper's delivery, as long-winded and pompous. What I found memorable were the settings and supporting characters: the dean dismissing Roark from architecture school; the stove where the frustrated architect burned his drawings; the rock drills in the quarry where he found work; the building committee tinkering with Roark's designs in the boardroom; admirers and critics gathered in a penthouse to praise the architect; and the courtroom where Roark defended his right to destroy as well as create. The mise-en-scène was always more vivid and intriguing than Roark, his designs, or Rand's philosophy.

This study foregrounds the mise-en-scène of the architectural profession. It is a challenge to what one architectural historian has called "Roarkism," our discipline's traditional focus on the architect as solitary creator to the exclusion of other narrators and narratives. This work also foregrounds the business aspects of practice that some scholars contend architectural historians routinely ignore or deny.[1]

My concern is with multiple participants, overlapping responsibilities, and the settings for design and building. I am interested in architecture as work and business, not in its typical guises as art or problem solving. The formation of the American architectural profession is one locus where these varied perspectives on architectural work converge. Nevertheless, the "Roarks" of both nineteenth-century American architecture and our historiography do have a part in this account. They were, after all, principal players in constructing professional identity and institutions. But I view them from unorthodox perspectives. Here they are not omniscient creators but collaborators, partners, entrepreneurs, merchandisers, educators, employers, and lobbyists. Their narratives are interwoven with those of modest, provincial, renegade, and failed architects. The first women and people of color to enter the profession contribute accounts. The viewpoints of architects' employees, assistants, rivals, and clients are also heard. The settings of both profession and practice—architectural organizations, schools, workshops, offices, ateliers, drafting rooms, building yards, and construction sites—are my subjects. Finally, I consider the architectural profession's place within the American building market and industry.

This is the first in-depth study of the American architectural profession. There are certainly publications on individual architects' practices, particular contractors and developers, building crafts, labor and the construction industry, and regional architects and builders. There are also accounts of the architect's role throughout history.[2] But until now there has been no work that weaves these diverse strands of American architecture and building together over an extended historical period. This study fills the need for what one commentator called "empirically based knowledge about what architects actually do."[3]

My subject is not architecture per se but why and how certain designers and builders chose to practice as professionals at a particular moment in American history. I do not argue, nor do I believe, that professionalization necessarily led to better design and construction. It was, instead, a response to a confluence of economic, social, and ideological issues in nineteenth-century America.

In my research I drew on new sources that reveal the interfaces between architecture and building, architecture and labor, and architecture and business. I have found materials on craft guilds, apprenticeships, mechanics' institutes, university programs, correspondence schools, single practices, partnerships, large offices, labor unions, and the building industry. Drawings and photographs of the physical spaces for architectural work as well as financial papers and accounting ledgers from offices are examined, too. A careful and detailed study of these archival, published, and visual materials is necessary to avoid lapsing into the generalities, anecdotes, publicity, and myths surrounding the architectural profession.

Since architectural history, my discipline, has traditionally privileged art and individual agency, I turned to social scientists' studies of contemporary practices and historians' accounts of the American professions for methodological models. These scholars examine the social, economic, and political assumptions underlying the professions, providing an alternative to "Roarkism."[4]

Emphasizing the architect as only an artist does an injustice to the richness and complexity of design and building. It distorts our understanding of architectural history, but it also profoundly affects those who practice, teach, and study architecture. Valuing architecture only as art and celebrating the architect only as designer can lead to frustration and disillusionment when real-life experiences fall so far short of these ideals. Furthermore, clients and the public then view the architect's role as an extremely circumscribed one. While this may not affect "star" architects, lesser practitioners find their services overlooked and discounted by those with mundane building needs. Architectural historians who teach and write only about the "Roarks" contribute to the disjuncture between professional and public expectations and realities.

American architects are now in the midst of a painful debate over the future of their profession. The relation between education and the profession is a particular flash point. One professional journal devoted an entire issue to "The Schools: How They Are Failing the Profession," warning that the "rift between the architectural schools and the profession has never been greater." This journal, one of only a handful covering the profession, itself became a symbol of architecture's troubles when it expired only a few months after the publication of this issue. Robert Gutman, a longtime observer of the profession, questioned the university control of architectural education, recommending more office training as the remedy for architectural students' dearth of practical knowledge and skills. The Carnegie Foundation for the Advancement of Teaching published a report on architectural education and the profession, pointedly subtitled "A New Future," in 1996. The Harvard Graduate School of Design organized a yearlong symposium to address the professional challenges of the nineties and beyond. Another sign of professional malaise was a *New York Times* story recounting the departure of architects from the field in 1996. Under the headline "Architects Scaling Back High-Rise Dreams," the reporter cited chronic unemployment in the profession as the cause of "defections" into areas like teaching, jewelry design, and even baking. Equally troubling was the 31 percent decline in the number of architectural graduates taking the examination for professional registration in 1995.[5]

Architectural historians, I noted, were usually absent from these discussions of the profession's future. Although two architectural historians did take part in the Harvard symposium, the Carnegie Foundation consulted only one architectural historian and then for information just on non-Western practitioners. Only two historical works on the profession were cited in the Carnegie report, and both were published more than forty years ago.[6] It is sociologists, critics, administrators, educators, and students who are the discussants and information sources. When professional practices and institutions are at issue, the hagiographies of architectural historians are not especially useful or insightful.

We must acknowledge and understand the origins and complex structures of architectural practice before we can reconfigure the professional forms and settings for the future. Otherwise we reduce the discussion to simplistic dichotomies like art and business, academy and profession, and theory and practice. These polarities bespeak our ignorance of the profession's origins and structures. Before implementing changes like more office training, we need to know how it and private practice historically functioned and evolved. As increasing numbers of women and people of color study architecture, we must learn how their predecessors adopted, accommodated, or resisted the ideals and norms of practice. Otherwise we risk idealizing or demonizing a past that we actually know very little about. My study will, I trust, provide a foundation for reclaiming this past and recasting the future.

This story of the profession focuses primarily on the nineteenth century because the conventions and institutions of American professional identity and values arose then. The nineteenth-century forms—private practice, professional societies, university programs, divisions and responsibilities of architectural work—still persist today. This account also delves back to earlier colonial traditions of design and building because they conditioned responses to professional architects in the nineteenth century.

Professional architects, latecomers on the scene, were always a very small part of the American building industry. During the nineteenth century the majority of those engaged in design and building were known as builders, carpenters, or building mechanics. Furthermore, the university programs, professional societies, certification of practitioners, and codes of ethics traditionally associated with professionalization did not exist until the late nineteenth century in American architecture. These are the years when scholars see the emergence of the architectural profession. In their accounts late nineteenth-century architects like Richard M. Hunt, Henry Hobson Richardson, Daniel Burnham, and Dankmar Adler are the founders of the architectural profession because they were formally educated, led professional societies, or wrote the first licensing laws.[7]

Nevertheless, in the United States architecture became a profession during the decades between 1820 and 1860 (the antebellum period). The founders of the profession—men trained in building workshops or architectural offices during the early nineteenth century—identified themselves exclusively as professionals. The late nineteenth century was a period of expansion and consolidation, not one of beginnings, in the evolution of architectural professionalism in the United States.

Early nineteenth-century figures like Asher Benjamin, Ithiel Town, Alexander Jackson Davis, William Strickland, Thomas U. Walter, James Gallier, and Richard Upjohn created the forms and settings of professional practice. They defined the professional architect as a designer and supervisor standing between clients who commissioned the work and artisans who constructed it. These men worked for professional organization, education, accreditation, and compensation. They recognized that a few isolated practitioners, however gifted, could not transform architecture from a craft into a profession. They experimented with partnerships and large offices as new forms for architectural practice.

Historically, however, the terms "architect" and "professional" have not been synonymous. Architects were designers, draftsmen, builders, or gentlemen without being professionals. Whereas the word "architect" came into use during antiquity, the professions were a premodern and preindustrial invention of eighteenth-century England. Subsequent nineteenth-century developments—capitalism, urbanization, and industrialization—both stimulated and challenged the professions.

In ancient Greece the term *architekton* originally meant a "master carpenter"; building artisans, shipwrights, and temple designers, all of whom worked in wood, were architects. Certain Greek artists also became known as architects—for example, Theodoros of Samos, renowned as a sculptor, metalsmith, and architect in the sixth century B.C. Roman architects, too, came from a variety of backgrounds: private training and apprenticeship; military engineering; and the civil service. Although the Emperor Hadrian dabbled in architecture, it was not really, Cicero had written, an appropriate calling for Roman aristocrats. Former slaves, released from imperial service, became architects. Yet Vitruvius, a self-made man with experience in military engineering, tried to dignify architecture, describing it as a learned career in his treatise. The architect alone, he wrote, combined firmness and utility with beauty.[8]

This discussion of the architect's position in society ceased during the Middle Ages, when the term "architect," meaning designer or creator, was rarely used. Master masons and builders, their identities now largely lost, were responsible for the monastic churches and cathedrals, and ecclesiastical patrons also played an important role in the creation of these buildings.[9]

The word "architect," however, came into use again in fifteenth-century Italy. The revival of antiquity created opportunities for those outside the traditional building crafts of masonry and carpentry. Italian goldsmiths, sculptors, and painters possessed a knowledge of antique forms. Thus Brunelleschi, Michelozzo, Bramante, Raphael, and Michelangelo all received commissions for buildings in the fifteenth and sixteenth centuries. Because they were not building craftsmen and did not belong to the construction guilds, these men were called architects rather than master builders. As the cult of the artist developed during the Renaissance, some commentators carefully distinguished architects from master builders and craftsmen. Giorgio Vasari, a biographer of Renaissance artists, maligned Giuliano and Antonio da Sangallo as designers because they were building craftsmen rather than painters or sculptors. Leon Battista Alberti, an intellectual and papal official, further distanced the architect from the building artisan. For him the architect was a scholar as well as an artist.[10]

The idea of the artist-architect spread along with Renaissance designs and theories throughout Europe. John Shute, a painter who traveled to Italy in 1550, was the first Englishman to call himself an architect when he subsequently became involved with building. Gentlemen like Lord Burlington, patron and designer of eighteenth-century Palladian architecture, were known as architects.[11]

In colonial and postrevolutionary America, "architect" was a more elastic term, but it ultimately carried the antique connotations of authority and responsibility. Master artisans who created basic architectural drawings and supervised construction were called architects, but they were also known as master builders, master mechanics, and artificers. Gentlemen who designed as a pastime, as well as planters and merchants who undertook building contracts used the title architect, too.[12]

The professions became associated with English gentlemen during the mid-eighteenth century when the word "profession" was identified with a learned vocation in the church, law, or medicine. Because they involved intellectual rather than manual work, the professions suited gentlemen, who demeaned neither themselves nor their class by entering a profession. A classical university education—a gentleman's course of study—gave professionals a refined and broad outlook. While a profession required expertise in a "professed" body of knowledge, specific training occurred after university, usually with an experienced practitioner. University-educated clergymen, barristers, and physicians were the true professionals in the ranks of English divinity, law, and medicine. Deacons, solicitors, surgeons, and apothecaries—whose instruction was narrow, technical, and practical—were neither gentlemen nor professionals.[13]

As a gentleman, the professional was a man of chivalrous instincts and refined feelings. His principal considerations, unlike those of merchants or tradesmen, were never financial. Honor guided his actions, and authority was his due. He was a paternal figure who advised his clients on what was best for them; he did not sell them goods or services. Women, certain ethnic groups, and people of color—who were clearly not gentlemen in English society—were barred from the professions. They called into question the professional's inherent right to honor and authority. White male supremacy in the professions was not challenged until university training became available to women and minorities in the late nineteenth century.[14]

In England a son almost always followed his father's occupation and did not rise above it. Economic necessity, however, made social mobility possible in the American colonies. Few gentlemen immigrated to the New World. The sons of merchants, planters, and even tradesmen became clergymen, physicians, and lawyers in the early eastern seaboard cities, but they were not gentlemen in the English sense of the word. Nevertheless, these early professionals still aspired to the status and privileges accorded English practitioners. The American elite came from the ranks of these early professionals, planters, and merchants who prospered in the colonies.[15]

The distinctions in English divinity, law, and medicine never took hold in the colonies because of a chronic lack of skilled labor. The Church of England failed to establish an elite clergy presided over by an American bishop. Legal practitioners in the colonies were simply lawyers. There were no barristers (who could argue before the highest courts) or solicitors (who could not). The hierarchy of physician, surgeon, and apothecary did not characterize early American medicine.[16]

The demand for professionals' specialized services first arose in urban centers. The history of the professions is, in part, a history of cities. It was in the early American cities like Philadelphia, New York, Boston, Washington, D.C., and then Chicago that a critical mass of professional architects and their institutions first developed. Thus I cover the East and Midwest more extensively than the South and Far West, where the profession developed only in the late nineteenth and early twentieth centuries. But the histories of southern and western professionals intertwine with those of eastern and midwestern architects. The latter settled in these new regional centers, bringing the culture and traditions of eastern and midwestern professionalism with them.

I begin by considering how American buildings were designed and constructed before the organization of the architectural profession. Building artisans were the first architects for the earliest settlements on the East Coast; gentlemen without craft training competed with these artisans only in the second half of the eighteenth century. I focus on these master craftsmen and their gentlemen rivals in the first chapter.

Benjamin Henry Latrobe, one of these gentlemen, immigrated to the United States in 1796. While he was an exceptional figure, unusually well educated in both architecture and engineering, Latrobe is pivotal because he introduced English ideas about the professions. Professionalism seemed to obsess him, and he frequently proclaimed himself the first professional architect and engineer to practice in the United States. Latrobe's career reveals both the achievements and the limitations of professionalism in the early American building market.

Although Latrobe introduced professionalism to the United States, he did not establish architecture as a viable profession. This was the contribution of the designers and builders before the Civil War who figure prominently in chapter 2, which examines the formation and goals of the first professional societies. Chapter 3 focuses on training and education, chapter 4 looks at the forms and settings of practice, and chapter 5 at the architect's assistants, clients, collaborators, and rivals.

Several issues constitute the core of this study. First, why did certain designers and builders decide to identify and organize themselves as professionals during the decades before the Civil War? Most of these men had trained and practiced as building artisans. Why did they reject the idea of architecture as craft in favor of architecture as profession? Did they, furthermore, completely abandon their artisanal roots, or did they meld certain craft traditions of training, collective action, and the marketplace with their new professional identities and institutions?

Second, all American professionals inherited a model of practice from eighteenth-century England. Did American architects modify these English ideas and forms of professionalism? Institutional commissions and government employment—mainstays of English practice—seemed to develop slowly and fitfully in early America. How, then, did capitalism, free markets, and industrialization—dominant forces shaping American building—affect architectural professionalization in the United States?

In 1848 Louisa Tuthill wrote the first architectural history to be published in the United States. Including an account of current American architecture, Tuthill urged young men to become professional architects. Architecture was both a "lucrative and honorable profession" in her view. This art, as she characterized it, "opens a fair field for laudable ambition." [17] Tuthill introduced a new element, money, into the European tradition of architecture as an honorable and artistic occupation. How nineteenth-century American architects coped with and resolved these disparate strands of professionalism is portrayed in the story that follows.

CHAPTER 1

THE FIRST PROFESSIONAL

In our new country indeed the profession of an Architect is in great measure new.
Benjamin Henry Latrobe, Letter of 12 July 1806 to Robert Mills

Benjamin Henry Latrobe, a young English architect and engineer, immigrated to the United States in 1796. After working in this country for ten years, he wrote to a former student:

> The profession of Architecture has been hitherto in the hands of two sets of Men. The first of those [gentlemen] who from travelling or from books have acquired some knowledge of the theory of Art, know nothing of its practice, the second of those [mechanics] who know nothing but the practice, and whose early life being spent in labor, and in the habits of a laborious life, have had no opportunity to acquire the theory. The complaisance of these two sets of Men to each other, renders it difficult for the Architect to get in between them, for the Building Mechanic finds his account in the ignorance of the *Gentleman-Architect,* as the latter does in the Submissive deportment which interest dictates to the former.[1]

Latrobe expected deference, not competition, from the gentlemen and building mechanics he encountered in the United States. He introduced and championed English ideas of professionalism and often claimed the distinction of being the first professional architect and engineer to practice in the United States. Only a professional architect's design, Latrobe explained to Thomas Jefferson, was a "simultaneous consideration of the purpose, the connection and the construction of his work."[2] The professional alone combined theoretical knowledge with a practical understanding of building.

From the outset Latrobe and other early professional architects found themselves embroiled in controversies over duties, authority, and compensation. Latrobe's twenty-four years in the United States were difficult and frustrating. Although proud that he could claim to be the first professional architect, he admitted that he had

> not so far succeeded as to make it [architecture] an eligible profession for one who has the education and the feelings of a Gentleman, and I regret exceedingly that my own Son . . . has determined to make it his own. The business in all our great cities is in the hands of mechanics who disgrace the Art but possess the public confidence, and under the false appearance of Oeconomy have infinitely the advantage in degrading the competition. With them the struggle will be long and harassing.[3]

Building craftsmen (usually called building mechanics in the eighteenth and early nineteenth centuries) and clients undoubtedly found Latrobe's claims for the professional architect's superiority ludicrous. Master builders had controlled the design and construction of public and private works since the earliest days of European settlement along the East Coast. To them, Latrobe was a prickly and arrogant interloper. Planters and merchants, the American elite, were equally unimpressed with his claims of gentility. They regarded him as a skilled surveyor and mechanic, but not their peer.[4]

MASTER BUILDERS IN
THE COLONIAL AND FEDERAL PERIODS

The trading companies and religious groups that settled North America in the seventeenth century encouraged skilled builders—known variously as mechanics, artisans, artificers, tradesmen, and craftsmen—to immigrate to the New World. Because these men possessed the skills needed to construct new settlements, they were promised passage, land, and exemption from taxes and military service. After London was rebuilt in the wake of the great fire of 1666, there was little work for either established masters or journeymen. Many building craftsmen decided to immigrate to the colonies.[5]

Carpenters were the preeminent building artisans in the colonies because of the abundance of wood for construction. One historian estimates that they outnumbered all other building artisans by four to one. There were, for example, about 13 carpenters in Philadelphia by 1690; a century later there were 450 carpenters in the city. Other building artisans—joiners, bricklayers, masons, glaziers, painters, and plasterers—joined carpenters in the major colonial centers of Boston, New York, and Philadelphia by the early eighteenth century.[6]

Master carpenters possessed both technical and supervisory skills. Timber frames were complicated assemblages of heavy, hand-cut members joined by mortise and tenon. Raising a frame for even a simple one- or two-room house required a crew of several men. Because carpentry was not only skilled but also dangerous and seasonal work, it commanded high wages in the colonies, where there was a chronic dearth of skilled labor. A carpenter in seventeenth-century Massachusetts earned more than twice as much as his counterpart in England. In 1663 Massachusetts Bay Colony judges established a ceiling of two shillings a day on carpenters' wages because of price gouging.[7]

The first building trade organizations in the colonies were associations of master carpenters. The Carpenters' Company of Philadelphia, the earliest organization, may date from the 1720s. It was exceptionally powerful because its members controlled the measurement and valuing of all building work through a secret price book. Thomas Jefferson so respected the Carpenters' Company that he insisted its price book be used for estimating construction costs at the United States Capitol.[8]

Other building associations, usually formed by carpenters, appeared elsewhere in late eighteenth-century America. There are references to a Society of House Carpenters in New York by the early 1770s, and Boston carpenters agreed on a price list and rules of work in 1774. Philadelphia bricklayers, by contrast, did not organize a guild until 1790. Apart from guilds organized around a specific craft, there were more inclusive organizations. New York City artisans, manufacturers, and tradesmen formed the General Society of Mechanics and Tradesmen in 1785, and ten years later the Associated Mechanics of Boston and the Massachusetts Charitable Mechanics Association were established. But southern craftsmen, both white and African American, were dispersed and relatively few in number. Moreover, white southerners would not have permitted African Americans to organize for any purpose. There were no craft guilds south of Baltimore and Washington, D.C.[9]

Early craft organizations were select associations of master artisans, men with workshops, apprentices, and journeymen. They were successful employers and businessmen who could afford the steep membership fees. The artisans, tradesmen, and manufacturers who composed the Massachusetts Charitable Mechanics Association organized around the issue of runaway apprentices. The twenty-five carpenters who became members represented only 15 percent of all master carpenters in Boston. The eighty members of the Carpenters' Company in Philadelphia in 1787 represented only one out of every six master carpenters in the city.[10]

Some master carpenters were also builders. Called "undertakers" for most of the colonial period, they were entrepreneurs as well as craftsmen. These men were the general contractors of their day, acquiring materials and labor and then directing work on the site. If they drafted basic architectural drawings and supervised, they were known as architects. The majority of master craftsmen, however, were not even employers, much less entrepreneurs. They worked alone, but they worked for themselves.[11]

Robert Smith (1722–77) was perhaps the most renowned master carpenter and master builder of the late eighteenth century. Apprenticed to a builder in his native Scotland, Smith was working in Philadelphia by 1749, remodeling Governor James Hamilton's residence, Bush Hill. He was responsible for Carpenters' Hall and the Walnut Street Prison in Philadelphia—the former the headquarters of the Carpenters' Company and the latter one of the first brick vaulted structures in the English-speaking colonies. Smith's practice as a designer extended from Rhode Island to Virginia. He specialized in institutional buildings: Nassau Hall at Princeton University, the College of Rhode Island (now Brown University), New College at the University of Pennsylvania, and the insane asylum in Williamsburg, Virginia. Yet Smith was also the undertaker for Benjamin Franklin's house and the Philadelphia Almshouse, and he invested heavily in local real estate. A member of both the Carpenters' Company and the American Philosophical Society, he designed fortifications for the Revolutionary Army at no cost. Nearly twenty years after his death Smith was honored with an exhibition of his architectural drawings at the Columbianum, an academy of fine arts in Philadelphia.[12]

During his lifetime Smith was described as a carpenter, house carpenter, and builder. But his design and construction of imposing public and private buildings set him apart from the typical master builder, and he was also called an architect. He was not, however, what an Englishman meant by a gentleman in spite of his standing and wealth. Bridging the divide between manual and intellectual vocations, Smith blurred the distinctions between gentleman and artisan, artist and tradesman. Philadelphia master carpenters like Smith synthesized design with supervision and execution with investment to a remarkable degree. No single artisan or group of masters elsewhere in the colonies could match their prominence, power, or wealth.[13]

Robert Smith was an unusual figure in early American architecture. In colonial Boston no master craftsman attained Smith's prominence as a designer and builder. Thomas Dawes (1731–1811) prospered as a master mason and builder, but he had only a modest career as a designer.[14] John Hawks (1731–90) was one of the first

Americans referred to as an architect. Trained originally as a carpenter and builder in England, Hawks prepared the most extensive set of architectural drawings—for the governor's palace in Tryon, North Carolina—to survive from the colonial period. But he drifted away from architectural work in North Carolina, a relatively poor and thinly populated colony with limited opportunities for architecture.[15]

William Buckland (1734–74) and Samuel McIntire (1757–1811) were the only other master craftsmen who attained substantial architectural reputations in early America. Their careers, however, were not as wide-ranging as Robert Smith's. While the Philadelphia master received commissions along the eastern seaboard, Buckland worked in northern Virginia and Maryland, and McIntire was based in Salem, Massachusetts. But Buckland and McIntire surpassed Smith in the variety and inventiveness of their designs. Trained as wood-carvers and joiners, Buckland and McIntire were specialists who created and assembled paneling, furniture, and architectural ornament. The drafting skills and knowledge of materials and styles necessary for joiners served them well as architects.

Apprenticed in London, Buckland immigrated as an indentured servant, engaged to finish George Mason's Gunston Hall in northern Virginia. After his servitude ended, he found clients among the planters, merchants, lawyers, and clergy scattered across northern Virginia and Maryland. He expanded beyond woodworking into architecture and contracting. Buckland married, acquired apprentices, hired journeymen, and purchased a house and slaves.[16] Samuel McIntire was descended from a family of Salem carpenters. His clients were the Salem merchants who grew wealthy from their near monopoly on trade with the Far East. Men like Elias Derby, the first American millionaire, provided McIntire with ample opportunities to refine his neoclassical designs in early nineteenth-century Salem and its environs.

But neither Buckland nor McIntire truly became his clients' peer. In 1774, the year of his death, Buckland commissioned a portrait from his friend Charles Willson Peale, who depicted him at work on an elevation for the Hammond-Harwood house in Annapolis, Maryland. Holding a drafting instrument above his sketch, Buckland wears no powdered wig and only a modest brown suit for his portrait. While Peale appropriated the grandiloquent architectural backdrop associated with English aristocratic portraiture, he presented his sitter as an intelligent workingman directly confronting the viewer's gaze. A Salem minister made a point of noting in his diary that McIntire was the son of carpenters and educated in that business. The architect was, the diarist continued, "a fine person . . . [who was] welcome but never intruded" in Salem society. McIntire was still a craftsman who knew his place, and he deferred to the merchants and clergymen of New England.[17]

Philadelphia master carpenters like Robert Smith were prominent in local political and cultural institutions, but they were exceptional figures in colonial society. Although they were artisans, they were also wealthy men who invested in foreign trade and real estate.[18] Because of their wealth, merchants and professionals accepted them as peers. However, as long as there were gentlemen who pursued architecture as an avocation, craftsmen-architects like Buckland and McIntire, who were not rich men, found acceptance into the American elite problematic.

During the second half of the eighteenth century, gentlemen like Peter Harrison (1716–55), Thomas Jefferson (1743–1826), Dr. William Thornton (1759–1828), and Charles Bulfinch (1764–1844) created architectural designs for their own pleasure. Occasionally, they acted as undertakers, organizing and financing building projects.[19] They were merchants, planters, lawyers, and physicians, the traditional American elite. Although such gentlemen-architects were never numerous, their designs for imposing private and public works had high visibility in their communities. They depended on master builders to execute their designs and rarely accepted any payment for their services. Jefferson and Bulfinch had regional and even national design reputations. Moreover, Jefferson possessed unusual influence as an architectural client and tastemaker because of his executive positions in state and federal government.[20]

Bulfinch was the only prominent amateur to turn to architecture as an occupation. Descended from a distinguished line of Boston merchants, he was educated at Harvard and then traveled abroad on an architectural itinerary suggested by Jefferson. A disastrous investment in one of his own residential designs, the Tontine Crescent in Boston, bankrupted Bulfinch in the early 1790s. Afterward his architectural interests became a way to earn a living. But even Bulfinch's talents and social connections, which led to commissions like the Massachusetts Statehouse, Massachusetts General Hospital, and Beacon Hill town houses, did not provide him with enough income from design and supervisory work. He was also a municipal administrator, serving as chair of the Boston Board of Selectmen and police superintendent for over twenty years.[21]

IMMIGRANT ARCHITECTS OF THE FEDERAL PERIOD

Bulfinch was not the only gentleman who found it necessary to work at architecture. In the years following the American Revolution, several Europeans tried to prosper as architects and supervisors for the private and public buildings being erected in the new nation. Some, like Stephen Hallet (ca. 1760–1825), George Hadfield (1763–

1826), and B. Henry Latrobe (1764–1820), had architectural training and experience before they immigrated to the United States. Others, like Pierre L'Enfant (1754–1825) and Maximilian Godefroy (1765–1840), had military backgrounds. L'Enfant, Hallet, Hadfield, and Latrobe were all involved with the federal building campaign in the new capital at Washington, D.C.

Despite the opportunities in the new federal city, these men's architectural careers in the New World were not easy. L'Enfant, the master planner of Washington, D.C., lost several positions because of his arrogance and insubordination. He became dependent on friends' charity and eventually died in poverty. Although Godefroy, a Frenchman like L'Enfant, won important commissions from the Catholic community in Baltimore, his sharp tongue and high fees alienated clients. Burdened by debts, in 1819 he returned to France, where he obtained only minor provincial commissions. Hallet lost the competition for the new federal Capitol building to Dr. William Thornton. Appointed to superintend the construction of the amateur architect's design, Hallet was dismissed for insubordination, laying foundations contrary to Thornton's plan. Although he remained in the United States, he never completed a single building. Hadfield, an Englishman, also worked as Capitol superintendent, quarreled with Thornton, and was dismissed. Unlike the three Frenchmen (L'Enfant, Godefroy, and Hallet), he worked steadily in Washington, D.C., for twenty-eight years, but his accomplishments there did not seem to fulfill his promise as a student at the Royal Academy and as an assistant in James Wyatt's London office. Despite Hadfield's work on buildings like the Treasury and War Offices, John Trumbull, the American painter, wrote that his friend Hadfield "had languished many years in obscurity in Washington."[22]

The three French architects found it difficult to accommodate their attitudes and working methods to an American building market dominated at one end by builders and at the other by a few master artisans and gentlemen-architects. Hadfield and Latrobe fared better. Both Englishmen were better educated and more experienced than their French colleagues. But they, too, struggled to build economically successful and artistically satisfying careers in the early nineteenth century.

THE FIRST PROFESSIONAL

Latrobe was the best prepared and most experienced architect to immigrate to early America. After training and working in both an engineering and an architectural office in London, he practiced there for five years. Yet when he arrived in 1796, he intended to live as a gentleman on income from his Pennsylvania lands. When this plan faltered, he "resolved to recommence [his] professional pursuits" as an architect and engineer. Latrobe entered and won the competition for a penitentiary in Richmond, Virginia, in 1797. That same year the directors of the Dismal Swamp Company in Virginia employed him as an engineering consultant. Architecture and engineering would now, he surely hoped, let him live like a gentleman.[23]

Since his father was a leading Moravian minister, Latrobe was undoubtedly familiar with the idea of professions as gentlemen's vocations. When he was twelve, his father planned a career in the church for his son and enrolled him in a Moravian academy on the Continent. There be pursued a gentleman's curriculum of the classics, mathematics, music, and drawing; his fellow students were German noblemen. Although religious doubts led Latrobe to abandon a career in the clergy, he did not reject the professional life of a gentleman. Returning to England when he was twenty, Latrobe entered the relatively new professions of architecture and engineering around 1786.[24]

He trained and worked first with John Smeaton and then with Samuel Cockerell, whose offices were centers for the professionalization of English engineering and architecture. Smeaton, a designer of harbors, bridges, and canals, was apparently the first Englishman to call himself a civil engineer. In 1771 he formed the Society of Civil Engineers for select colleagues to discuss theory, practice, and professional ethics. Cockerell, a designer of imposing churches and residences, was a founder in 1791 of the Architects' Club, one of the first architectural societies in England. Only members of the Royal Academy or another fine arts academy were eligible for admission.[25]

John Soane, whose severe neoclassicism profoundly influenced the young Latrobe, was also an original member of the Architects' Club. In his *Plans, Elevations, and Sections of Buildings,* published in 1788, Soane took up questions of architectural professionalism. The architect, he wrote, occupied a position of "great trust" between the client and the mechanic; he protected the former's interests but also defended the latter's rights. The architect was a gentleman, like the clergyman, physician, and barrister, who must be above crass commercial interests. If the architect worked as a builder, Soane continued, he jeopardized his honor and authority as the wise paternal figure mediating between client and mechanic.[26]

RIVALS AND COLLABORATORS

Latrobe was steeped in professional ideas a full decade before he left for the United States. He alone among the immigrant architects of the late eighteenth century came with both a highly developed ideology of professionalism and extensive experience in architecture. Latrobe blamed gentlemen-architects and building mechanics for his difficulties. But whatever the real reasons, his position as a professional architect and engineer was complicated because amateurs and builders were his collaborators as well as his competitors. Although his education and experience were exceptional, Latrobe is still pivotal to any history of American practice because he defined professionalism in his actions and writings. He also educated the next generation of professionals, architects like Robert Mills and William Strickland.

Latrobe had extensive dealings with Jefferson, the most prominent gentleman-architect in the United States. In 1803 President Jefferson appointed Latrobe his surveyor of public buildings with principal responsibility for completing the Capitol. Their clash over how to illuminate the House of Representatives chamber was, for Latrobe, a classic example of the amateur's interference with the professional.

Jefferson wanted long, wedge-shaped skylights, like those he had admired in the Halle aux Blés in Paris, for the dome over the House chamber. Latrobe advised his client that skylights would leak, drip with condensation, and admit a harsh light. Instead he proposed a glazed lantern over the dome to illuminate the space below. Jefferson strongly disliked Latrobe's idea, objecting to it because he knew of no antique precedent for a lantern over a dome. Latrobe disagreed, writing Jefferson: "Nothing in the field of good taste, which ought never to be at warfare with good sense, can be beautiful which appears useless or unmeaning." The lantern's functionality for Latrobe was, in fact, part of its architectural beauty. Unconvinced, Jefferson responded that Latrobe's "passion for the lantern" caused him "real pain." After several months of wrangling, Jefferson asserted his presidential prerogative, and Latrobe acquiesced. The skylights were used, and, as he had predicted, they leaked and admitted a harsh light.[27]

But Latrobe did prevail in the end, if only because the British burned the Capitol in 1814. James Madison, the new president, was not an amateur architect, and Latrobe had a glazed lantern erected over the new chamber for the House of Representatives. If he ever mused on Jefferson and Madison as architectural clients, Latrobe might have recalled his earlier comparison of the two men's presidential styles: "Mr. Jefferson is a man *out of a book*. Mr. M[adison] is more a man of the world. . . . I think the latter will adopt his measures more to the actual state of the world and of opinions, while the former seems to have in many cases attempted to force the state of things into the mould of theory."[28] Jefferson was, for Latrobe, as much an idealist in matters of architecture as in affairs of state.

Although Latrobe played the pragmatist in the skylight imbroglio with Jefferson, he understood architecture to be an art and the architect an artist. He joined the early fine arts societies and displayed his drawings alongside the work of other painters and sculptors. William Dunlap, who wrote the first history of the American arts in 1834, described Latrobe as an artist who never left home without his sketchbook.[29] Nevertheless, Latrobe knew that "a picture is not a design." This was why he considered an amateur like Dr. Thornton a kind of idiot savant, "a Man wholly ignorant of Architecture having brilliant ideas but possessing neither the knowledge accessory to their execution, nor the capacity to methodize and combine the various parts of public work."[30]

His professional differences with builders, his other nemesis, came to the forefront during the Baltimore Cathedral commission. Acting like a gentleman-architect, Latrobe donated his designs to the building committee and had no intention of becoming involved with site supervision. In 1806 John Hillen, a merchant who was the cathedral contractor, and George Rohrbach, the building superintendent, decided that Latrobe's foundation walls were not thick enough. They changed his drawings, without consulting him, to include a shallower crypt, wooden rather than stone vaulted spans, thicker walls, and columnar supports.[31]

Latrobe characterized their changes as the amateur's "happy fancy" and the builder's "knack of guessing improved by experience." While it was logical to assume that foundation walls should be thick and "too much strength does no harm," his original structure was not a guess but a calculation using "scientific principles." Before arriving at his design for the crypt, he had spent three weeks studying the foundation walls—"their stress and perpendicular action of the lateral pressure upon them . . . their weight and solidity." The result was a sound foundation wall, Latrobe insisted, that was also the most economical use of material. The professional's opinion was not "formed by *guess* or *habit*"; it was based on "*theory* confirmed by practice."[32]

Latrobe's theoretical knowledge of structure and materials came from such published works as John Smeaton on lighthouses and Bernard Belidor on hydraulic architecture. This was not modern theory, deriving general principles from controlled experimentation and mathematics, but empirical knowledge based on studying successful constructions, usually executed by the authors of the theory texts. These books, Latrobe's training with Smeaton, and his own practice familiarized him with diverse materials and structures. While his theory was based on experience, it drew on a broader and more complicated range of examples then either Hillen's or Rohrbach's. Latrobe possessed, in one scholar's opinion, a unique ability to visualize structural problems in a systematic and comprehensive fashion. Furthermore, he had the drafting ability to work his ideas out on paper. During the early nineteenth century, no American mechanic, contractor, architect, or engineer was his equal in drawing or structural knowledge.[33]

Latrobe's Baltimore difficulties were caused by his clients' misunderstanding about the role of drawings and their builders' limited experience of structure. But his absence from the building site did not help matters. Design by correspondence was always risky, especially if the client and builder were unfamiliar with the professional architect's role and regarded his drawings as guides, not binding contracts, for execution. Furthermore, Latrobe was donating his designs like a gentleman-architect. Thus his beneficiaries assumed he was content to leave the details of execution to their builders.

His pro bono work for the cathedral ultimately proved very costly, in terms of Latrobe's time and peace of mind. The Baltimore cathedral went through seven major design revisions because of changes made or demanded by the building committee. At one point Latrobe threatened to withdraw and deny all association with the building.[34] It was a learning process for the building committee. After the cathedral was essentially completed, the trustees wrote Latrobe: "It is true, that objections were sometimes made to parts of your plans, the propriety and correction of which, their [building committee's] inexperience did not permit them at the time to discern clearly."[35] This frequent need to educate clients was a responsibility that Latrobe, as self-proclaimed first professional architect, did not relish and apparently neglected.

The Baltimore commission made clear that supervision and inspection of work were often necessary for establishing the architect's authority with clients and builders. A dispute with the building superintendent had troubled Latrobe's first American commission, the Virginia State Penitentiary, in 1797. He met with daily "opposition and insult" from the builder as he conscientiously tried to "direct everything from the first shovelful of earth to the position of the last brick" at the penitentiary.[36] Thus Latrobe sought other ways to control the execution of his designs.

Latrobe subsequently used detailed drawings and specifications to enforce his authority on the building site. The 1799 marble contract for the Bank of Pennsylvania—signed by the bank directors, masons, contractors, and architect—specified that all work must conform to Latrobe's drawings or written directions. The architect must sign off on any design changes in writing or on the drawings. Both the architect and the contractors inspected and measured the work. If disputes arose, outside referees settled them. Perhaps these contractual guarantees of his authority were another reason Latrobe considered the Pennsylvania bank his masterpiece; the process as well as the design was a triumph for him.[37]

Yet it was more difficult to control the contracting process for private houses. Unlike the bank commission, an unusual and ambitious vaulted structure at the time, house design and construction were controlled by master carpenters. In Philadelphia the Carpenters' Company wielded great power because of its control over building prices. Latrobe outmaneuvered the company at the bank probably because of its limited experience with marble and masonry vaulted structures. Everyone (client, masons, and builders) depended on Latrobe's exceptional expertise at the bank. Houses were the carpenters' turf, however, and they clearly had clients' trust and confidence there. Latrobe claimed that Sedgeley, a house he designed for William Cramond in the late 1790s, had run five thousand dollars over budget because of the carpenters' secret price list. This was Cramond's fault, Latrobe later wrote, for ruling it out of his architect's "profession to judge of Carpenter's work."[38]

PARADOXES OF PRACTICE

But Latrobe confused clients and artisans because his actions often contradicted his professional claims. He did not always exercise what he defined as his professional rights of supervision. After winning a bitter fight to supervise the penitentiary work in Richmond, he left the city in late 1798 to devote himself to the Bank of Pennsylvania, promising the governor he would return to supervise completion of the penitentiary. But he never did, sending only some written instructions for the workmen. Latrobe's abandonment of the very responsibilities he had fought for so fiercely surely puzzled and exasperated the penitentiary client, superintendent, and workmen. It also further confused the professional architect's role in supervision. In this light, Latrobe's complaints about subsequent alterations to the penitentiary seem disingenuous.[39]

The Richmond penitentiary work certainly paled by comparison with the Philadelphia bank and waterworks commissions he had in hand by the spring of 1798. Philadelphia, with a population of fifty thousand, was then the largest city in the United States; its wealth and sophistication clearly suited Latrobe's ambition.[40] The Bank of Pennsylvania was a fireproof building constructed of masonry vaults. The facade, sheathed in marble, used the first example of the Greek orders to be built in the United States. It was, along with Bulfinch's Massachusetts Statehouse, the first complex vaulted structure east of the Mississippi River.[41] The waterworks were the most extensive and ambitious municipal system then designed in the United States, with innovative steam engines pumping water from the Schuylkill River through a brick vaulted conduit to the city.[42]

Important private commissions like William Cramond's Sedgeley (the first Gothic Revival villa in the United States) and speculative row houses on Walnut Street followed in 1799. These works established Latrobe as the leading designer of architectural and engineering works in Philadelphia and the United States. His comment that "for my professional reputation I should have done enough had I only built the Bank of Pennsylvania and supplied the city with Water" suggests how much he had accomplished in only a few years.[43] But, ironically, he was soon to despair of his career. He complained to his father-in-law in 1803: "But as it is I have absolutely nothing to do there [Philadelphia]. . . . Of other public works, even on a moderate scale, there is no prospect; and since the Cramond house I have not even had a transitory application to design a private building."[44] His plight was so desperate that James Traquair, who had worked as stonemason on the bank commission, asked Thomas Jefferson if he had any work for Latrobe. With no commissions in sight, Traquair explained, the architect was planning retirement to a farm.[45]

Latrobe's troubles were a result of the expense of his high-profile commissions. The final costs for both the Bank of Pennsylvania and the Philadelphia waterworks far exceeded his original estimates. Sedgeley's bloated budget of forty thousand dollars made prospective home owners wary of Latrobe,[46] and this reputation for financial extravagance followed him to Washington. When some fifty-one thousand dollars in unauthorized expenditures for the Capitol came to light in 1807–8, a congressional committee investigated and considered dismissing Latrobe for professional misconduct. He was ultimately exonerated but only because the legislators concluded artists like Latrobe "were not very nice about calculations in money matters."[47] Although he supported Latrobe publicly, Jefferson chastised him privately for his faulty cost estimates and chronic inattention to the building accounts. This mismanagement, he wrote Latrobe, "has done you great injury, and has been much felt by myself."[48]

Latrobe had only a limited understanding of the American building economy. Both private and public sector works were severely undercapitalized. Banking reserves were small, and the financial system was local and fragmented. Public revenues were limited, consisting only of customs duties. The government preferred to raise funds from private sources for many public works. Private investors were adamant about short-term gains whether they financed public projects like canals and waterworks or private undertakings like speculative housing. They wanted to limit costs rather than build the impressive but expensive structures that Latrobe advocated. Public officials faced the wrath of both political opponents and the electorate if building projects proved more expensive than the original estimates.[49]

Latrobe had to become a peripatetic architect and engineer because the American building market was so localized and thinly capitalized. During the remaining seventeen years of his career, he traveled throughout the country in search of enough challenging and lucrative work to sustain his professional practice and genteel life.

In Delaware he laid out the Chesapeake and Delaware Canal and surveyed the town of Newcastle during the early 1800s. He also became the chief architect for the federal government in Washington, D.C., and then an engineer for the navy in 1803–4. His federal salary was apparently insufficient because he also undertook private and commercial work in both Philadelphia and Washington, D.C. When he received a commission for the customhouse and waterworks in New Orleans, he spread his attentions over an even greater geographic area. Congress suspended work on the Capitol in 1811 as the threat of war with Britain grew. Latrobe shifted his focus to the New Orleans work, but the war eventually suspended building operations there as well. A year later Latrobe was on the move again, resettling in Pittsburgh to design steamboats for Robert Fulton. But this enterprise collapsed, too, and he returned to Washington, where friends secured his reappointment as architect to rebuild the burned Capitol in 1815. After bitter quarrels with the supervising commissioner, Latrobe resigned this position in 1817. He moved to Baltimore, where he oversaw work on the cathedral and the exchange, the latter designed with the cantankerous Maximilian Godefroy, with whom he quarreled. In 1818 he resumed work on the New Orleans water system. The constant search for work ended when he succumbed to yellow fever there in 1820.

Latrobe's far-flung practice made it necessary, he wrote in 1803, to "act on many occasions by proxy."[50] John Lenthall, an experienced English mechanic, became the clerk of the works (building superintendent) at the Capitol. He was, in Latrobe's opinion, a good assistant. A clerk like Lenthall, Latrobe wrote, directed and combined the work of all the mechanics so that they worked "without loss of time or waste of material or dispute among themselves." He also made working drawings and, in Latrobe's absence, determined whether contracts for labor and materials were being faithfully fulfilled.[51] Because of Lenthall, Latrobe wrote that he could work on the Capitol with "only an occasional personal attendance." Consequently, the architect did not move his family to Washington for several years after accepting the federal appointment in 1803.[52]

But Latrobe's confidence in Lenthall was ultimately too great. In 1808 his clerk was killed when the vault covering the Supreme Court in the Capitol collapsed and fell down on him. The fatality occurred as Lenthall and his workers took down the temporary supports for the vault. Although Latrobe accepted responsibility, in public statements he did allude to Lenthall's premature and clumsy removal of the wooden centering.[53] In a private letter to Jefferson, Latrobe's explanation of the events leading up to the collapse was more candid than his public accounts. Lenthall had redesigned the vault to use less material and centering in order to economize, and Latrobe had consented to these "bolder and more dangerous vaults" against, he confessed to Jefferson, his better judgment.[54] Jefferson must have wondered why Latrobe, given his doubts about the vault's structural integrity, was not there to supervise the removal of the centering. This was a serious dereliction of his often vaunted professional responsibilities, which proved fatal to Lenthall. As with the Virginia penitentiary commission, Latrobe seemed far more zealous in asserting his supervisory rights than in actually attending to them.

As Latrobe's practice spread beyond Philadelphia, he needed assistants in his office as well as clerks on the scattered building sites. Frederick Graff, the son of a bricklayer and a carpenter's apprentice, began working for him in 1799. William Strickland and Adam Traquair, whose fathers had worked on Latrobe's Bank of Pennsylvania, were sent to his office in the early 1800s. Lewis DeMun, a former French military officer, came around 1802, followed by Robert Mills, previously a student of James Hoban and draftsman for Jefferson, in 1803.[55]

Latrobe's assistants helped to prepare the extraordinary number of detailed working drawings and written instructions required to execute his innovative structural and architectural designs. These documents were especially necessary because Latrobe was so often absent from the building site. Scaled plans, elevations, sections, and details in building had become more common with the advent of costlier structures designed with vaulted spaces and in new styles like neoclassicism during the second half of the eighteenth century. Drawings for engineering projects, by contrast, were still rather primitive. Master mechanics on engineering projects rarely used scaled drawings and often simply chalked full-size details on boards. Thus, either Latrobe or his assistants had to teach them how to decipher and use scaled engineering drawings. "I must indeed work hard," Latrobe wrote his brother, "having to make the Men who are to execute, as well as the designs of my work."[56]

As Latrobe juggled commissions, he sent his assistants to construction sites with drawings, documents, and contractors' payments. DeMun, Mills, and Strickland also helped Lenthall prepare working drawings for the Capitol. As they grew more experienced, they assisted in surveying the site and executing feeder lines for the Delaware Canal project. Mills supervised work on the Bank of Philadelphia and the William Waln house when Latrobe finally moved to Washington, D.C., in 1807.[57] But managing a staff was time-consuming and frustrating. John Barber, a chief clerk, and Thomas Breillat, a draftsman, absconded with office papers, books, and monies in the summer of 1800. Strickland, only an adolescent when he entered Latrobe's office, sometimes disappeared for days without a word.[58]

Furthermore, some clients objected to Latrobe's staff arrangements. Accustomed to a master builder who charged a single fee for design, contracting, craftsmanship, and supervision, they especially balked at hiring a superintendent like Lenthall and then paying Latrobe too. The architect often found it necessary to explain just what he did and did not do. "To execute the work either by myself or by proxy, is wholly out of my profession," he wrote to William Waln. "It is not necessary that I should oversee or superintend the workmen as they are at labor." Even if he were willing to supervise the construction of Waln's house, Latrobe continued, no one could afford such a costly use of his time.[59]

Latrobe's fees were indeed high, and he found it difficult to collect them. Although he tried to charge 5 percent of the building budget, the standard professional fee in his view, he rarely got it. This was not surprising when one considers that his better-established professional mentors in England had trouble receiving this amount.[60]

LATROBE'S LEGACY

Latrobe was not stoic about his professional difficulties. He complained regularly about "the indignities . . . which I must suffer in the prosecution of my profession" and about his "great misfortune to be born and educated a *Gentleman,* at least on this side of the Atlantic."[61] Since the nineteenth century, critics and historians have generally accepted Latrobe's own interpretation of these events. In 1834 William Dunlap described Latrobe's career as proud but painful because of Americans' ignorance of art and science. Talbot Hamlin, who won a Pulitzer Prize for his 1955 biography of Latrobe, saw the architect as a tragic figure. He died destitute and nearly forgotten, Hamlin wrote, because of the national suspicion of artists and experts.

Today architectural historians routinely acclaim Latrobe as the father of the architectural profession in the United States. During the last twenty years, he has received what in the academic community passes for canonization: an exhaustive and expensive project devoted to the publication of his correspondence, journals, travel sketches, and architectural and engineering drawings.[62] Yet his legacy to the architectural profession is far more problematic than such assessments suggest. Latrobe was imperious, temperamental, inconsistent, and improvident—qualities the public still associates with the professional architect. Other architects like L'Enfant, Hallet, and Godefroy exhibited these same traits, but they never identified themselves as fully and vociferously as Latrobe did with professionalism. Nor were they as successful as Latrobe.

In a letter to Jefferson, Latrobe stated that his task was "to dictate in matters of taste" to the president, Congress, and the public. He clearly had little patience or respect for the leaders of the new Republic when they became involved with artistic or architectural issues. Congress was an assembly of clowns and buffoons, he wrote, who could appreciate only the architectural literalism of his corncob capitals in the Capitol.[63] Jefferson advised him to moderate his tone and his designs if he wished to practice in a republic—"The object of the artist is lost if he fails to please the general eye." But Latrobe seemed to relish his own arrogance: "There is perhaps among all the *persons* holding employment under government, not one, so unpopular as myself. . . . I believe that I have the despotism of manner which belongs to all artists, and appears to be inseparable from some degree of reputation."[64]

Although Latrobe asserted that he was a "man of business and account," he was clearly out of his depth in financial matters. All his major commissions—the Bank of Pennsylvania, the Philadelphia waterworks, Sedgeley, and the Capitol—cost far more than the original estimates he gave the clients. But he transformed this reputation for extravagance, as he did his arrogance, into a point of pride, writing that "the fault which the public have found with my professional character, is that my ideas and projects are too extended to be practicable for some centuries to come."[65]

He managed his personal finances as poorly as he did his building budgets. In pursuit of wealth he repeatedly made highly speculative and ultimately disastrous investments: in land, a steel mill, a gold mine, power looms, and steamboats. His canal commissions were also risky; like other early engineers, he gambled and took his salary in stock shares. If the canal company failed, as the Chesapeake and Delaware did in 1805, Latrobe received nothing. He often had to borrow from family and friends. Ever the gentleman, he also signed notes guaranteeing others' debts. In 1817 he finally had to declare personal bankruptcy. Risky investments and imprudent loans surely had as much to do with his precarious finances as American philistinism.[66]

Although Latrobe's professional difficulties were partly of his own making, they were also the result of basic economic realities of early nineteenth-century America.[67] There was simply not enough capital to underwrite the ambitious private and public projects that Latrobe and other immigrant architects like L'Enfant, Hallet, Godefroy, and Hadfield considered worthy of their training and talent. Even Bulfinch, a well-connected Bostonian, could not make a living from his architectural practice. Although Latrobe was quick to proclaim himself the first professional architect, he had little insight into what that meant in harsh economic terms. Architectural scholars simultaneously gloss over Latrobe's responsibility for his own financial predicament and obscure its systemic causes.

On only one occasion did Latrobe cease his railings about persecution of the professional architect and reflect more dispassionately on his American career: "Had I, in England, executed what I have done here, I should now be able to sit down quietly and enjoy *otium cum dignitate* [leisure with dignity]. But in England the croud [*sic*] of those whose talents are superior to mine is so great, that I should perhaps never have elbowed through them. Here I am the only successful Architect and Engineer."[68]

Latrobe's legacy to the next generation of professional architects was not just a corpus of buildings. He had identified the professional architect with public buildings of artistic and structural excellence. Less positively, he had associated the architect with arrogance, temperament, and fiscal imprudence. Unlike Latrobe, L'Enfant, Hallet, Godefroy, and Hadfield, antebellum architects worked during an unprecedented period of opportunity and economic expansion in the four decades before the Civil War. Growth and prosperity made cooperation and organization, the next phase of professional development, possible for them.

CHAPTER 2

PROFESSIONAL ORGANIZATIONS

AND AGENDAS

How far the founding of an institution of architects may contribute
to a birth of genius for the profession, we may well doubt: but as a
"nursing father," it may foster and rear: watchful as a chief duty,
to discourage mediocrity and put down pretension.
Alexander J. Davis, Letter of 1841 to Thomas U. Walter

Writing to a friend in Europe in 1811, Benjamin Henry Latrobe stated that he was
at the head of a profession that had no body. Even a gifted architect steeped in professionalism like Latrobe could not single-handedly establish the profession. Before
this could happen, a critical mass of professional architects needed to prove their
design and supervisory capabilities over a period of time.[1] Professionalization was a
collective effort requiring organization and cooperation. The appearance of the first
architectural societies in the antebellum period signaled that Latrobe's ideas of professionalism were finally taking root. The body of the profession was beginning to
materialize.[2]

The antebellum period was an era of both expansion and dislocation. After the
War of 1812, steam technology created new manufacturing and industrial capabilities. Canal and railroad transportation networks led to the formation of regional
and national markets, upending the traditional monopolies of local economies and
forming unprecedented capital reserves. In the late 1820s and 1830s, suffrage was extended to all white males who owned property, and Andrew Jackson, a populist candidate, was elected president. Evangelical Protestantism emphasized a personal and
emotional experience outside of the established religions.[3] These developments all
challenged traditional hierarchies in economics, politics, and religion.

In this climate of leveling and egalitarianism, the professions of law, medicine, and divinity came into question. Populists excoriated professionals for restricting access to these occupations. Medical licensing acts and educational requirements for the practice of law, enacted during the colonial and Federal periods, were almost completely swept away by 1860. Technical training at proprietary schools supplanted the classical education of early American lawyers and physicians. Even ministers, especially in the rapidly growing Baptist and Methodist denominations, did not necessarily have college degrees.[4]

But a paradoxical desire to rise accompanied this assault on traditional rankings and privileges. A hunger for status and dignity was reflected in the American use of the title "gentleman" by all white males, a practice that shocked European visitors. Far from abolishing the professions, those attacking rank and privilege eliminated barriers restricting access to them. Furthermore, apothecaries, architects, and engineers now sought professional recognition. Natural ability—not birth, education, and wealth—was the criterion for admission to the professions.[5] The first professional architectural societies appeared during this turbulent time.

THE AMERICAN INSTITUTION OF ARCHITECTS

In December 1836 twenty-three architects from New York, Philadelphia, Boston, Baltimore, Washington, D.C., and New Orleans met to create the American Institution of Architects at the Astor House in New York. After electing officers and drafting a constitution in early 1837, they met again at the Pennsylvania Academy of the Fine Arts in May 1837.[6] Thomas U. Walter, a Philadelphia architect, was responsible for organizing the new institution. He had studied architecture and engineering with William Strickland, Latrobe's former student. Strickland, Robert Mills, and John Trautwine, another Strickland pupil, were also charter members.[7] The prominent roles played in the American Institution by the first and second generations of Latrobe's professional progeny undoubtedly would have pleased him. But the presence of so many former master builders among the institution's founders would surely have dismayed him.[8] Ignored by scholars until now, the American Institution of Architects is crucial for an understanding of the architectural profession. Its history reveals the complex and contradictory forces that simultaneously drove and undermined professionalization in antebellum America.

Among the institution founders were men like Asher Benjamin, Minard Lafever, Alexander Parris, and Ithiel Town. Trained in the building crafts, they had previously identified themselves with artisanal culture. They joined elite craft organizations like the Bricklayers' Company of Philadelphia, the Associated Housewrights

Society, the Society of Housewrights, and the Massachusetts Charitable Mechanics Association.[9] Unlike their colonial and Federal predecessors, these master builders were no longer primarily house carpenters. Both government officials and private individuals now had previously undreamed of capital reserves from the national markets created by the canal and railroad systems, and they invested much of this money in real estate.[10] Master builders, as well as Latrobe's professional heirs, received commissions for ambitious buildings like customhouses, state capitols, hotels, banks, exchanges, universities, schools, hospitals, asylums, and penitentiaries in the antebellum period.

Responsibility for large-scale work was, in fact, the common bond between the master builders and the office-trained architects who established the American Institution of Architects. The traditional association of master builder with design had facilitated the rise of gifted artisans like Benjamin, Town, and Lafever. Like Latrobe and his heirs, these men now found it advantageous to distinguish the architect from other competitors in the antebellum building market. Thus Asher Benjamin, who had identified himself as a carpenter and housewright in early Boston city directories, called himself only an architect after 1830. Benjamin, a prolific author of builders' guides, adopted a decidedly less fraternal tone toward his artisan readers with his publication of *The Practical House Carpenter* in 1830. Sounding like Latrobe, Benjamin now wrote that mechanics were dependent on the architect's instructions. He also lambasted private individuals and building committees who "cramp the invention of the architect by their economy or pervert it by their fancies."[11]

Master builders like Benjamin had compelling economic and social reasons to distance themselves from their artisanal roots. The traditional solidarity of master, journeymen, and apprentice was crumbling amid the alternating economic booms and busts of the 1820s and 1830s. Organizing and staffing a workshop was an expensive and risky undertaking in an overheated, competitive building market. Fewer and fewer journeymen now made the transition from employee to independent practitioner. They became a new proletariat, part of the nearly three hundred thousand wage earners who joined trade unions in the 1830s. Masters were no longer surrogate fathers or mentors; they were employers who had to bargain sharply with journeymen in order to survive. Between 1833 and 1837 there were thirty-four strikes over wages and working hours in the New York and Boston building trades. Masters and journeymen became adversaries as labor became unionized.[12]

The strikes and lockouts associated with the antebellum labor movement were costly and violent. The rise of militant trade unionism alarmed many middle- and upper-class Americans, who believed it undermined the position of respectable mechanics and jeopardized the very existence of the American Republic.[13] Successful master builders like Benjamin and Town undoubtedly grew uncomfortable with their old artisanal identities. Professionalism simultaneously associated them with their middle- and upper-class clients and distanced them from militant trade unionism.

The American Institution of Architects was only one of the many professional organizations formed during the 1820s and 1830s. In spite of populism and egalitarianism, professionalism appealed to many early nineteenth-century Americans. Disenchanted with the dilettantism of early American art societies, the artists who founded the National Academy of Design pointedly excluded amateurs from this new organization in 1826. Samuel F. B. Morse, the first president of the academy, feared the growing populism and materialism of American life and saw professionalization of the arts as a solution. William Dunlap, chronicler of the American fine arts, described Morse's organization as "a real academy, governed by artists, with artists for teachers, having an exhibition which supported their school." The National Academy of Design included architects as well as artists. Town, Davis, Strickland, and Haviland—all founders of the American Institution of Architects in 1836—were early members of the National Academy of Design.[14]

Engineers as well as artists organized a professional association before the Civil War. Populist state legislators and congressmen called for the abolition of West Point during the Jacksonian era, arguing that it created an elite caste of engineers who were not really soldiers. In 1838 forty engineers, including Strickland, discussed founding an association to advance "professional knowledge" and elevate "the character and standing of the Civil Engineers of the United States." This ambitious national organization, however, foundered after only a few meetings.[15]

Architectural Science

The purpose of the American Institution of Architects was to promote "architectural science." Architectural historians, however, have never understood the political and social implications of this term in nineteenth-century America. Science— that is, reason—had a particular meaning and resonance in early America. Alexander Hamilton believed it was the basis of all professional work. Science allowed professionals to mediate between competing interest groups in American society.[16] By invoking science, the American Institution's founders were carving out a special place for the professional architect, between the client and mechanic, in the building market. This is undoubtedly why the 1837 constitution of the American Institution enjoined members from measuring and valuing any work but their own and from accepting money from builders and tradesmen whom they supervised.

The professional architect had to somehow stand apart from commercial pressures but still compete within the market.[17]

But the word "science" had also acquired an egalitarian connotation by the 1830s. It then became understood as any systematic learning that was accessible and useful. Science stood in contrast to the idle learning of aristocratic virtuosos and the secret arts and mysteries of master craftsmen. Mechanics' institutes, formed in Europe and America during the 1820s, offered free lectures, evening classes, libraries, and exhibitions. Their programs were intended to educate "scientific mechanics" for an industrialized and technologically innovative economy. Dedicated to practical learning open to all, the mechanics' institutes were the schools of antebellum populism. Unlike American colleges that taught classical languages and literature to gentlemen's sons, the institutes educated American mechanics for the worlds of commerce and industry.[18]

The founders of the American Institution of Architects were familiar with the mechanics' institutes and their scientific curricula. While Davis exhibited his work at the New York Mechanics' Institute, Strickland, Haviland, and Walter all taught at the Franklin Institute, a mechanics' organization, in Philadelphia. Furthermore, Benjamin, Haviland, and other authors of antebellum builders' guides gathered their discussions of history, classical orders, construction, materials, manual skills, and taste under the rubric of architectural science. They set forth "scientific" principles for everything from sawing wood to drawing a classical order.[19]

By embracing architectural science, the founders of the American Institution identified professional practice with a rational and egalitarian basis for privilege and distinction. Science as the basis for professional qualifications and privilege mitigated the charges of exclusivity professionalism inevitably raised in the populist period before the Civil War. The American Institution was not an exclusive gentlemen's club but a professional society with rigorous but impartial standards based on architectural science.[20]

Proficiency in architectural science became the basis for admission to the institution. Walter, Davis, and Haviland, who wrote the constitution, required prospective members to pass an examination devised by the professors (founders) of the institution. The areas of expertise tested were familiar from the architectural science of any antebellum builders' guide: architectural history, principles of design and composition, principles of construction, and the nature and property of materials. The only new subject was professional etiquette.[21] The founders proposed what was, in effect, the first architectural licensing examination.

While associate members were required to demonstrate their abilities, professors, or senior members, were a self-selected elite. They had a minimum of five years of practice and were described as being "regularly educated for the profession."[22] Only one institution founder, Karl Reichardt, had any formal training in architecture. Several men had office training, but the majority were former master builders educated through craft apprenticeships.

"Regular education" was a term Latrobe had used, defining it as knowledge of "what has been done before in the Same line," gained by working with an established practitioner and by studying books and drawings.[23] The founders of the American Institution simply blurred Latrobe's distinction between a craft apprenticeship and office training. They saw both as "regular education" because they involved work with an experienced designer and supervisor. Defining regular education in this way allowed both office-trained architects and master builders to become professors of the institution.

The founders also provided for the study from books and drawings that Latrobe had listed as a part of "regular education." They pledged to collect and to preserve the culture and artifacts of architecture. The institution was to house a library, a drawings collection, and a cabinet of casts and models. But only professors and their students had access to these materials, thus restricting learning to a select circle.[24]

The Gentlemen's Club

A desire for recognition persisted even in the midst of the concern for leveling and egalitarianism in early nineteenth-century America. Fraternal organizations with ceremonies and regalia, bestowing dignity and office, were popular during this period. The American Institution of Architects fulfilled these fraternal needs, too. The members elected officers: Strickland, president; Davis, vice president; and Walter, secretary. Each professor was to receive a signet ring, used to affix a mark to each of his original drawings. The stamped drawings then became material evidence of his status as an institution member and a notarized document of his authority on the building site.[25]

The American Institution members never convened again after their May 1837 meeting. Davis later attributed the demise of this national organization to rivalries between Philadelphia and New York architects, but he also believed that the institution lacked popular support; its library, exhibitions, and lectures should have been open to the public.[26] But the financial panic and depression of 1837, the most severe economic crisis yet experienced, meant members had no discretionary funds to support the society or time to organize and attend meetings. The organization rose and fell on antebellum contradictions of populism and exclusivity and economic expansion and contraction.

Twenty years passed before American architects again tried to organize another professional society. In the winter of 1857 Richard Upjohn convened a group of twelve New York architects at his office in lower Manhattan. They agreed to establish an organization for the discussion of all the "branches of the arts and sciences" pertaining to architecture. The American Institute of Architects (AIA), the name eventually chosen for this new association, surely referred to the earlier organization.[27] This midcentury association, like the American Institution, has attracted only passing notice in the histories of American architecture until now.

Conditions at the time of the institute's founding were hardly auspicious. Populist opposition to the professions had not abated. The country was in the midst of another economic depression, and competition for architectural work was fierce. Henry Van Brunt, a young architect and early institute member, later recalled the 1850s as a period when architects were set against one another. They regarded books and drawings, he continued, as trade secrets to be kept hidden from competitors.[28]

Upjohn, the first president of the AIA, surely agreed with Van Brunt's gloomy assessment of this period. He was originally a cabinetmaker who left England for the United States in 1829. When he founded the institute in 1857, Upjohn had worked for nearly two decades as the leading architect of the medieval revival in the United States. But he had labored, Upjohn told institute members, "under the most adverse circumstances when the profession was in its infancy . . . [and] in an isolated position."[29]

Part of the problem, Upjohn believed, was that American architects pursued their "individual interests, alone and [each] separately endeavoring to advance." The institute, he continued, was a "means of interchange" to "promote the scientific and practical perfection of its members and elevate the standing of the profession." As a young craftsman in New Bedford, Massachusetts, Upjohn had believed in collective action; he was a charter member of the local mechanics' institute and fought for reduced working hours.[30] The AIA was a continuation of the earlier tradition of collective action that Upjohn had known from the artisanal world.

A Select and Local Society

Upjohn knew that the American Institution of Architects, an ambitious national organization, had already failed. He put his faith in a select group of local architects. Early AIA members, like his son and partner Richard Michell Upjohn, his son-in-law and partner Charles Babcock, and his assistant Leopold Eidlitz, had ties to his own office. Others, like Jacob W. Mould, Frederick Peterson, and Upjohn himself, belonged to the expatriate architectural community in New York. Richard M. Hunt, an American by birth, had recently returned from Europe after living and studying abroad for many years. Almost all the founders were associated with the medieval revival that Upjohn had initiated with his 1839 design for New York's Trinity Church. Hunt, educated at the Ecole des Beaux-Arts, was the sole exception.[31]

Although the institute's founders obsessed for many years about how many and which architects to admit, the membership qualifications and professional standards that they codified were never very explicit. The first draft of the AIA constitution in 1857 required only that candidates for admission be recommended by the founders. An amendment in 1858 stipulated that senior members be principals of architectural firms with three years of consecutive experience. Associate members were students who had three years of office training. There was never any suggestion that the institute members certify areas of professional expertise with an examination like the one the 1836–37 institution proposed. It was not until 1869 that AIA members were required to be in "honorable practice," which meant refusing bribes from builders or suppliers.[32]

In the spring of 1857 the founding members staged a solemn ceremony, rather like the initiation rites of a fraternal order, to mark the adoption of their constitution. Those members present all signed their names to the document in the Gothic Revival chapel at New York University (Fig. 1). Appropriately, this space was the work of Alexander Jackson Davis, a founder of the earlier association and a new member of the AIA.[33]

Thomas U. Walter, another link between the 1836–37 and 1857 organizations, praised the idea of selectivity at this ceremony. Institute membership was a mark of great distinction, Walter stated, that the public would soon recognize as an honor. An institute member would be assured of respect and deference. Architects were also an artistic elite, he continued, because their works were totally imaginative. Painters and sculptors, by contrast, merely copied nature, but architects created anew.[34] Leopold Eidlitz, another founder, echoed Walter's ideas, but he also criticized architectural science, the touchstone of the 1836–37 organization, as an outmoded and mindless system of generic solutions. While science was accessible to "practical architects," who were only common carpenters, artistry was the mark of the professional architect.[35] Eidlitz, a central European who had trained in Vienna, had no patience with the populist and egalitarian ideas that were the hallmark of antebellum architectural science.

Thus the AIA, like the early Institute of British Architects, now became an exclusive gentlemen's club—so much so that even Eidlitz, joined by Hunt, complained

FIGURE I. Alexander Jackson Davis, perspective view of proposed New York
University Chapel, ca. 1837 (New-York Historical Society).

that it was a "sort of mutual admiration society" where only members' friends gained admission. Although the AIA was urged to mount lectures and exhibitions open to all because the public "are the ones who really hold the reins . . . [and] require to be enlightened," the institute members focused on themselves.[36] There were no public programs. The library and collection of drawings and models proposed in the constitution were open only to members. The AIA members, a writer charged, were either ignorant or indifferent to "the influence which they are capable of wielding in favor of the profession."[37] In the contradictory impulses toward both populism and exclusivity that characterized antebellum America, the AIA clearly favored the latter.

Younger members like Hunt and Peterson did, however, persuade Upjohn and Walter to admit more architects and practitioners from outside New York City. Yet the AIA always had a limited geographic representation during the nineteenth century. Thirteen years after Upjohn founded the institute, there were 2,000 architects practicing in the United States, only 140 of whom were institute members. Furthermore, northeastern architects represented 65.5 percent of these 140 members. Architects from the Midwest accounted for 17.3 percent, those from the Southeast 16.5 percent, and from Canada 0.7 percent. A network of local chapters was created in 1867, but—except for Chicago and Cincinnati—they were all on the East Coast nine years later.[38]

Office training was now the "regular education" for institute members. Upjohn was the only architect among the original thirteen members with artisanal training. This continued to be true thirteen years later, when four-fifths of the members were still trained in offices, and did not change with the establishment of the first architectural schools at universities in the decades after the Civil War. Office training continued to be important in the early twentieth century. In 1912, when there were thirty-two university programs, two-thirds of all AIA members had still received some instruction in a practitioners office.[39]

Fees and Competitions

The two issues that preoccupied the AIA during the nineteenth century were fees and competitions for public work. Although members presented papers at their annual conventions, education was never a high priority. After drafting a constitution, AIA members took up the pragmatic issue of architectural charges. Upjohn stated that the principal goal of the AIA was "the establishment and maintenance of a perfect understanding as to prices and methods of conducting business." These were the concerns of architects who were businessmen running their own offices.[40]

The institute members, like Latrobe, advocated a percentage fee tied to building costs. Such payment set the architect apart from mechanics who received a daily wage. Unlike a lump-sum payment, the percentage fee did not lock the architect into a figure that might prove incommensurate with his time and effort. It created a formula that assumed the architect's labor rose along with costs and also gave the architect an incentive to drive up the budget.[41]

Arguments over a voluntary or mandatory payment schedule dragged on for nine years before members adopted the 5 percent fee in 1866. They then agreed to a staggered schedule of charges ranging from a 1 percent charge for preliminary design studies to a full 5 percent for studies, working drawings, specifications, detail drawings, and superintendence. The architect was paid in increments as each phase of the working process was completed. The 1866 schedule noted that all drawings belonged to the architect; the client did not purchase them. "Our merchandise," Upjohn told the 1869 convention, "is our brain, we sell our ideas."[42]

Many members, however, simply could not collect a 5 percent fee. Even prominent architects like Davis and Upjohn had charged by the drawing or by the day in the early days of their practice. When Davis and Upjohn used a percentage fee in the 1850s, they sometimes reduced the rate to less than 5 percent, especially if the building costs greatly exceeded their original estimates. A member from Baltimore claimed in 1897 that not more than one architect in ten in that city received the 5 percent fee. The Baltimore architect with the largest practice, this member claimed, collected only 3 percent.[43]

Thus the 1866 schedule was really only a suggested rate of charges. Furthermore, a professional society did not coerce the gentlemen who were its members. Such a mandatory fee schedule, moreover, raised the issue of price-fixing and reminded the public, as Upjohn and Walter admitted, of trade unions' "trying to put up prices" through "highly objectionable processes." Like the 1836–37 institution, the AIA was determined to distance itself from the building trade unions.[44]

But controversial competitions for public buildings did motivate the institute to enact a binding code. After the Civil War, the building market in the North and Midwest began to rebound. There were competitions for important public buildings like the New York State capitol (1866) and the New York City post office (1867). But AIA members felt victimized by these competitions because building committees did not compensate entrants for their labor. Committees also cobbled together a design from several submissions or entrusted the execution to a builder rather than to the winning architect. Nonetheless, competitions could elevate an unknown designer who won into the front ranks of the profession. Whereas young and inexperienced draftsmen and architects saw competitions as opportunities, the established architects of the institute regarded them as insulting to the profession. Thus they adopted an institute code in 1870 that prohibited members from participating in competitions where entrants received no compensation, architects were not appointed as jurors, winners were not guaranteed supervision of their designs, and fees were not a percentage of building costs.[45]

Six years later, however, the institute shifted the emphasis from policing its members' involvement in competitions, evidently an unpopular and thankless task, to reforming the process. The federal government was emerging as an important client for large-scale building, and the institute lobbied for legislation to award all federal government commissions through competitions run according to the 1870 code. The first bill, introduced in 1876, failed to pass, marking the beginning of a protracted campaign.[46]

The very insularity of the early AIA and its attention to bread-and-butter issues like fees and public competitions helped it to endure during a time that was openly hostile to the professions. Where an ambitious national organization like the 1836–37 institution failed, the AIA, with its limited agenda and select membership, survived into the late nineteenth century, a period more favorable to all the professions. Sheer survival was the AIA's greatest accomplishment in its first twenty years.

WESTERN ASSOCIATION OF ARCHITECTS

As African Americans, immigrants, laborers, and women pressed their claims in the last decades of the nineteenth century, other Americans now saw regulation and constraint as necessary to preserve national unity and social order. Furthermore, doctrines like social Darwinism made inequality seem acceptable because it was inevitable. Large-scale commercial, industrial, and governmental enterprises created new and complex hierarchies in which deference to authority ensured smooth functioning. Professional claims of expertise and authority seemed less anomalous in an atmosphere where there was a general concern for order, standards, and deference.[47] The professionalization of architecture, building on foundations laid during the antebellum period, now developed and expanded. Numerous local, regional, and national organizations for architects appeared and pursued ambitious, if not always successful, agendas.

The Western Association of Architects (WAA) was a powerful new organization, established in 1884 at a Chicago meeting of a hundred architects from fourteen midwestern states. The majority of these architects, over sixty, were from Chicago;

Dankmar Adler, Daniel Burnham, William LeBaron Jenney, John Root, and Louis Sullivan were all instrumental in forming and then directing the WAA. These men were disgruntled with the AIA, which had admitted them but, they contended, denied them real leadership roles. WAA members asserted that their association was run democratically by its members, not by a board of trustees, like the AIA.[48]

The WAA founders did not envision their organization as a sedate and select gentlemen's club. Charles Illsley, a Saint Louis architect and the first WAA president, hoped that over six hundred architects would attend the second meeting: "We should not let this association lay [*sic*] along in its early stages as the AIA unfortunately did. Among other ends in view is the making of a powerful and favorable impression on the public, and nothing tells on them like numbers."[49] To get these telling numbers the WAA founders adopted a liberal admissions policy, admitting anyone who was already a member of the AIA or a state architectural society. But any architect currently practicing in the United States was eligible to apply; after examining applicants' backgrounds the board recommended new members at the annual convention. In 1885, the WAA admitted Louise Blanchard Bethune, the first woman practitioner elected to an American architectural association.[50]

Bethune, who was from Buffalo, was also appointed to a committee whose purpose was to establish state organizations as feeders into the WAA. There were no distinctions, unlike in the AIA, between senior and junior members. All successful applicants became fellows.[51] But the leadership soon retrenched on this expansive admissions policy because of complaints that too many builders and contractors were joining. One Wisconsin architect was dismayed that a former bricklayer who could barely draw plans and accepted any compensation rather than a percentage fee was a fellow.[52] A revised membership policy required all fellows be "a professional person whose sole occupation is to supply all data preliminary to the material, construction and completion of a building and to exercise administrative control over contractors supplying material and labor . . . and [over] the arbitration of contracts stipulating terms of obligation and fulfillment between proprietor and contractor."[53]

This definition is striking for its studied avoidance of the term "architect" and of the masculine pronoun. Moreover, while it made clear that a member did not become involved with contracting, it did not refer to the artistry and imagination that Thomas U. Walter had extolled at the AIA ceremony in 1857. Architectural drawings were merely preliminary data for a building, and the architect was a professional person who supplied them. The only traditional element was the description of the architect as a mediator between builder and client in negotiating contracts.

The WAA definition of an architect was perfectly attuned to certain late nineteenth-century developments in business, perhaps because its authors (Adler, Jenney, and William W. Boyington, another Chicago architect) were all building large commercial practices at the time. Their clients directed the new railroad, insurance, retail, and real estate conglomerates.

The WAA leadership clearly valued these clients' opinions. In 1888 candidates for membership were required to submit client testimonials to their proficiency and character. Applicants to the AIA, in contrast, needed recommendations only from institute members during the late nineteenth century.[54] The WAA reconfigured the architect's role in terms that heads of hierarchical business organizations understood and appreciated. The architect they described was a practitioner who comprehended and functioned in this new world of large rationalized bureaucracies. However, the WAA's deference to big business may have been just as irrelevant to architects with modest or provincial practices as the AIA's emphasis on percentage fees and public competitions.

Licensing

The WAA leaders rationalized the architect's role in the building market, but they realized that rhetoric alone could not secure widespread acceptance of professional authority. The WAA, Adler explained at the 1885 convention, intended to "fix throughout the states of the Great West the legal status of the architect." The large membership and allied state organizations were part of a WAA plan to lobby legislatures on architectural licensing. Adler put the case to his fellow members (whom he addressed as all male):

> We wish our fellow citizens to concede that we possess superior knowledge in
> our profession and to submit to our guidance in all matters relating to their
> building interests. . . . [Yet] the public knows us as only a body of business-
> men, self-styled architects, who have by their executed works, demonstrated
> at the risk of their clients, their greater or lesser justifications for assuming the
> title of architect. . . . Let no man practice architecture without a license from
> a competent state tribunal.[55]

Similar discussions on state certification of architects' qualifications were then taking place in France. In 1885 French architects proposed government review of their technical qualifications. Their artistic abilities, however, were not subject to review. Richard Norman Shaw led a group of British architects who bitterly opposed state regulation in 1884 because standardized requirements and uniform examinations could never assess their aesthetic qualifications. Prussia, however, had required state certification of its municipal architects since the early nineteenth century to ensure public safety and welfare. This was the kind of certification that Adler had in mind for American architects.[56]

Uniform standards and licensing established a mechanism to test and certify practitioners. Such a review did not necessarily privilege breeding or class or degrees. The process, open to all, effectively meant that society sanctioned professionalism as being in the public interest. The WAA did not assume authority as an inherent right of architects as gentlemen or artists. Its members wanted a legal basis for their status.

But when WAA supporters introduced licensing bills in the Illinois, Missouri, Iowa, Texas, and Kansas legislatures in 1886, none of them passed. Many legislators still believed that architectural licensing was a special-interest bill. They feared that builders, contractors, artisans, and home owners would be prohibited from designing and supervising construction if architects were licensed. The WAA hunkered down for a long campaign.[57]

The national leadership of the AIA did not support the WAA campaign for licensing. It regarded regulation as demeaning. The institute, as an exclusive organization, had no real interest in increasing the number of professional architects through legislation. Its officers shared the views of Shaw and other British architects that state bodies could never evaluate artistry, the touchstone of architectural ability.[58]

Merger

Licensing aside, the AIA and WAA did hold common views on several issues. For instance, in 1886 they both supported legislation awarding federal commissions to private architects through regulated competitions. But the combined numbers of the AIA and WAA memberships did not impress Congress. Like the earlier 1876 proposal, this bill failed to pass.[59] There were other points of accord, as well. The WAA adopted the AIA schedule of charges. Like the AIA, it also demonstrated very little interest in educating either the public or draftsmen or younger architects. Although Louis Sullivan chaired a WAA committee to draft a code of ethics in 1887, its members could not agree on standards of practice. The WAA architects seemed to have as little desire to legislate professional ethics as their AIA colleagues. Finally, a clique of Chicago architects dominated the WAA councils just as a few northeastern architects did the AIA leadership.[60]

It was not a complete surprise when the two organizations began contemplating a merger in 1887. The leaders of the WAA and the AIA believed success in reforming competitions and federal government work required a united professional front. Consolidation occurred two years later, with the new association adopting the older's organization's name. The AIA nearly doubled its membership to 465 with the merger. Hunt became president of the new organization, Root was named secretary, and Root and Adler were appointed to the new AIA executive board.[61]

THE AMERICAN INSTITUTE
OF ARCHITECTS AFTER 1889

Public Architecture

In 1893 the AIA finally achieved its agenda on public architecture when Congress passed legislation regulating competitions for federal buildings. Climaxing a campaign the AIA had undertaken in the 1870s, the passage owed much to the popular and critical acclaim of the Chicago World's Fair of 1893. The exposition buildings, designed on a monumental scale and integrated into a master plan, demonstrated what professional architects could accomplish. The fair architects included Daniel Burnham, Richard M. Hunt, Henry Van Brunt, George B. Post, Charles F. McKim, and Dankmar Adler, all AIA leaders. The exposition gave them clout and access to political and business leaders who promoted the AIA policy on public buildings with Congress.[62]

The Tarsney Act, the AIA bill on public architecture that Congress passed in 1893, established limited competitions for federal commissions. Institute members were to advise the Treasury secretary, the federal official responsible for all government building appropriations, and serve as competition jurors. The winning architect supervised construction and received compensation according to the institute schedule. The Supervising Architect's office, responsible for design and construction of government buildings since 1853 and derided by the AIA since the 1870s, was stripped of all powers except supervision and certification of payments.[63] But the institute's victory proved short-lived. The Tarsney Act provisions were advisory, not compulsory, and the sitting Treasury secretary refused to implement them. Not until Lyman Gage, former president of the Chicago World's Fair board of directors, became Treasury secretary were they fully applied. Gage, who knew and respected the AIA leaders because of the fair, instituted the first competitions. By 1906 over twenty-two architects from Baltimore to San Francisco had received commissions for important buildings like Cass Gilbert's New York Custom House. Some younger men like William Boring and Edward Tilton of New York, who won an early competition for the Ellis Island Immigration Center, also benefited. But winning architects often had ties to the AIA leadership who were the competition advisers. Gilbert, Boring, and Tilton had all worked in the McKim, Mead and White office.[64]

But the AIA never persuaded Congress to make the Tarsney Act provisions mandatory. Furthermore, legislators repealed the act in 1912, finding that private architects' services were too expensive. The AIA leaders countered with their own statistics vindicating private architects, but Congress reinstated the supervising architect as the government's chief designer. The stereotype of the extravagant architect, familiar on Capitol Hill since Latrobe's days, still had currency.[65]

Public commissions remained the AIA's principal concern throughout the late nineteenth and early twentieth centuries. In 1897 George B. Post, then AIA president, exhorted members to undertake "better and more important work than the regulation of institute organization . . . [and] of professional practice." He recommended they pursue "public architecture and urban planning." Less prominent architects also internalized this agenda. In an 1889 institute paper entitled "Professional Conquest," J. W. Yost of Columbus, Ohio, recommended pro bono service on advisory boards to architects because it often led to important public commissions.[66]

In 1900 AIA members held their annual convention in Washington, D.C., and resolved to lobby for a special congressional committee to plan buildings, parks, and art in "accordance with a comprehensive artistic scheme." A year later Senator James McMillan asked Burnham, McKim, and other Chicago fair artists to join his Senate Park, or McMillan, Commission. They accepted his invitation and eventually drafted a comprehensive plan for redeveloping the capital along the Beaux-Arts lines of the Court of Honor at the Chicago World's Fair.

Other institute members were advising public bodies considering similar City Beautiful plans in Baltimore, Boston, Buffalo, Chicago, Cleveland, Detroit, New Orleans, New York, Philadelphia, Saint Louis, and Saint Paul by 1904.[67] Such commissions gave architects the opportunity to display their professional expertise. President Theodore Roosevelt and other leaders of the Progressive movement believed in expert advice as a tool of reform. They saw professional advisers as well versed in balancing self-interest against community welfare, reconciling the private and public realms. Although Roosevelt did not personally care for the "very broad and entirely straight mall" the McMillan architects designed for Washington, D.C., he insisted that his secretary of agriculture defer to architectural expertise. The secretary complied and set the new agriculture building back from the McMillan architects' broad mall.[68]

Since the early nineteenth century, professional architects like Latrobe had contributed designs to fledgling educational and religious institutions. But AIA leaders, in privileging large-scale public buildings as the touchstone of professional work, served their own interests too closely. They validated only the traditional concept of architect as artist and planner on a grand scale and demeaned the modest incremental role architects might play in community welfare.[69]

Licensing Redux

Although the former WAA members pressed architectural licensing as an issue in the AIA councils, they did not convince the leadership to adopt it as a priority. But some local AIA chapters and state organizations continued to lobby for licensing. Under Dankmar Adler's direction the Chicago chapter drafted licensing bills and lobbied for their passage. Adler believed that the scale and complexity of late nineteenth-century buildings like skyscrapers made licensing imperative. He warned AIA members that unqualified architects, builders, and artisans were a menace to "the safety of life and limb and to health and finances" in an era of tall buildings. Consequently, many critics saw licensing as a boon only to architects associated with large commercial practices rather than to average practitioners.[70]

N. Clifford Ricker, dean of engineering and director of the architecture program at the University of Illinois, joined forces with Adler on licensing. They succeeded after an inexperienced architect's flawed structural design caused a fatality on a Chicago construction site. The building trade unions, as well as tradesmen, contractors, and real estate agents, now formed a coalition with architects on licensing. This broad support convinced Illinois legislators that licensing was about public safety rather than about granting a monopoly to architects, and they passed the first licensing law in 1897.[71] This law established a state board to examine architects or engineers who prepared working drawings for most kinds of construction; contractors, however, were exempted. But then only licensed practitioners could call themselves architects. Practicing architecture without a license brought fines ranging from fifty to five hundred dollars a week. Incompetence, recklessness, or dishonest practices were grounds for revocation. Licensed architects and engineers stamped all their drawings and specifications with a seal signifying liability for defective construction, injuries, and death.[72]

Adler and Ricker, who served on the first board of examiners, agreed to grandfather all architects practicing before July 1897, on the condition that they supply client testimonials and examples of two buildings erected before January 1898. Ricker later conceded this loophole allowed many incompetent architects to receive licenses. This was the price he and Adler paid for the support of prominent architects who considered any examination humiliating.[73] All other candidates had to submit evidence of their education and work. If these credentials were deemed insufficient, the candidate took a written examination on materials, construction, sanitary laws, and supervisory duties. Ricker emphasized that the examination questions tested what any architectural graduate, office apprentice, or experienced mechanic or supervisor should reasonably know. No particular form of education or training was privileged.[74] Licensing still had to skirt sensitive issues of occupational barriers and class privilege during the late nineteenth century.

After nine years of operation, the board reported that 704 licenses had been granted, 501 to grandfathered applicants and 203 to applicants who passed the examination. Ricker observed that one of licensing's most important effects ran counter to original expectations: "Country practice, excepting courthouses and large school buildings, . . . is passing into the hands of local architects instead of Chicago architects." State licensing made provincial practitioners more competitive with their urban colleagues, but only for the bread-and-butter work of architecture. High-profile commissions in the hinterlands still went to architects from major cities just as they had to the Towns, Stricklands, and Upjohns before the Civil War.[75]

Only four other states, primarily in the Far West and Southeast, where the profession was relatively young, followed Illinois's example and passed licensing laws in the early 1900s. Opponents of licensing argued that long-standing building codes and municipal building departments adequately protected the public from defective construction. They also wanted to preserve the rights of builders, mechanics, and even home owners to design and build. Many architects, for their part, still considered licensing degrading. As a young architect, Frank Lloyd Wright complained that it put him on equal footing with banana peddlers and chiropodists. AIA members agreed and voted against licensing in 1904 and 1906.[76]

Registration supplanted licensing after 1900. Fifteen states passed architectural registration laws, and even Illinois repealed its licensing act to pass a registration law. AIA members supported registration as a more dignified form of regulation. At a time when government standards had begun to regulate all aspects of American life from meatpacking to industrial trusts, registration now seemed less sinister to the public. It was still similar in operation to licensing: the state examined architects and then registered those who qualified; only documents stamped by registered practitioners (architects and engineers) were legal documents for certain kinds of construction. Today the act granting the privilege of practice is registration, while the license is a certificate or other official document indicating registration.[77]

FIGURE 2. Cover of *Architectural Sketches* by Alfred Zucker,
New York, 1894 (The Avery Architectural and Fine Arts
Library, Columbia University).

Codes of Ethics

The leaders of the AIA dragged their feet on another central issue of professionalism: a code of ethics. In fact, they seemed to take pride in their failure to enact standards of professional conduct. Richard Upjohn noted in an address of 1869 that only members' "moral relations to one another" kept their practices honorable. Twenty-five years later Daniel Burnham, then AIA president, echoed these sentiments. Since architects were gentlemen, he asserted, conscience and peer pressure were enough to ensure their honorable conduct. Typically, he associated codes of conduct with trade unions' mandatory standards.[78] If AIA leaders were complacent about ethics, many builders were critical of architects' behavior. Paul Starrett, a job superintendent for Burnham and later a general contractor himself, revealed that certain architects took advantage of builders. According to Starrett, Ernest Graham (Burnham's assistant in the 1890s) purposely misled contractors with his written specifications. They submitted low bids, won the contract, and then discovered the basis for their bids was incorrect. Then Graham held them to the contracts and bragged to clients about his tough negotiating tactics.[79]

An architect like Graham was no longer John Soane's impartial mediator between client and contractor. Frederick Baumann, a pioneer in Chicago skyscraper develop-

FIGURE 3. Cover of *Recent Buildings by Sidney A. Guttenberg, Architect*, Mount Vernon, New York, 190?
(The Avery Architectural and Fine Arts Library, Columbia University).

ment, attributed sharp dealings like Graham's specifically to large offices. He wrote that, expanding "beyond rational limits," these offices "stoop[ed] to unethical behavior to secure commissions because of their high overhead costs." Architects like Burnham, Holabird and Roche, and Stanford White who held equity positions in buildings they designed faced even stronger temptations to browbeat contractors.[80] But the AIA turned a blind eye to such questionable behavior.

When the AIA did take a stand on architects' relations with contractors in the 1890s, it condemned the practices of less prominent architects who circulated souvenir sketchbooks and monographs to prospective clients. Unlike builders' guides or house pattern books, these publications were solely advertisements for an architect's practice. Their formats ranged from paper pamphlets with crude wood engravings to hardbound volumes with embossed covers. The numerous illustrations were reproductions of renderings and photographs of completed buildings and office staffs (Figs. 2, 3, 4, and 5). The text was minimal, consisting of the architect's vita, building lists, and client testimonials. Printing and publishing houses throughout the United States specialized in producing these advertising materials for architects.

FIGURE 4. Reception room of Ferry and Clas, Milwaukee, Wisconsin, from *A Book of the Office Work of George Ferry and Alfred Clas,* 1895 (The Avery Architectural and Fine Arts Library, Columbia University).

FIGURE 5. Drafting room of Ferry and Clas, from *A Book of the Office Work of George Ferry and Alfred Clas,* 1895 (The Avery Architectural and Fine Arts Library, Columbia University).

FIGURE 6. Harvey Ellis, renderer, residence designed by Eckel and Mann in Saint Joseph, Missouri, from *Selections from an Architect's Portfolio: George R. Mann,* 1893 (The Avery Architectural and Fine Arts Library, Columbia University).

Although the architects who used souvenir sketchbooks were not nationally prominent, many were well-educated, successful architects like George R. Mann of Missouri. Trained at the Massachusetts Institute of Technology (MIT), Mann worked in the office of McKim, Mead and White in New York. But Mann moved to Missouri in search of opportunity, establishing a successful regional practice in Saint Louis and Saint Joseph, and became an AIA member. He employed as a renderer Harvey Ellis, whose work in Mann's 1893 souvenir sketchbook is exceptional. Even the advertisements in Mann's sketchbook were tastefully executed (Figs. 6 and 7).[81]

Purchased by building suppliers and contractors, advertisements underwrote the cost of producing these publications, which architects distributed free to potential clients. According to the editors of a leading construction and real estate

F I G U R E 7. Advertisement for St. Louis Cut Stone Company from *Selections from an Architect's Portfolio: George R. Mann,* 1893 (The Avery Architectural and Fine Arts Library, Columbia University).

journal, the whole system was rife with fakery and blackmail: "Every building house which furnishes so much as a nail . . . is besieged for advertisements. . . . The innuendo is that a refusal to contribute will, in the hereafter, prejudice the firm that refuses to 'stand and deliver.'"[82] In 1895 the AIA tried to address the problem, but its efforts were fumbling. It proscribed members from association with any publication containing advertisements—unintentionally including professional journals as well as promotional sketchbooks. There was no further clarification, and architects continued to publish souvenir sketchbooks with advertising well into the twentieth century.[83]

On the local level the Boston AIA chapter did enact a code of ethics in 1895, but it was not binding and had no provisions for dealing with violators. It defined the architect's rights and set out guidelines for behavior toward other architects, but it failed to mention professional responsibilities to builders, clients, or the public.[84] The AIA finally adopted a detailed code of practice in 1909. Like the Boston code,

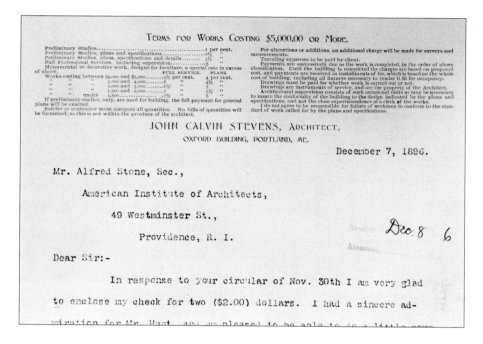

FIGURE 8. Letterhead of John Calvin Stevens, Portland, Maine, with schedule of charges, 7 December 1896 (The American Institute of Architects Archives).

it was merely advisory. The members drafted these recommendations at a time when Progressives were demanding accountability from the professions (the American Bar Association also drafted its first code of practice in 1908). In this climate the AIA code finally made reference to architects' duties to educate students, deal fairly with contractors, and safeguard public welfare. But public service was still defined as designing only large-scale buildings and comprehensive urban plans.[85] Nevertheless, the code indicated members' awareness of something beyond their own rights and privileges. But the institute was still unwilling to make its code mandatory, impinging on what it regarded as a member's private business. The architect was a self-employed gentleman, and the institute trod lightly.

The AIA's first and most important professional accomplishment was the fee schedule, which became the standard document for practice when the courts accepted it as the basis for customary charges in 1894. One member even printed the complete schedule at the top of his letterhead (Fig. 8). There were to be no misunderstandings over charges with his prospective clients. But this consuming interest in fees was unseemly in an organization that did so little for professional and public education.[86] When institute leaders from New York (McKim and Post) tried, albeit unsuccessfully, to increase the 5 percent fee in 1896, Adler disgustedly described the institute as a clique of eastern architects who wanted to pocket big fees from clients.[87] For all the AIA's talk about the professional practitioner as artist, it did very little to promote quality design for more humble work. The focus was always on large-scale commissions. The scope of architecture as an art was highly restricted.

When Alexander Jackson Davis wrote about a professional society in 1841, he was dubious about its ability to nurture architectural genius. Instead he hoped it would raise standards for all and educate the public as well as the profession. By concentrating on fee schedules and public work during its first half century, the AIA seemed obsessed with providing opportunities for only a select group of architects. It left education to other institutions that arose during the nineteenth century.

CHAPTER 3

TRAINING AND EDUCATION

*There may be good building without it [instruction], but there can be no
good architecture unless it is taught and taught well.*
William Robert Ware, An Outline of Architectural Education, 1866

During the late nineteenth century, William Robert Ware and other educators
founded the first degree programs in architecture at public and private universities.
While Ware argued that such instruction was a prerequisite for good architecture,
it was not always necessary for good building. Yet the very mechanics whom Ware
credited with creating sound building without instruction were, in fact, hungry for
knowledge. Although architectural historians have concentrated on university programs, they were, in fact, not the first institutions to offer architectural training.
Master builders and artisans were responsible for the first American organizations
and publications to provide instruction in design and construction. In early America architectural learning was first a part of artisanal culture.

ARTISANAL LEARNING

Since the origins of architectural professionalism are traditionally associated with
late nineteenth-century Beaux-Arts architects, craft training as a basis for architectural practice has never been studied. But apprenticeship to a craft like carpentry or
bricklaying was the background for many of the first professional architects in
America. Such training also affected the curricula of some of the first American architectural schools. Thus craft apprenticeship must be understood as a foundation
for early American architectural education.

   Young men entered an apprenticeship between the ages of twelve and twenty-
one. Bound or indentured to a master craftsman for a term of seven years, the apprentice was initiated into the art (special skills) and mysteries (special knowledge)

of a given trade. Although he received no wages, an apprentice was supplied with food, clothing, lodging, and (if necessary) the rudiments of reading, writing, and ciphering. Through this system adults supervised and controlled potentially idle, rebellious, and even violent male adolescents. After leaving his master, the apprentice became a journeyman who received payment for his work. An ambitious journeyman honed his skills and saved to buy tools and to set up his own workshop.[1]

Apprenticeship was a path into design and construction for both white and African American males. Slave owners like Thomas Jefferson considered craft apprenticeship a sound investment in their human property. Although slave artisans worked principally for their masters, they were also loaned or hired out. The slave master usually appropriated all of the wages his craftsman earned. Robert Jemison, an Alabama entrepreneur, operated a school for slave artisans during the antebellum period. In the 1840s Jemison emancipated Horace King, an African American designer and builder, who later specialized in covered bridges. King and other free African American artisans practiced throughout the South before and after the Civil War.[2]

Gender was more of a barrier into the building trades than race. Restrictions on women's legal status and ownership of property circumscribed their roles in the workplace. The colonial, Federal, and antebellum periods provide references to women in trades like baking and tailoring; these women were usually the widows or daughters of bakers or tailors. But I have found no evidence then of women building artisans, who appeared officially in the building trades only much later in the nineteenth century, when they began entering the workforce in unprecedented numbers. The first census to record women in the building trades was the 1890 survey, which listed 198 women carpenters and joiners and 41 women brick- and stonemasons. By the 1900 census their numbers had grown to 545 women carpenters or joiners and 167 women masons. Women of color in the building trades were counted separately in the 1900 census. There were 46 carpenters and joiners and 16 brick- and stonemasons who were African American women. One Chinese woman was either a carpenter or a joiner and one American Indian woman was a mason.[3]

Although an English statute of 1564 stipulated a seven-year term for colonial apprentices, it proved impossible to enforce because of mobility, the absence of regulatory agencies, and chronic labor shortages in the New World. American apprenticeships usually lasted only a few years. Revolutionary War ideas and experiences further eroded the master's authority over his apprentices during the late eighteenth century. Amos Lincoln, indentured at the age of fourteen to a Boston carpenter, obtained his master's permission to serve in the Revolutionary Army. After the war Lincoln, who had risen to the rank of captain, did not return to his master but opened his own workshop.[4]

Industrialization further transformed American apprenticeship. Young men went into factories, where they received little training but earned wages for even unskilled labor. Masters now had to pay something in order to compete with the factories. Indentures became informal verbal agreements; apprentices could leave, but the master could also turn them out. Such casual arrangements suited the boom and bust cycles of the antebellum economy.[5] Apprenticeship had almost completely disappeared from the industrialized cities of the North and Midwest by the late nineteenth century; it survived only in thinly populated and unindustrialized areas in the South and Southwest. An 1888 report issued by the National Association of Builders explained:

> Fifty years ago and perhaps even twenty-five years ago the employer in the building trades worked with his own hands, and . . . could give proper instruction to his apprentice. He took the boy to board in his house . . . and could control his general conduct to the end that a good mechanic should be the result. . . .
>
> Employers [today] seldom work at the trade for the reason that there is a great increase in the volume of business. . . . the time of the employer is fully occupied attending to business details and in general direction; he seldom or never takes into his own hands or remains long enough upon actual work to instruct in that practical way which was possible formerly.[6]

The master was now an employer; his former apprentice was simply an employee who learned on the building site or went elsewhere for instruction.

Drawing Schools and Builders' Guides

Drawing schools and builders' guides, alternative sources for instruction in design and construction, appeared as early as the eighteenth century. Enterprising masters like Thomas Nevell and Asher Benjamin were among the first instructors to take paying pupils. After teaching drawing privately for five years, Nevell, a master carpenter in Philadelphia, opened a school between 1771 and 1773. In an advertisement he still used the language of apprenticeship and indentures, promising to teach "the art of architecture, . . . so necessary a mystery to the carpenter's business." Nevell's course of study included "the right use and construction of lines for the formation of regular or irregular arches, groins for vaults or ceilings, . . . the most expeditious and approved method of diminishing columns and pilasters; [and] the readiest rule for laying out the flutes and fillets." Claiming that his two-month course was suitable for anyone of "common capacity," he taught three sessions between 1771 and 1773 before the Revolutionary War forced him to close the school.[7] In an 1801 advertisement Asher Benjamin, then a New England carpenter, offered instruction in "the art of drawing plans and elevations [and] any other figure perspectively" to "young carpenters, joiners, and all others concerned in the art of Building." The design and construction of "the five orders of architecture, proportions of doors, windows, and chimneypieces, construction of stairs, methods of framing timbers; tracing of groins to angle brackets, circular soffits in circular walls; plans, elevations and sections of Houses with all ornament" were other subjects of study.[8] Nevell and Benjamin were not unique. Louise Hall, who studied early American artisans, found newspaper announcements for drawing classes as early as 1735.[9]

Changes in American design and construction as well as apprenticeship created a demand for courses like Nevell's and Benjamin's during the late eighteenth and early nineteenth centuries. In a 1773 advertisement William Williams, a Philadelphia master carpenter, assured prospective clients that he designed "in a new, bold, light and elegant taste" popularized by English neoclassical architects like Robert Adam.[10] Designers, builders, and artisans wanted to design and build new features like vaulted interiors, slimly proportioned classical orders, circular staircases, and round and oval room plans. Written instructions and references to existing buildings, the traditional means to convey design ideas, were inadequate guides for artisans working in unfamiliar styles like neoclassicism. Drawings became increasingly necessary. Immigrant architects like Stephen Hallet and John Haviland taught drawing to both artisans and amateurs, stressing their knowledge of modern European styles in newspaper announcements.[11]

Some master artisans like Theophilus Burr, a Boston housewright in the early 1800s, had no interest in the new styles. He was "content to be old-fashioned" and indisposed to "look with favor upon those constantly seeking after 'some new thing.'"[12] Others, like John Holden Greene, a prominent Providence, Rhode Island, designer and builder, were probably too preoccupied with business, which in Greene's case also included real estate and a manufactory for prefabricated ornament. Thus Hiram Hill, Greene's apprentice for four years in the early 1820s, wrote that while his master trained him to be a "good workman and capable of doing almost any kind of carpenter's work," he also attended evening classes during his apprenticeship. These studies gave him, Hill wrote in his diary, "a considerable proficiency in architectural skill," including a knowledge of drafting, classical orders, and "the theory of circular stair building."[13] Designing these intricately framed staircases, one architect later recalled, "was thought at the time a great achievement and every young architect had to be able to lay out the requisite geometrical lines and intersections from which to build a flight of circular stairs."[14] Hill's evening classes gave him a competitive edge that Greene could not provide.

Publications with basic and advanced instruction in drafting, design, and construction also became available in the late eighteenth century. Asher Benjamin was the first American to publish one of these so-called builders' guides, *The Country Builder's Assistant,* in 1797. Information on drafting, descriptive geometry, materials, structure, the classical orders, ornament, and scaled designs of houses, schools, and churches was all gathered under the rubric of science, with its overtones of accessible learning.[15] Benjamin used the patriotic- and egalitarian-sounding title *The American Builder's Companion* for his second builders' guide of 1806. In the preface to *The Rudiments of Architecture* (1814), his third publication, Benjamin explained that his "treatise on architecture, fully explaining the rudiments of the art," was so inexpensive that it was "within reach of every apprentice." *The Elements of Architecture* (1843), his final book, reiterated the republican ideal of architectural science "which all may read and understand without the aid of an instructor."[16]

The republican overtones of Benjamin's writings were not unique. Edward Shaw entitled his 1855 book *The Modern Architect or Every Carpenter His Own Master* and described his audience as "every mechanic . . . who may have a desire to become his own master."[17] The builders' guides not only informed mechanic-readers but also empowered and liberated them. Knowledge purportedly led to economic and social mobility in nineteenth-century America. Self-help books proliferated in other crafts and trades during the late eighteenth and early nineteenth centuries: Oliver Evans, *The Young Mill Wright and Miller's Guide* (1795), William Lapsley, *The Taylor's Instructor* (1809), Cornelius S. Van Winkle, *The Printer's Guide* (1818), and Cornelius Molony, *The Practical Dyer* (1833).[18]

The genre of builders' guides evolved into elaborate home study courses in the late nineteenth century. *The American Architect and Building News,* a professional journal founded in 1876, published long-running series on drafting, architectural history, sanitation, office management, and building law.[19] The International Correspondence School Company in Scranton, Pennsylvania, offered an eight-volume architectural course and self-administered examinations in 1899. Architectural educators and experts like William Robert Ware of Columbia University contributed to a curriculum that covered drawing, mathematics, geometry, architectural history and ornament, heating and ventilation, estimating, contracts, specifications, and superintendence. Students who passed the examinations were issued a certificate. The Scranton school also published editions of Ware's *American Vignola* (1902–6), a guide to designing classical architecture.[20] During the late nineteenth century, the first women artisans may have learned from these textbooks and correspondence school courses.

Mechanics' Institutes

Mechanics' institutes, like craft apprenticeship, have not previously figured in the history of American architecture. But they, too, offered training in architectural drafting, design, and history during the nineteenth century. Educating the scientific artisan became the mission of these organizations established in the United States and Great Britain during the first half of the nineteenth century. The New York Mechanic and Scientific Institute was formed in 1822. Two years later the Franklin Institute, named after Benjamin Franklin, the most famous of all American apprentices, was established in Philadelphia. Mechanics' institutes appeared in Glasgow and London in 1823 and 1824, respectively. Governing boards in the United States commissioned imposing institute buildings from prominent architects like John Haviland, who designed the Franklin Institute, and Alexander Jackson Davis, who designed Mechanics' Hall in Newark, New Jersey.[21]

These mechanics' organizations were neither protectionist guilds for masters like the Philadelphia Carpenters' Company nor welfare organizations like the Massachusetts Charitable Mechanics Association. Mechanics' institutes were centers for lectures, evening classes, libraries, drawing and model collections, and trade exhibitions. Their programs were either free or, as one magazine noted, "at a charge within the reach of his [the mechanic's] income."[22]

Practical subjects like mathematics, chemistry, machinery, and drafting were offered. But lectures on poetry, language, and literature were also popular at some American and English institutes. Charles Quill, who wrote *The American Mechanic* (1838) for young working men, argued, "There are other and higher purposes to which hours may be devoted than the earning of so many dollars and cents . . . Who shall say that the poorest journeyman may not reach forth his hand in the garden of the muses?"[23] Yet Quill also emphasized that institutes educated a scientific mechanic who "has knowledge; he learns to investigate; he applies a little science to his work, and he becomes a discoverer. His methods are the fruit of reflection and they save labor, time, materials and money." Such a mechanic was not an imitator, "who turns out good work, but precisely as his old master did fifty years ago." The scientific mechanic had principles, exercised reason, and made improvements.[24]

Some early professional architects taught at the mechanics' institutes. William Strickland, the first professor of architecture at the Franklin Institute in 1824, presented a weekly series of evening lectures during the 1824–25 terms. John Haviland was appointed professor of drawing there in 1824 and taught until the end of the decade. The Franklin Institute offered several programs in drawing: architectural drawing, mechanical drafting, lettering, and landscape and ornamental drawing. Fifty students enrolled during the first year, and demand continued to grow throughout the nineteenth century. Thomas U. Walter studied architectural drawing with Haviland at the Franklin Institute, then went into Strickland's office for further study. After he established his own architectural career, Walter returned to the institute as a professor of architecture.[25]

Although the Franklin Institute charged tuition, many institutes like the New York Society of Mechanics sponsored free evening classes for apprentices and journeymen. The courses in New York included freehand sketching, architectural drawing, mechanical drafting, and ornamental modeling. These classes met four times a week for seven months. Before there were public libraries, the mechanics' institutes made collections of books, drawings, and prints available to workingmen; in 1823 the New York society had a collection of five thousand volumes.[26]

In the decades before the Civil War, mechanics' institutes were part of the paradoxical culture of populism and republicanism. Belief in social and economic mobility was a central tenet of republican America. Some mechanics like Thomas U. Walter did succeed; his Franklin Institute courses and contacts certainly played a part in his ascent. The rhetoric of antebellum America extolled men like Walter as "enlightened, respectable and useful citizens" whom the mechanics' institutes saved from "intellectual and political slavery" to the upper classes. Yet Walter was "saved" because he left the manual trades behind and became a professional.[27] Furthermore, mechanics' institutes were a way to control and order working-class life. Master artisans' preoccupation with business and the end of formal indentures meant that organizations like the mechanics' institutes had to socialize as well as educate apprentices and journeymen. A reader of *Mechanics' Magazine* praised the institute classes, lectures, and libraries because they kept workingmen away from "the vices and temptations of a large city." Labor unions and job actions were just as threatening to some Americans as saloons, whorehouses, and gambling dens. Charles Quill advised his artisan readers to avoid "the entangling alliances" of labor unions and instead join a mechanics' institute or lyceum.[28]

The popularity of mechanics' institutes endured beyond the antebellum period into the late nineteenth century. The Franklin Institute continued to offer classes and other educational programs after the Civil War. But to survive, it and other mechanics' institutes now emphasized general-interest lectures and courses for middle-class audiences of both sexes. The institutes' commitment to the working classes began to wane. Late nineteenth-century organizations like the Young Men's Christian Association, settlement houses, public high schools, and proprietary trade schools took over the practical curricula of the mechanics' institutes. They offered working-class students foundation courses in drafting, mathematics, design, and construction into the twentieth century. Again these late nineteenth-century schools may have educated women artisans. Yet the prospects of these students' becoming a latter-day Thomas U. Walter were virtually nonexistent. These courses no longer commanded respect in professional circles like the AIA, and professional leaders no longer taught in these organizations.[29] Other kinds of training for aspiring architects displaced them.

Office Training

As craft apprenticeship waned, assisting an established architect became the accepted path into the profession after the Civil War, and was the common bond shared by prominent and lesser architects. Study with a practitioner was the traditional way of preparing for the professions of law and medicine in England and the American colonies. The student paid a pupilage fee for office instruction with prominent and well-educated practitioners commanding the highest fees. Such arrangements, like those for apprenticeship, were more casual in the United States. Harold van Buren Magonigle, who was only fourteen when he studied in Calvert Vaux's office in 1881, recalled: "I was entered as a 'student' which meant that I got no pay and was able to be snooty to friends who were mere office boys. I wasn't articled, paid no fee and didn't live in the mahster's [sic] house. . . . I was not supposed to work on office work except for my education."[30]

Magonigle's situation was not unusual; architectural students usually did not pay pupilage fees in the United States. Apparently Latrobe did not charge students he took into his office, nor did he indenture them as apprentices. Instead, they were assistants as well as students. Although Latrobe claimed to receive two hundred guineas from a prospective student, he waived this fee if the boy proved to be talented and of good character, but his students usually received no compensation during the first or second year. After they learned enough to be useful in preparing materials, copying and making drawings, and assisting with land surveying and site supervision, Latrobe purportedly paid them an annual salary of as much as one hundred dollars.[31] Seven men are known to have studied with Latrobe, remaining with him for periods ranging from one to five years. Strickland and Mills stayed the longest and became the most renowned architects to "graduate" from Latrobe's office. Whereas Strickland began his study when he was only an adolescent, Mills was twenty-two.[32]

Writing to Mills in 1804, Latrobe explained that what a pupil studied depended on the architect's commitments and the office schedule: "Winter is the best season for studying the theory as summer is to attend to the practice of our profession, and as I shall spend most of my time for the next four months in the office, you will perhaps not find that period uselessly or unpleasantly spent with me."[33] There were more mundane tasks like cleaning the office and running errands, but as an assistant grew more proficient and experienced, he received, as noted previously, more challenging assignments. Mills took the first steps to independent practice while still in the office. Latrobe arranged for him to serve as clerk of the works for his Bank of Philadelphia. He also allowed Mills to accept private work and helped the younger man with his designs and client negotiations.[34]

Assistants like Mills were a source of abundant and cheap labor for both Latrobe and his clients. Latrobe negotiated a salary for Mills to superintend construction on the Bank of Philadelphia. He later bragged to the bank directors that Mills's salary was $150 less than what his superintendent was paid at the earlier Bank of Pennsylvania. But the architect believed he had served Mills's interests well. The younger man wanted the experience and did not need the money, in Latrobe's opinion, to live on. When Latrobe began rebuilding the Capitol, burned during the War of 1812, he realized just how necessary his student assistants were. It was now very difficult to produce the sketches, drawings, and detailed estimates because Latrobe had only one assistant in his office in 1814.[35]

Latrobe's students, for their part, had differing views of their experiences with him. Mills praised him as the teacher who had freed him from "the shackles of ignorance, [that] habits of education and prejudice" had imposed. Strickland's experience with Latrobe was decidedly less positive.[36] While Mills was a student who came into the office with prior training and experience, Strickland was a green apprentice. According to Latrobe, Mrs. Strickland complained that he "cruelly ill treated" her son. The architect refused to buy William a winter coat and shoes and gave him only menial tasks like washing out the watercolor plates, leading Strickland's parents to abruptly remove their son from Latrobe's charge.[37]

Years later Strickland provided his own account: "I dusted the portfolios, washed the brushes and looked around for a chance of promotion—at length *ground plans* were given me to copy. The study of architectural style and history took place "at night [when] I copied the engraved plates and read the letter press of [James] Stuart's Athens, Ionian Antiquities, etc; and [I] was soon enabled by contrasting these works with Batty Langley, [Abraham] Swan . . . to discover the graceful forms of Grecian architecture." Nevertheless, Strickland became "acquainted with the use of tools in my father's shop," while he was in Latrobe's office.[38] After seeing Latrobe's professional and financial difficulties for himself, the boy and his father undoubtedly decided it prudent to master carpentry as well as architecture.

Summing up his studies, Strickland wrote: "I came out of Latrobe's office at the age of 19 years pretty well stocked with a knowledge of drawing *plans, elevations and Sections,* but rather scantily supplied with mathematics; this branch of science I soon found to be indispensable to my further progress in the practice of architecture." He corrected this deficiency with his next employer, a Philadelphia surveyor and street regulator. While laying out the "lines of streets, lanes and alleys," Strickland found that he "had an excellent opportunity to study Geometry, Algebra, and apply the results." [39]

In both offices Strickland learned principally what the work in the office required. Anything else he had to learn by himself. He claimed, for example, that he taught himself perspective by studying Dr. Brook Taylor's *New Principles of Linear Perspective of the Art of Designing on a Plane.*[40] While Latrobe may have taught him little about mathematics, it seems incredible that Strickland, whom Latrobe deemed "an excellent draftsman," learned nothing from his first master's considerable gifts as a perspectivist. But Latrobe may have seen the young Strickland as only a copyist. There was no reason or time to instruct such a young boy in the intricacies of perspective views.[41] Latrobe needed construction documents, not perspectives, from his assistants.

Although Latrobe did not charge his students, some architects did collect fees for instruction. When Ithiel Town and Alexander Jackson Davis formed their first partnership in 1829, Davis announced that he would, "if desired, give instructions on drawing, perspective and architecture." A month later his first pupil arrived. According to diary entries, Davis accepted seventeen pupils, from as far away as Rhode Island and Louisiana, between 1829 and 1861. Their terms of study varied between two months and one year, and their pupilage fees ranged from ten to two hundred dollars.[42]

John Stirewalt came from North Carolina in 1832 to study with Davis. In the opinion of Patrick Snadon, a Davis scholar, Stirewalt drew and "improved" designs for existing buildings already drawn by Davis.[43] Although no sketches survive, perhaps Davis sent his student out into the streets to study and draw real buildings as well.

Town must have taught, too. In a second partnership agreement drafted in 1842, the two men divided the student fees, with Town receiving one-third and Davis two-thirds of the proceeds. When they first formed an association in 1829, it was, as Davis scholar Jane B. Davies notes, an extraordinary opportunity for a newcomer like Davis as well as his students. Town was an established figure in the Greek Revival and Gothic Revival and an inventor who designed a wooden lattice truss widely used in covered bridge construction. Apart from Town's knowledge and experience, his library, numbering many thousands of volumes, was available to the students.[44]

There were indentured apprentices as well as paying students in Town and Davis's office. Since both partners emerged from the artisanal world, they continued the tradition of apprenticeship in their office. Surviving indentures for two young men show that they received no wages during the first two years in the office. Thereafter they were paid a salary, beginning at a rate of one hundred dollars, with increments for each additional year they remained. While Town and Davis paid a draftsman six hundred dollars annually in the 1830s, an apprentice earned only two to three hundred dollars after five years. Under the indenture terms Town and Davis were not surrogate fathers; they supervised the apprentices only during office hours.[45]

By the 1850s and 1860s architects who had been formally educated began to accept pupils in their offices. Richard M. Hunt, the first American architect to study at the Ecole des Beaux-Arts, was perhaps the most renowned teacher. Hunt accepted his first students in 1857, only two years after his return from Paris. His students included Frank Furness, Charles Gambrill, George B. Post, Henry Van Brunt, and William Robert Ware, generally older men with university degrees, engineering training, or prior office experience. They paid him a fee and occasionally assisted with office work.[46] Hunt first taught in his rooms at the University Building on Washington Square. In 1858 the atelier moved to the Studio Building, designed by Hunt as living, working, and exhibition space for artists. There the students, Furness recalled, worked in a large room surrounded by Hunt's collection of casts, engravings, drawings, books, and objets d'art (Fig. 9).

Hunt deliberately separated his teaching studio from his office. Dismayed by the usual office training that reduced students, in his opinion, to drafting machines for working drawings, Hunt tried to re-create the Paris studio where he had studied. The Ecole ateliers, he emphasized, taught the student to compose as soon as he drew a line: "The day he enters they give him a simple problem to do and let him work it out alone. That exercises his mind. And then the professor corrects the work . . . in that way they teach him to cultivate his imagination from the very start."[47] Hunt was the atelier *patron,* a practicing architect who taught his students by criticizing their design problems.

Besides a study of the classical orders, Furness said Hunt gave his students a design problem, which they first sketched and then developed into more detailed and elaborate drawings over the course of a month. Hunt commented on their designs, Furness recalled, "with a critical bludgeon, with now and then between the blows a very small dose of praise." He once devastated William Robert Ware by calling his

design for a fountain a washtub. Yet he then showed Ware "how it should be done" and rekindled the young man's enthusiasm for the project.[48]

But Hunt's most important lesson was, in Furness's opinion, to "draw, draw, draw, sketch, sketch, sketch . . . it doesn't matter [what], it will ultimately give you a control of your pencil that you can the more readily express on paper your thoughts in designing." Hunt believed that "the greater facility you have in expressing these thoughts the freer and better your design will be."[49] Van Brunt's sketchbooks indicate that the students drew from the engravings in Hunt's library (Fig. 10). They also studied Hunt's Ecole projects and the sketchbooks he had kept while traveling in Europe, the Middle East, and Egypt.

FIGURE 10. Henry Van Brunt, sketch of Order of the Court of Lions, Alhambra, ca. 1858 (The Avery Architectural and Fine Arts Library, Columbia University).

Hunt had no patience with the midcentury battle between classical and medieval revival styles. "Our experience was a liberal education in the fullest sense," Van Brunt later recalled. "We left him [Hunt] with our imaginations no longer sterilized by prejudice and partisanship, but enlightened by his influence." He made them, Ware believed, missionaries for architecture who were taught "to hand along to others the light that we were receiving." [50]

Chicago architects also offered office training. William LeBaron Jenney was a renowned teacher in the Midwest. He too had trained in Paris, but he had studied engineering at the Ecole Centrale des Arts et des Manufactures rather than architecture at the Ecole des Beaux-Arts. Jenney was one of the few formally educated architects to practice in Chicago before the great fire of 1871. His students included Daniel H. Burnham, William Holabird, Martin Roche, Normand S. Patton, and H. Van Doren Shaw.[51] His formal lessons seemed rudimentary, rather like those of a builders' guide: "I taught them to look over the illustrated books and study the different styles until they could easily distinguish one from the other," Jenney later wrote, "then to study and draw out the several orders until they were sure not to mingle them in their work." Although Jenney claimed that his instruction was like that of the Paris ateliers and referred to his office as his studio, there is no indication that he gave his students monthly design problems. Nor did he segregate them from his office as Hunt did. While Jenney's students paid no fees, they "earn[ed] their keep" by doing office work.[52]

Office instruction was often variable and haphazard. Dankmar Adler, who described such training as "graduating from the drawing board," learned from an assistant, not the principal architect, in the Detroit office where he was a student. This man taught him, Adler later recalled, "a systematic study of architectural history and of the philosophy of architectural design" and techniques for "rendering drawings and watercolors."[53] Harold van Buren Magonigle, a student in the Vaux office, was not so lucky. Although Downing Vaux showed him how to "grind India ink . . . and how to use a ruling pen and trace a drawing in ink on tracing paper," Magonigle enrolled in an evening class at Cooper Union to learn more about architectural drawing.[54] What Vaux taught him was only what Magonigle needed to help with working drawings. Even self-study in an office could be hard. "The poverty of the [Vaux] office library," Magonigle remembered, "was amazing." Many Boston architects, Henry Van Brunt recalled, regarded their drawings as "personal secrets" and "concealed [them] . . . from the rest as if they were the pages of a private diary. Even books and prints were carefully secluded from inspection by any rival. Pupils, . . . as in my own case, often looked with eager and unsatisfied eyes through the glass of their master's locked bookcases."[55]

This was exactly why, in Charles Babcock's opinion, office training was a "deplorably bad system." Babcock, who trained in Richard Upjohn's office, felt that a student "rarely learns more than drawing and construction" in an office because his master is "too much absorbed in his professional work to attend thoroughly to the education of his students." Anything that pertained to taste, design principles, and architectural history the student, he continued, had to learn in "his leisure hours . . . without guidance or direction."[56] Nevertheless, architects like Dankmar Adler, Stanford White, and Bertram G. Goodhue were among the more prominent graduates of the drawing board. It was a system that served the interests of both architect and student. The former got cheap labor and occasionally pupilage fees; the latter received firsthand experience and often wages while he learned.

University Programs in Architecture

Charles Babcock was critical of office training, and he did something about it. He returned to architecture, after leaving it for the Episcopal clergy, and became the first director of the Cornell architectural program in 1871. His program and William

Robert Ware's at MIT, established in 1868, provided the first systematic courses in architectural study at American universities. Both Babcock and Ware believed that university training objectified the distinctions that early professionals had unsuccessfully drawn between architects and builders.[57] Academic credentials also bestowed social status. As Thomas Davidson, a nineteenth-century educator and philosopher, observed, "Whatever is taught in school will soon become respectable and gentlemanly." If architects studied at universities, then young men would not have to argue with their fathers, as the Washington, D.C., architect Glenn Brown did in the 1870s, that an architectural career was suitable for a gentleman. As William Robert Ware later wrote, his goal as a university educator was to train "a body of generously educated architects, gentlemen, and scholars."[58]

But educators believed that university training had implications for the design of contemporary American architecture. It tamed what Ware described as the "chaos" of styles in nineteenth-century American architecture.[59] American degree programs, like the old royal academies of art, could establish uniform artistic standards by rewarding or rebuking future practitioners. Ware's faith that education could create and disseminate a national style of architecture was boundless and rather naive. Stylistic uniformity was elusive even in nineteenth-century France, where established institutions like the Ecole des Beaux-Arts, the Académie des Beaux-Arts, and the Conseil des Bâtiments Civils wove together architectural education and practice.[60] The first academic programs—at MIT, Columbia, Cornell, the University of Illinois, and Tuskegee Institute—would be just as diverse and eclectic as the chaotic American architecture that Ware so deplored.

Ware's dream of order and uniformity was widespread in the professional community. One of the first architectural schools proposed in America was more inclusive and comprehensive than the Ecole des Beaux-Arts. In 1867 AIA members endorsed the idea of a "grand central school of architecture," an amalgamation of American and British mechanics' institutes, central European polytechnical institutes, and the Ecole des Beaux-Arts. The AIA school was to consist of evening classes in drawing, modeling, and construction for building mechanics; a three-year technical curriculum of drawing, mechanics, astronomy, construction, and civil engineering; and a two-year academic program of drawing, aesthetics, and the history of art and architecture. These three programs represented the collective training of the AIA membership in 1867.[61] Educating everyone involved in design and construction, the proposed school put the architectural profession at the center of the building process. The "grand central school of architecture" prepared and conditioned mechanics, builders, and engineers to work under the architect's direction;

it institutionalized the professional ideal of architect as head and authority. While the school was open to all, it was a hierarchical institution, with architecture privileged as the only academic course of study.[62]

The AIA, not surprisingly, never secured the funds for this ambitious "grand school." Instead its members decided to support Ware's MIT program, just then getting under way.[63] The AIA vision, moreover, of placing architecture at the center of the curriculum did not materialize at any of the early university programs. Architecture was taught within the context of engineering or industrial arts programs at MIT, Cornell University, the University of Illinois, Columbia University, and Tuskegee Institute. It deferred to practical building concerns in the academy just as it did in the real world.[64]

Engineering, unlike architecture, had been formally taught since the early nineteenth century. Considered a part of military training, it was taught at West Point beginning in 1816. But it was soon recognized as integral to private economic development as well; canals, bridges, turnpikes, and then railroads were needed to transport both agricultural and manufactured goods. Schools like Rensselaer Polytechnic Institute taught the theory and methods of experimentation required to design and build an infrastructure for the public and private sectors.[65]

Congress gave further encouragement to engineering programs with the passage of the land-grant act in 1862. Proceeds from the sale of federal lands were set aside for the establishment of agricultural and mechanical arts institutions. The first architectural programs—MIT (1868), Cornell University (1871), and the University of Illinois (1873)—were all established at land-grant institutions. Tuskegee Institute, a historically black college and university, also received funds under the second land-grant act in the 1890s. Columbia, a private institution, founded its program as part of the School of Mines in 1881. Architecture, administrators at these institutions reasoned, could share faculty, facilities, and courses with existing engineering schools. Two programs could be economically created from just one course of study.[66]

William Robert Ware was the father of American architectural education. He opened the MIT program in 1868 and then created the Columbia course thirteen years later, remaining there until his retirement in 1903.[67] Before entering Richard M. Hunt's atelier, Ware had received a liberal arts degree from Harvard and then studied engineering at the Harvard Lawrence Scientific School. When he and Henry Van Brunt opened a Boston office in the 1860s, they formed an atelier like Hunt's for students. Thus Ware was well qualified for his position at MIT. Nevertheless, he insisted on traveling abroad between 1866 and 1867, enrolling briefly in an Ecole atelier, visiting the Kensington Museum design program in London, and purchasing books, prints, casts, and photographs for the MIT collection. Ware's first architectural students arrived in 1868.[68]

His experiences with Hunt and in Paris profoundly affected the programs at both MIT and Columbia. The Beaux-Arts method of working a design up from a sketch of the *parti,* the basic concept, became key for him. This process, Ware wrote in an 1865 letter, "encourage[d] a habit for simplicity and frankness, . . . a habit of working up from the requirements of the problem to the *ensemble* and thence to the detail, and not vice versa." Designing from the *parti,* Ware continued, "would put new character and expression into our building, and could not fail to provide the only originality of style that is possible and desirable."[69] In 1872 Ware hired Eugène Létang, a Frenchman and former student in Emile Vaudremer's atelier, to teach at MIT. According to William Rotch Ware, William Robert's nephew and an MIT student, Létang's constant cry was "Oh simplifiez ça," as he "wean[ed] them away from the worship of the false god of American designers—overelaboration."[70]

While design was a key element, Ware believed his first-year students were too immature and inexperienced to begin studio work. He and his fellow students in the Hunt atelier had all been older and experienced when they first tackled design problems. Thus Ware required lectures and recitations in English literature and composition, mathematics, science, and modern languages during the first year of study at both MIT and Columbia. After this liberal arts training, he introduced the classical orders in drawing, theory, and history classes during the second year. Every student owned a copy of Vignola's *Rules of the Five Orders of Architecture* (1564). While MIT students took design studio in the second term of their second year, Columbia students, who were generally younger, were ready only by the third year.[71]

Ware came to the conclusion that the Ecole system, emphasizing only "artistic training [and] the development of the powers of design," was inappropriate for educating men with "intellectual character and professional culture . . . and broad education."[72] Lectures in structure, materials, design theory, and architectural history that Ware considered fundamental were never required for Ecole students. Furthermore, there was no general training in the arts and sciences at the Ecole, where the focus of training was the design studio.[73] It was, Ware wrote, the "ideal development of the apprenticeship system" where the "newcomer is thrown in among his elders and betters to pick-up what he can, as fast as he can."[74] While the Ecole educated a handful of architects who would ultimately design monumental buildings for the French state, it primarily produced superb draftsmen for the government architectural bureaucracy. Furthermore, Ecole students knew little about designing and erecting the modest building types required to sustain most American architectural practices. "The architecture it teaches," Ware wrote, "is largely an architecture of paper and pencil."[75] At MIT and then Columbia he struggled to combine a polytechnical curriculum and a liberal arts education with the Ecole design studio in only four years. Ware's goal seemed a synthesis of his own training—Harvard College, the Lawrence Scientific School, and Hunt's atelier—into a single university program.

Charles Babcock, like Ware, institutionalized his own experiences in the Cornell program. Although Babcock later condemned office training, the medieval revival styles and attention to craftsmanship and construction he learned in Upjohn's office profoundly affected his teaching.[76] The views of architecture and practice Babcock brought to the Cornell program were formed twenty years earlier in Upjohn's mid-century office. Like Ware at MIT and Columbia, Babcock was, in essence, the Cornell architectural program. He was the only instructor until 1880 and served as director until his retirement in 1897.[77]

As American architects grew fascinated with classical and Renaissance styles, Babcock still stressed medievalism and architectural craft, which he had learned from Upjohn. Although he included Renaissance examples in his history lectures, he taught that Gothic was the apex of architectural creativity. Babcock encouraged his students to learn French so they could read Viollet-le-Duc, French champion of medieval structure and architecture, in the original.[78] Medievalism permeated the design studios, as seen in published examples of Cornell student work, all done in Victorian Gothic—then a waning, if not dead, style in major American cities.[79]

Like Ware, Babcock devoted the first year to general studies. Drawing was the only instruction related to architecture for first-year students. Second-year students dealt with building materials, mechanics, heating, and construction. "Before the architect can become a true artist," Babcock wrote, "he must master the art of building." This did not mean training in the building crafts, he continued, but learning "how to design good masonry and good carpentry and be able to pass judgment on completed work." There was no shop work at Cornell, but students visited building sites.[80] Design, which Babcock believed was fundamentally impossible to teach, was postponed until the third year of the four-year program. He and Ware shared a skepticism about the bravura drafting skills of the Ecole. The best designer, Babcock wrote, was too "intent upon expressing an idea . . . [to] stop to refine his means of expression."[81]

A basic pragmatism lay at the core of Babcock's curriculum, distinguishing it from Ware's programs. A Cornell graduate was not Ware's gentleman or scholar but still the antebellum "man of science" and "master of the art of building" who could "at once get employment." After learning the business of architecture in an office for two or three years, a Cornell student established his own practice. Professional independence was Babcock's goal.[82]

The University of Illinois program, like those at MIT, Cornell, and Columbia, was essentially the work of one man, N. Clifford Ricker. He was first a student at Illinois, like MIT and Cornell a land-grant institution, taking architectural drafting, descriptive geometry, and projection drawing in the engineering curriculum. Since there was no architectural course of study in 1869, Ricker devised his own and became the first graduate of an American architectural program in 1873. He was then asked to teach and become director of the program.[83] Ricker was the sole architectural instructor until 1885 and taught until his retirement in 1915. Because Illinois was the only architectural program outside of the Northeast until 1889, Ricker's impact was enormous. By 1900 he had reputedly taught one-quarter of all American architectural students.[84]

Ricker's background, which encompassed artisanal training, office experience, university education, and travel abroad, was the most diverse of all the early architectural educators. His personal history is surely one of the most spectacular but last ascents of an ambitious and enterprising "scientific mechanic" in nineteenth-century American architecture. After working in his father's New England shingle mill, Ricker became a partner in an Illinois wagon and blacksmith shop. He then studied in the Chicago office of J. W. Roberts, a former Upjohn student. After earning his Illinois degree, Ricker, like Ware, traveled abroad. His itinerary was rather different, including London and Paris but also Vienna and Berlin. The international exposition in Vienna especially interested him, as did the Bauakademie in Berlin.[85]

Architectural history was important to Ricker just as it was to Ware and Babcock. He always taught the history courses at Illinois himself and prepared illustrated lecture notes for his students. While Ware was wedded to Vignola and the classical orders and Babcock to Viollet-le-Duc and medievalism, Ricker stressed the standard German texts. Although he did translate Viollet's writings for his students, he also gave them Rudolf Redtenacher's *Architektonik* (1883) and later Otto Wagner's *Moderne Architektur* (1895).[86]

Germanic influences pervaded other aspects of Ricker's curriculum. The sequence of courses at Illinois was similar to the architectural curricula at the central European polytechnical institutes. His midwestern students and their employers, Ricker believed, wanted "scientific principles applied to building," so mathematics, science, materials, construction, and sanitary engineering were taught in the first and second years. Ricker delayed drawing classes until the second year and design studio until the final year of the four-year Illinois program.[87]

Unlike either Ware or Babcock, Ricker was intent on synthesizing architecture and engineering. His program alone thoroughly integrated architecture into the engineering department. Graphic statics, a method for solving structural problems, was first taught in the United States at Illinois in 1875. Ricker instituted the first program in architectural engineering at an American university in 1890. Given his own background and the prominence of architects with German roots like Dankmar Adler and Frederick Baumann in Chicago, Ricker's interest in central European precedents is understandable. The merger of the Berlin academies of architecture and engineering into a single technical college in 1879 surely influenced Ricker's thinking about the Illinois program.[88]

As a former artisan himself, Ricker believed that manual training provided the basis for architectural learning. Thus shop practice was an essential part of the Illinois program. Students enrolled in three different workshops (carpentry and joinery, cabinetmaking, and scaled models) during their first year. The Russian imperial system of vocational training, exhibited in Vienna while Ricker was there in 1873, inspired the Illinois workshops. They were the first American example of the Russian system of drawing and models.[89] Yet Ricker insisted his students needed theoretical understanding of materials and construction as well as workshop experience. The program offered theory courses in timber, brick, stone, iron, steel, tile, and terracotta during the second year. All this recalled the early nineteenth-century emphasis on the "scientific mechanic" who combined theory and practice. Ricker even included a section on stair building, the antebellum building mechanic's litmus test of ability, in his construction theory course.[90]

Illinois students waited longer than their MIT, Cornell, and Columbia counterparts to enter the design studio. During their fourth and final year, Ricker eased them into studio with exercises in designing a building detail and then a small building. A complete set of working drawings and specifications for the building were also required. He stressed real-life problems in his studio assignments rather than the monumental public buildings associated with Ecole programs. Thus the student works chosen to illustrate the 1888 *American Architect* article on Illinois were an iron railing and a water tower.

Ricker, like Babcock, was intent on preparing his students for the realities of architectural practice. He openly admitted that he slighted the "aesthetical side" in favor of "the practical and scientific" in order to "send out graduates [as] well fitted for office work" as any school could equip them.[91] Unlike Babcock, however, Ricker moved beyond his personal experience in building craft and office work. The Illinois engineering department and his own interests in central European polytechnical education and Russian shop helped him shape a new field: architectural engineering. While he did not neglect design and architectural theory and history, he placed the study of materials, structure, and construction at the center of his curriculum. Ricker shaped the perfect school for the Chicago architectural offices and general contracting firms involved with skyscrapers and other commercial building types in the late nineteenth and early twentieth centuries.

Ricker simulated the experiences of the workshop and office at Illinois. Yet he, along with Ware and Babcock, strongly advised students to complete their education by working in offices over school vacations. But African American architects trained at Tuskegee Institute in Alabama never had to leave the campus to experience the architectural office and construction site. From 1881 until 1901 students there worked on almost forty campus buildings. The Tuskegee architectural faculty designed the buildings and landscaped the grounds of the campus and Greenwood, an adjacent two-hundred-acre planned community.[92] Babcock and Ricker had designed several campus buildings (Babcock did six buildings at Cornell and Ricker five at Illinois), but their commissions were limited in comparison with the work created by Tuskegee faculty members. Furthermore, Babcock's and Ricker's campus works never became an integral part of the architectural curriculum as they did at Tuskegee.[93] The Tuskegee educational programs and campus buildings exemplified the philosophy of self-help and self-sufficiency espoused by the school's founder, Booker T. Washington. Tuskegee, founded in 1881, stressed learning by doing as well as studying. Students raised their food on the campus model farm, made bricks at the campus brick kiln, helped with campus housekeeping and maintenance, and constructed campus buildings.[94]

While a student at Hampton Institute in Virginia, Washington may have worked on the Second Empire and High Victorian Gothic buildings Richard M. Hunt designed for the campus. The memory of one Hampton building caused Washington to write later: "If the people who gave the money to provide that building could appreciate the sight it had upon me, . . . they would feel all the more encouraged to make such gifts. It seemed to me to be the largest and most beautiful building I had ever seen. The sight of it seemed to give me new life."[95] When he founded Tuskegee, Washington recalled architecture's power to uplift and inspire. Created only twenty years after emancipation, the architecture of Tuskegee became a powerful symbol of racial achievement and pride. In *Working with the Hands* (1904), Washington called the Tuskegee buildings "an object lesson" that "students are able to equip a large building from top to bottom." The campus was, he continued, a "city in itself built by young coloured men, most of whom were totally ignorant of systematic mental or menial training when they asked to be admitted to Tuskegee." The campus and the community of Greenwood remain, Richard Dozier notes, the largest collection of extant buildings designed, built, and used by African Americans in the United States.[96]

Tuskegee was also the first southern institution to offer a comprehensive course in architecture and building. Unless they entered the profession through craft apprenticeship or office experience, white southerners left the region to study architecture during the nineteenth century. While John Stirewalt, a North Carolinian, studied with Alexander Jackson Davis during the 1830s, Louisianans like Henry Hobson Richardson and James Freret went abroad to the Ecole des Beaux-Arts in the late nineteenth century. Tulane University in New Orleans offered an architectural engineering course in 1894, but it was soon discontinued.[97]

The Tuskegee architectural program developed within the mechanical industries department, which taught carpentry, brick masonry, sawmilling, blacksmithing, and wagon and carriage construction. Washington, like Ricker, drew on the Russian system of manual training, with its emphasis on mechanical drafting and scaled models. But he departed from the Russian model with his insistence that the student actually "do everything we teach," not just draft and build models.[98]

In 1892 architectural drafting was added, and Washington hired Robert Taylor, who taught thirty-five students in his first year at Tuskegee. Taylor, the son of a free builder in Wilmington, North Carolina, was the first African American to earn an architectural degree, graduating as the valedictorian of his MIT class in 1892. After seven years Taylor developed a four-year course of study at Tuskegee that encompassed instruction in materials, drafting, design, history of architecture, estimates, and specifications. Students also learned about materials and supervision by working in the industrial workshops. Finally, as the catalog for 1899–1900 noted, "buildings [were] constantly in operation on the school grounds," and students could observe "work in progress of erection and . . . enter competitions for buildings to be erected."[99] It appears, however, that students primarily assisted faculty like Taylor with their designs and worked on construction for campus buildings like Thrasher Hall, the physical sciences building, which was Taylor's first commission at Tuskegee. In 1897 Washington asked the architect to design his home on a site in the Greenwood community.[100]

Tuskegee was significant because its administrators and faculty were all African Americans. This was not the case, for example, at Hampton Institute, where Washington had studied. White philanthropists like Julius Rosenwald, Andrew Carnegie, George Eastman, and John D. Rockefeller were trustees and donors who financed the Tuskegee buildings, but black professionals like Taylor, David Williston (Taylor's student and also a Cornell graduate in landscape architecture), and Wallace

Rayfield (a Howard University graduate who studied architecture at the Pratt Institute) designed and supervised.

Taylor, Williston, and Rayfield taught and inspired the next generation of African American professionals, including Vertner Tandy, William S. Pittman, John Lankford, and Charles Bowman. These Tuskegee alumni went on to teach architecture: Pittman at Tuskegee, Lankford at Shaw University and Wilberforce University, Bowman at Western University. William Hazel, a former Tuskegee professor, became the first director of the Howard University architectural program. Although Paul Revere Williams studied architecture at the University of Southern California, Tuskegee affected him, too. Williams, a prominent twentieth-century Los Angeles and Hollywood architect and the first African American to become an AIA fellow, remembered that Pittman was one of the first architects he knew.[101]

The Tuskegee synthesis of craft training, architectural education, and building experience was unique in American architectural education. It was set against the backdrop of a building industry becoming increasingly specialized and fragmented during the late nineteenth century.[102] Few American architects were as thoroughly trained and experienced in both architecture and building before they left school as Tuskegee graduates. Photographs commissioned by Booker T. Washington from photographer Frances Benjamin Johnston illustrate how Tuskegee students spanned the worlds of drafting room and building site (Figs. 11 and 12). Tuskegee and Illinois were the only early American schools to preserve the artisanal origins of architectural training and professionalism in the United States.

Tuskegee and other historically black colleges and universities like Howard University, Hampton Institute, Claflin College, Alabama State University, and Shaw University received revenues from federal lands with the passage of a second land-grant act in 1890. Furthermore, the federal government withheld these funds from white land-grant institutions that refused to admit students of color. Thus Robert Taylor graduated from the MIT program in 1892 and Vertner Tandy from Cornell in 1907.[103]

Some land-grant institutions already had more liberal admissions policies in place before the 1890 legislation. As A. D. White, the first president of Cornell, proclaimed in 1862, his institution (in part a land-grant college) was "open to all—regardless of sex or color."[104] Cornell, MIT, and Illinois were the first architectural programs to accept women. Three women had graduated with honors from the Cornell program by 1888, seventeen years after its foundation. Sophia Hayden, who designed the Women's Building at the 1893 Chicago exposition, was the first woman architect to graduate from MIT in 1890. According to Louise Bethune, a Buffalo architect who

FIGURE 11. Class in mechanical drawing, Tuskegee Institute (Frances Benjamin Johnston, photographer, Frances Benjamin Johnston Collection, Prints and Photographs Division, Library of Congress).

declined admission to Cornell in favor of office training, twelve women had graduated from American architectural schools by 1891. No women were admitted to the Tuskegee architectural program in its early years. American women were pioneers abroad as well as at home. Julia Morgan, who had studied engineering at the University of California, became the first woman admitted to the Ecole des Beaux-Arts in 1898. Higher education at universities funded by the federal government was the point of entry for white women into the architectural profession. But traditional paths into the profession like building trades and office training, with a few exceptions like Louise Bethune, were largely closed to them during the nineteenth century. Many women, white and black, were shunted away from architecture into allied fields like drafting but also interior design and landscape architecture, decoration and gardens being considered appropriately feminine spheres. While the census

FIGURE 12. Tuskegee students framing the roof of a large building (Frances Benjamin Johnston, photographer, Frances Benjamin Johnston Collection, Prints and Photographs Division, Library of Congress).

for 1890 recorded only 22 women in architecture, it listed 305 women as "designers, draftsmen, and inventors." By the 1900 census there were a hundred women architects, out of nine hundred women involved with design, drafting, or inventing.[105]

Architectural programs at private universities, which traditionally educated sons of the privileged classes, were very slow to admit women, Jews, Catholics, and people of color. With the exception of Cornell, which was both a private and a public institution, private universities were unaffected by federal legislation requiring liberal admissions policies (Fig. 13). In the early twentieth century architects of color breached the walls of the Ivy League schools. Julian Abele and John Lewis Wilson were the first African American architects to graduate from the University of Pennsylvania in 1902 and from Columbia University in 1923, respectively. However, Harvard, Columbia, and the University of Pennsylvania did not accept white or black women architectural students until the 1940s, when World War II had siphoned off the male student population.[106]

Because the first women and African American architects generally had university degrees, their credentials were more imposing than those of their white male colleagues. The overwhelming majority of students in university architectural programs

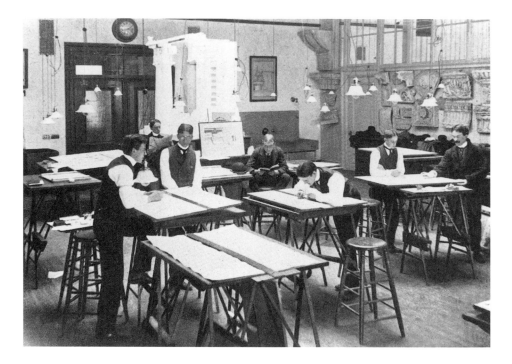

FIGURE 13. First-year students in drafting room, Havemeyer Hall, Columbia University, 1900, from Architectural Record, July 1900 (Fine Arts Library, Cornell University).

left without a degree after only a year or two of study. From 1867 until 1898, 3,250 students matriculated in architectural courses of study, but only 650 students completed their degrees. A four-year university degree was often too expensive for many students. While a year at Columbia in the 1880s cost seven hundred dollars for tuition, fees, and room and board, the annual charges at Illinois were three hundred dollars. When no state or professional society required an architectural degree in order to practice, "a great many students," a writer for the *American Architect* noted, "are not willing to give so much time to the study of architecture." [107]

Faced with such a small pool of candidates for degrees, MIT, Cornell, Illinois, and Columbia devised two-year programs for "special students." At the eastern schools these were essentially the four-year curriculum stripped of general courses in arts and sciences. Special students, who tended to be older draftsmen, concentrated on courses in drawing, design, materials, construction, surveying, mechanical systems, history of architecture and ornament, specifications, and working drawings. Illinois's special program was, as usual, unique. Ricker developed a one-year course to train building craftsmen and mechanics. The program offered instruction in basic building materials (wood, brick, stone, and iron) and shop practice (carpentry, joinery, stair building, and cabinetry), with some classes in architectural drawing, graphic statics, and architectural design. The goal of the Illinois program, Ricker emphasized, was to educate, not architects or draftsmen, but foremen and builders.[108]

Ricker believed that the two-year special programs at MIT, Cornell, and Columbia were an educational travesty and a professional disservice. The public blurred the distinctions between degree candidates and special students because both had university training. Babcock came to agree with him; the Cornell special program was discontinued in 1888 because the faculty concluded its students "must be thoroughly equipped . . . to rise to high positions in the profession." This meant a four-year program.[109]

Both Illinois and Cornell could disdain special students because they had many regular degree candidates. While Cornell had nineteen special students out of forty-eight degree candidates and Illinois had eleven out of forty-four in 1888, MIT had only seventeen degree candidates but forty-eight special students in that same year.[110] Urban schools like MIT probably lost students to offices. But a growing number of Americans also attended the Ecole des Beaux-Arts for architectural training in the late nineteenth century. Charles McKim, who studied at the Ecole after dropping out of Harvard, urged young men to go to Paris. In his opinion the Ecole was "by far the best and most thorough" preparation for architectural practice. McKim so admired the Beaux-Arts institution that he established the American Academy in Rome in 1894, basing it on the French Academy in Rome, as a course of advanced design in classical and Renaissance surroundings.[111] So many Americans sought admission to the Ecole that French administrators restricted the number of foreign students, principally Americans, admitted beginning in 1905. Former Ecole students in New York organized the Society of Beaux-Arts Architects in 1894. They created an open design competition, the Prix de Paris, and sent the winner to the Ecole des Beaux-Arts.[112]

The Ecole transfixed many Americans because it represented architecture as a fine art. The Ecole students, buildings, books, photographs, casts, drawings, and exhibitions awed young architects like A. L. Brockway, a student there in 1888. "A loftier conception of architecture results," he recalled, and "a devotion to one's chosen work is aroused" at the Ecole. Brockway later taught at Syracuse and modeled the curriculum there after the Ecole. Even Ware, skeptical about the relevance of the Beaux-Arts curriculum to American education, encouraged his MIT and Columbia students who wanted advanced training in design and composition to attend the Ecole.[113]

Yet Ecole-inspired training was available in the United States through evening classes and private ateliers taught by former Ecole students. Sketch clubs like the Boston Architectural Club, the T-Square Club of Philadelphia, and the Architectural Leagues of New York and Pittsburgh sponsored design and drawing classes taught according to Beaux-Arts precepts. They also staged exhibitions and juried competitions. The Metropolitan Museum of Art offered classes to prepare students for the Ecole entrance examinations. The cost of the year-long course was twenty-five dollars, and many draftsmen who never intended to go to Paris took the course.[114]

This widespread enthusiasm for the Ecole affected university architecture programs. After Babcock retired from Cornell in 1897, Alexander Trowbridge, a former Ecole student, was hired to institute a Beaux-Arts curriculum.[115] Babcock's emphasis on the sciences, materials, construction, and medieval architecture gave way to a curriculum stressing the classical orders, architectural drawing, and design studio. In 1903 Ware was forced to retire from Columbia. Ateliers and design competitions became the focus of the curriculum, and Ware's liberal arts courses were eliminated. Practicing architects like Charles McKim and Thomas Hastings, former Ecole students, taught studios downtown near their offices rather than on the Columbia campus.[116]

New York architects with large offices were apparently responsible for Ware's ouster. McKim, Hastings, George B. Post, and John Carrère complained that Ware's gentlemen-scholars were of little use to them in the 1890s.[117] They needed men who could prepare the drawings and documents necessary for large-scale commissions, and Ecole methods, as even Ware himself admitted, produced superb draftsmen. Architects with large drafting staffs considered the Beaux-Arts curriculum a practical course of instruction. It served the needs of the modern office as much as it did those of the fine arts.

American education was as diverse as the architectural practices it served during the nineteenth century. Continuing the traditions of craft apprenticeship and professional pupilage, the practitioner's office was the principal educator of American architects. But it was rarely considered complete in itself. Drawing schools, builders' guides, and mechanics' institutes supplemented the office during the late eighteenth and early nineteenth centuries. After the Civil War, correspondence schools, architectural periodicals, private ateliers, sketch clubs, and charitable institutions continued this tradition.

University programs had a limited impact during this period. Few American architects enrolled in their degree programs. Moreover, many of the most influential architects—H. H. Richardson, Charles McKim, John Root, Dankmar Adler, and Stanford White—attended the Ecole des Beaux-Arts or studied engineering or graduated from the drawing boards. Louis Sullivan, who studied briefly at MIT before going to the Ecole, was the exception. Public universities were more influential in opening up the profession to women and people of color. Formal training and academic credentials were a necessity for them given the obstacles to learning and working in mainstream offices.

The first university programs at MIT, Cornell, and Columbia followed the English tradition of a liberal education for professionals. The student's mastery of a broad curriculum as well as drafting, design, history, materials, and construction demonstrated the professional integration of design and building under the architect's direction. The curricular structure itself was a symbol of this ideal of architectural authority.

The University of Illinois and Tuskegee Institute privileged different strands in the complex weave of American professionalism. They recalled and honored the artisanal roots of the early American profession. Both schools were pioneers; they were virtually the only centers for formal study of architecture and building in their respective regions. They trained not only architects but also builders and artisans. At Illinois Ricker developed a two-year course for builders and contractors and an innovative architectural engineering program. He alone among the early architectural educators recognized the profound technological changes that were transforming late nineteenth-century architecture. Taylor's and Ricker's programs recall, if anything, the AIA's dream of a grand central school where artisans, builders, engineers, and architects would be trained together. As a result, Tuskegee graduates like John Lankford were able to work as architects, builders, and real estate developers, profoundly shaping the new African American communities that arose after emancipation.

However, the paradigm for twentieth-century education emerged in architectural schools like Columbia, Harvard, and the University of Pennsylvania that adopted a Beaux-Arts curriculum organized around studio projects, competitions, and design juries. These programs shaped the future of American architectural education, offering a design methodology and a focus on architecture as a fine art but pragmatically producing facile draftsmen for the large architectural offices. The architectural office dominated American professional life throughout the nineteenth century. Its evolution from a single-person shop to a large corporate office would affect not only professional education but also the direction and character of American architectural work.

CHAPTER 4

FORMS AND SETTINGS

OF PRACTICE

Though a thorough artist, Richardson was a very good businessman
and a man of the world. He knew that the business of the profession
was of as much importance as the art of it.
John B. Gass, RIBA Journal *(1896)*

English professionals had traditionally held themselves aloof from the marketplace. They were their clients' peers and advisers; they were not businessmen selling and trading for a profit. American architects, as Europeans like Latrobe and L'Enfant soon discovered, worked within a very different economic and ideological context. Architectural opportunities for American practitioners depended primarily on the marketplace. Private patronage was feeble, and ongoing institutional employment was rare. American architects lived from commission to commission unless they had private wealth or other sources of income. The early professional landscape was filled with frustrated architects like Latrobe and Hadfield and failed ones like L'Enfant, Hallet, and Godefroy.

But the economic expansion and populist movements of the decades between 1820 and 1860 fueled new hopes for artistic freedom and financial success among American artists and architects. Although entrepreneurial practice contradicted a fundamental tenet of traditional professionalism—aloofness from commerce—it did free architects from the constraints of either private patrons or government officials and became the touchstone of American professionalism during the entire nineteenth century. Artisans-turned-professionals like Ithiel Town and Richard Upjohn as well as Ecole-educated architects like H. H. Richardson and Charles McKim embraced the entrepreneurial model. While eastern and midwestern architects might disagree over the priority given to aesthetics or tectonics in design, they agreed that American architects were businessmen creating opportunities to ensure the survival of their practices. This conception of architect as artist, constructor, *and businessman* was uniquely American. To succeed at the business of architecture, Americans evolved new forms and settings for practice throughout the nineteenth century.

ARTISTS AND ARCHITECTS

AS ENTREPRENEURS

Between 1820 and 1860 (the antebellum period), American artists and architects became independent entrepreneurs in new markets created by an unprecedented prosperity in trade, manufacturing, and agriculture. William Dunlap praised American artists and architects in the 1830s as men of "industry, virtue, and talents" who "exchanged the product of their skill and labor for the money of the rich."[1] The arts were now part of a robust market economy in the United States. Entrepreneurial initiative and resourcefulness supposedly brought artists honor and wealth. Bold marketing schemes created new and larger audiences for the arts. In the decades before the Civil War, American artists mounted their own exhibitions and toured the country with them, charging admission and lecturing for a price. Lotteries sponsored by the American Art Union promoted art for the middle classes in the 1830s and 1840s. Incorporating drawing and design classes into the public school curriculum created future art consumers as well as artists.

But this popularization of the arts did not meet with universal approval in the artistic community. Samuel F. B. Morse saw it as simply the commodification of the fine arts, yet another sign of the vulgarity and materialism of antebellum American life.[2] Others, however, welcomed American artists' entrepreneurial spirit and saw it as a democratization of the arts. Alexander Jackson Davis endorsed teaching everyone from the sailor to the gentleman how to draw when he lectured before the Apollo Association, the forerunner of the American Art Union. He also urged universities to move beyond "a drilling in Latin and Greek" to teach modern and practical subjects like architectural science.[3]

Davis put his ideas into practice. He exhibited his architectural drawings at Morse's National Academy of Design, but also showed them at the well-attended fairs of the New York Mechanics' Institute. At the institute fairs his New York University designs were exhibited beside cabinets displaying false teeth, engraved plates for bank notes, and examples of penmanship. Taking rooms in the University Building on Washington Square, which he had designed with his partners Town and

Dakin, Davis invited the public to "conversaziones," where he made his books, drawings, and other collections available and discussed his work with prospective clients. He advertised his conversaziones and architectural services in the newspapers. Finally, around 1838, he began publishing a projected six-part series of his designs under the title *Rural Residences*.[4]

House Pattern Books

Although Davis never completed the *Rural Residences* series, he initiated a new publishing genre, later known as "house pattern books," that profoundly altered the course of architectural practice. These publications created a taste for architectural consumption and marketed architects' services to new clients. They were a response to the opportunities and challenges of American entrepreneurial practice. *Rural Residences* presented a collection of principally domestic designs, ranging from a farmhouse with a portico of unpeeled tree trunks to a castellated Gothic Revival villa. A perspective view and simple plan accompanied each design. In the text Davis discussed how each design was appropriate for only certain clients, sites, and materials. The plates were lithographs (an expensive graphic process at the time), and they were even hand-colored in some editions.[5]

Davis's readers were not Asher Benjamin's "scientific mechanics." They were prospective home owners, those who could afford only the "economical farmer's house of wood," wealthy clients able to indulge in the fantasia of an Oriental villa, and middle-class families seeking comfort and taste in bracketed wooden cottages. Each design visually encoded the social and economic gradations of American society, suggesting the tasteful and appropriate for what Davis called the "proper pride of republicanism." But these designs were only recommendations, Davis emphasized, not drawings for actual construction. All clients needed to employ an architect to create a building suited to a particular site, needs, budget, and materials.[6]

Davis's ambitious publishing project foundered during the economic disruptions of 1837. It was Andrew Jackson Downing, a landscape gardener and Davis's collaborator on several residential projects along the Hudson River, who capitalized on the idea. Using comparatively inexpensive wood engravings, Downing created mass-market versions of *Rural Residences* during the 1840s and 1850s under such titles as *Cottage Residences* (1842) and *The Architecture of Country Houses* (1850). His publications combined theoretical discussions of picturesque landscape and architecture with practical suggestions for plans, gardens, and household gadgets for country cottages and villas. Downing, like Davis, emphasized that the small-scale perspectives and simple plans in his books were not models but suggestions; he advised the reader that a professional architect must develop the designs further and supervise construction.[7]

Although pattern books of church and school architecture subsequently appeared, house designs (first country and then suburban) always dominated the genre, becoming popular promotional tools for architects like William Ranlett of New York and Samuel Sloan of Philadelphia during the 1840s and 1850s. These publications brought Ranlett and Sloan clients from around the country. Whereas Davis and Downing wrote about their duty to improve American taste, later architects were blunt about wanting new clients and increased revenues from their pattern book ventures. J. H. Kirby, a Syracuse architect in the 1880s, wrote in the introduction to his collection of house designs that it had "no missionary purpose" but was to "be of some profit . . . in a business way."[8]

By the 1860s, however, some architects questioned whether pattern books really helped them and the profession: "Well, our artistic merchant has found something to suit him; all he wants now is a good mechanic. . . . An architect? Pooh! Who wants an architect when he buys Downing?" As this architectural writer observed, home owners purchased pattern books for house designs that a builder could execute.[9] While Downing and Davis regarded their books as lessons in architectural taste, their readers saw them as yet another example of American practical guides and manuals. Like the builders' guides before them, pattern books empowered readers and diminished the role of expert advisers. Publishers and writers catered to this market for practical guides by providing complete sets of scaled architectural drawings, specifications, and cost estimates for pattern book designs. The small-scale perspectives and plans of Downing's books disappeared. George Woodward claimed that the drawings and information in his *National Architect* "can at once be placed in the hands of the builder for execution." This volume alone went through ninety-five editions from 1869 until 1877.[10]

Periodical publishers also recognized the potential of pattern book designs. Beginning in the 1880s *Scientific American Builder's Monthly* (1885–1905) and *Shoppell's Modern Homes* (1886–1904?) provided complete working drawings (reproduced as elaborately colored chromolithographs) and specifications for low- and moderate-income housing. Robert Shoppell wrote that his large office of "specialists in design, construction and specification writing" produced construction documents for houses that cost only a quarter of what an architect charged. The expertise and specialization of the modern architectural office, he claimed, were now available to every home owner.[11]

Some architects introduced further refinements to the pattern book phenomenon by specializing in selling plans and specifications through mail-order catalogs rather than publishing pattern books. Benjamin D. and Max Charles Price of Pennsylvania and New Jersey and George F. Barber of Tennessee were particularly successful mail-order practitioners. Nothing is known about the Prices' training and background, but in their publications they called themselves architects. Specializing in churches between 1867 and 1907, they claimed that over seven thousand congregations in Canada, Mexico, and the United States used their designs. Plans, "ready for the builder to estimate on and build without the supervision of an architect," ranged from simple, wooden gabled boxes to elaborate, brick Gothic Revival structures. The Price brothers also sold imitation stained glass on adhesive paper (Figs. 14, 15, and 16).[12]

George F. Barber, who first worked as a carpenter, opened an architectural office in Knoxville that employed thirty draftsmen and twenty secretaries by 1900. His was probably the largest practice in Tennessee, and he was the leading mail-order architect in the United States. Concentrating on residential work, Barber published eight hundred designs in some nine catalogs and a monthly magazine between 1888 and 1903. He claimed clients from the United States, Canada, South Africa, Europe, Japan, China, and the Philippines. Barber, like the Prices, was willing to customize designs for his clients, at an additional cost. Real estate developers also used his services; one Baltimore developer built forty-seven homes from Barber plans. However, Barber houses were usually constructed in communities where there were local contractors but no architects. Whereas the Prices' most expensive set of plans and specifications cost $150, Barber's was only $60.[13]

Selling drawings at a flat rate challenged the AIA and WAA idea of the professional architect who directed both design and construction for a percentage fee. The professional relationship between the client and architect, Leopold Eidlitz wrote, was not a onetime business proposition where cash was exchanged for a product or service. The professional architect had a continuing relationship with a client whom he advised and guided through the entire design and building process. Mail-order practice, while commercially innovative in the mode of Sears and Roebuck, diminished the architect in the professional societies' view. It eliminated the comprehensive and personalized service that was the hallmark of traditional professionalism. By selling standardized designs to a mass market, however, the Prices and Barber affected the way more Americans lived and worshiped than an architect with a conventional practice.[14]

Church Plans

BENJAMIN D. PRICE
MAX CHARLES PRICE
ARCHITECTS

FIGURE 14. Cover of *Church Plans* by Benjamin D. and Max Charles Price, 1901 (The Avery Fine Arts and Architectural Library, Columbia University).

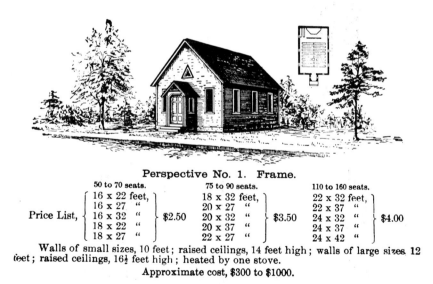

Perspective No. 1. Frame.

	50 to 70 seats.		75 to 90 seats.		110 to 160 seats.	
Price List,	16 x 22 feet,		18 x 32 feet,		22 x 32 feet,	
	16 x 27 "		20 x 27 "		22 x 37 "	
	16 x 32 "	$2.50	20 x 32 "	$3.50	24 x 32 "	$4.00
	18 x 22 "		20 x 37 "		24 x 37 "	
	18 x 27 "		22 x 27 "		24 x 42 "	

Walls of small sizes, 10 feet; raised ceilings, 14 feet high; walls of large sizes 12 feet; raised ceilings, 16½ feet high; heated by one stove.

Approximate cost, $300 to $1000.

FIGURE 15. Frame church, *Church Plans* by Benjamin D. and Max Charles Price, 1901 (The Avery Architectural and Fine Arts Library, Columbia University).

FIGURE 16. Price's paper imitation of stained glass, *Church Plans* by Benjamin D. and Max Charles Price, 1901 (The Avery Architectural and Fine Arts Library, Columbia University).

Professionalism in the United States was a delicate balancing act. American architects had to be entrepreneurial but remain dignified. It was the tone of mail-order practices, with promises of low prices, that offended many in the profession. The hapless J. Q. Ingham of Elmira, New York, enraged the AIA with an advertisement for a discounted sale of his discontinued plans in the 1890s (Fig. 17). Making it clear

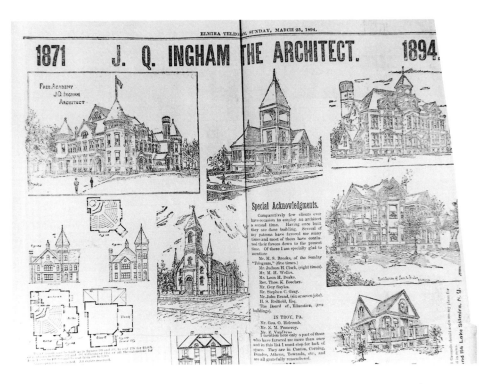

FIGURE 17. Detail of advertisement for J. Q. Ingham from *Elmira Telegram,* 25 March 1894 (The American Institute of Architects Archives).

that he sold the same plans again and again, Ingham promised very cheap prices for everything from a "lakeside cottage to a colonial revival mansion." The AIA secretary chastised him for using advertising that savored "more of the quack medicine and ready-made clothing" than "a dignified card of a professional man." [15]

The issue of rote design that Ingham's case raised was a sensitive one. As pattern books and mail-order catalogs grew in popularity, some architects countered by emphasizing that only the professional provided unique solutions tailored to a client's specific needs. Yet architects like Ingham clearly sold the same designs repeatedly, while Barber and the Prices were willing to customize their generic designs.

Apparently, the repeated sale of generic designs was common enough for the popular journal *Puck* to satirize the practice in verse and drawings during the early 1890s. After purchasing a lot in the new suburb of Eden City, an earnest couple pore over books of house plans and architectural history and then sketch out a dream house resembling the capacious gate lodge that H. H. Richardson designed for the

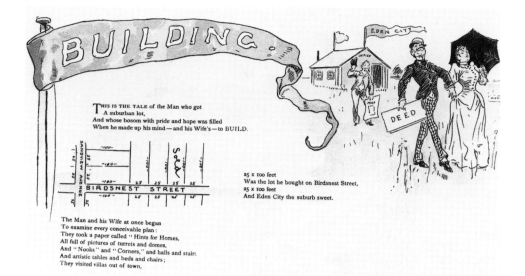

THIS IS THE TALE of the Man who got
   A suburban lot,
And whose bosom with pride and hope was filled
When he made up his mind — and his Wife's — to BUILD.

25 x 100 feet
Was the lot he bought on Birdsnest Street,
25 x 100 feet
And Eden City the suburb sweet.

The Man and his Wife at once began
To examine every conceivable plan :
They took a paper called " Hints for Homes,
All full of pictures of turrets and domes,
And " Nooks " and " Corners," and halls and stair
And artistic tables and beds and chairs ;
They visited villas out of town,

The Man then went to an architect,
And said : " Dear sir, if you don't object,
I would like to give you a hint or two
As to the house I expect from you.
   Ah — hm !
The Front Hall is n't a very large place ;
But I want to get the effect of space —
You understand, as an architect,
I don't want space ; but a spacious effect —
And here, at the end, I want a Nook,
Where a fellow can lie and read a book ;
The Drawing-room ought to be large and bright,
With three bay-windows and lots of light ;

And hereabouts ends the tale of the Man :
He bought that plan.
And this is the sort of house he got
On his eligible suburban lot.
It was finished a year ago last May,
And this is the sort of kind of way
That suburban residence looks to-day.

wealthy Ames family (Figs. 18 and 19). Consulting their architect, the husband presents their plan. Pointing to the "libraree," he explains: "That mark doesn't mean a bed; / It shows there's a skylight overhead—I got the idea (it's rather bright,) / From a house at Newport by Stanford White" (Fig. 20). After listening sympathetically, the architect directs his clerk to take down from the shelf stock plan number 637, a Queen Anne house exploding with turrets, gables, porches, and bay windows yet narrow enough to be slotted into the cramped Eden City site (Fig. 21).[16]

The *Puck* verses poke fun at both the architect's cynicism and the client's pretension and gullibility. They recall an editor's comments from an 1870s building journal: "It is very much with architects as it is with doctors, our ignorance helps them far more than their knowledge or capacity. . . . The truth is that in all ordinary cases of house construction, the architect is only as serviceable as would be the fifth wheel to a coach."[17]

When Davis and Downing first urged American workers and farmers to retain an architect for their houses, they were at odds with prevailing wisdom and traditional practice. Since the colonial and Federal periods, the majority of Americans had turned to master artisans and builders for designs and building construction. An editor wrote that architects' fees limited them to "building churches and houses

FIGURES 18–21 (*opposite and left*), "Building" (*Puck,* 10 June 1891).

for rich people, who have nothing to do with their money but to throw it about." A clergyman in Scuppernong, North Carolina, put it more positively when he wrote in 1859: "I want a *Church,* not a meeting house or a barn and therefore I want to engage an *architect.*" [18]

House pattern books and mail-order designs further democratized architectural taste and created a mass market for design. But they also undermined the professional architect's traditionally contested control over American housing, an especially important market for modest and provincial practitioners. Architects like the Prices and Barber who tried new marketing methods achieved popular success but professional disdain. Those who were more timid entrepreneurs, however, risked losing business yet again to builders and mechanics. The line between appropriate and inappropriate enterprise and marketing was often difficult for architects to discern. Some, like J. Q. Ingham, eventually resigned from the AIA because they could not determine what was professionally acceptable or could not finesse the divide between traditional professionalism and American entrepreneurship. Furthermore, professional societies were always more zealous about policing the conduct of rank-and-file practitioners. [19] They tended, we shall see, to turn a blind eye when prominent architects engaged in questionable activities.

GOVERNMENT ARCHITECTURE

Professional architects in France, Germany, and England had traditionally found employment, and often permanent situations, with the state. American government was always a hesitant and reluctant architectural patron, but it did offer some opportunities, especially for large-scale public buildings, throughout the nineteenth century. Since the establishment of Washington, D.C., in the 1790s, ambitious architects and planners had gravitated to the new capital. In the early 1800s North Carolina employed William Nichols and South Carolina Robert Mills as state architects. But American architects grew wary of government commissions. Latrobe, soured by his Washington experiences, wrote in 1811: "The service of a republic is always a slavery of the most inexorable kind, under a mistress who does not give to her hirelings civil language." Thomas U. Walter, who undertook additions to the Capitol in 1851, would surely have concurred with Latrobe. He had prolonged disputes about his fees with federal officials. Walter's heirs, in fact, continued to press his claims against the government long after his death. [20]

During the second half of the nineteenth century, almost all federal work became institutionalized in the Supervising Architect's Office of the Treasury Department. The first supervising architects emphasized economy and efficiency through uniformity in plan and style. While their efforts pleased parsimonious legislators, they brought only disdain from the professional community. One AIA member complained that Federal design was "very military, but it was not art and the monotony became unendurable."[21] After the Civil War, the widespread abuses of the spoils system further tainted the Supervising Architect's Office. Political considerations, not architectural expertise or excellence, reputedly dictated staff appointments. John Root wrote that he turned down a federal appointment to supervise Chicago building because it would have taken him "away from my own legitimate business, [and] would have identified me with politics."[22]

Prominent late nineteenth-century architects like Richard M. Hunt and John Carrère refused appointments as supervising architect. While they feared becoming embroiled in politics, they also did not care to sacrifice their lucrative private practices. Dankmar Adler observed that the supervising architect "performed[ed] for a salary equal to one tenth that of a private practitioner."[23] H. H. Richardson, too, did not long for a state position. He felt that officially sanctioned styles and formulas constrained European architects who held government posts. Although American architects faced public indifference and economic uncertainty, Richardson believed they did not have to contend with bureaucratic interference. He reportedly returned from his last trip abroad with a "renewed sense of intense delight in the freedom of his own path." The antebellum belief in independent practice as the path to professional honor and personal success still held for late nineteenth-century American architects.[24]

FORMS AND SETTINGS OF PRACTICE

Independent Practice

Latrobe and other early architects had survived through a combination of private and public commissions. This mode of working was also familiar to the antebellum craftsmen who embraced architectural professionalism; the master artisan had traditionally functioned as an independent businessman presiding over his own workshop. But finding enough work to sustain an architectural practice proved a challenge for many practitioners throughout the nineteenth century. It often involved compromising the traditional view of the professional architect as only the designer and supervisor of construction. American architects had to devise a number of strategies to survive and to prosper in a market-driven economy.

Drafting   Many early architects earned a living by selling designs and drafting services to craftsmen and speculative builders. These draftsmen for hire included both struggling young architects and prominent practitioners in the decades before the

Civil War. James Gallier, an Irish immigrant in New York, recalled that developers applied to bricklayers and carpenters for building plans. They, in turn, hired "some poor draftsman, of whom there were half a dozen in New York at that time to make the plan, paying him a mere trifle for his services." James Dakin and Minard Lafever, both founders of the American Institution of Architects, were, Gallier continued, caught in this "horse-in-the-mill routine of grinding out drawings for the builders." Thomas U. Walter sustained his Philadelphia practice by selling drawings at five to ten dollars per sheet to speculative builders. The imposing buildings that he is remembered for today represented only a small percentage of his work and income.[25]

However, there were sellers' markets for drafting in less established antebellum cities like Chicago. John Van Osdel, known as Chicago's first architect, had a lucrative and exclusive arrangement with city builders. Trained as a mechanic in the East, Van Osdel moved to Chicago, a booming new city, in the late 1830s—a time when mechanics still chalked drawings and full-size details on trestle boards. Chicago builders and speculators employed Van Osdel, concluding it was more efficient and inexpensive to buy designs and drawings from him. They promised him they would "not make any drawings, or construct any important buildings without a plan." The architect was put on a daily retainer, a minimum of two dollars. Such arrangements continued into the 1880s, when William W. Boyington claimed many Chicago architects still "were largely supported by contractors."[26]

Drafting work was abundant for two reasons during the decades before the Civil War. Builders, speculators, and clients now needed architectural drawings to demonstrate compliance with municipal building codes. Written instructions or chalked instructions on trestle boards were not documents of record.[27] Moreover, as house pattern books created a widespread taste for architectural novelty and diversity, facility in design and drafting became a selling point for American architects. A New York mechanic testified in a lawsuit (a dispute over fees between Richard M. Hunt and a real estate speculator) that if you wanted a house different from any other you needed a professional architect. The average builder or artisan, he continued in his testimony, could not supply the novel designs or quantity of drawings necessary to execute unfamiliar work. Only a trained architect like Hunt could provide such services.[28]

Building   Other architects worked in construction to supplement their professional income from design and supervision. Leading architects, many former craftsmen, worked as builders, suppliers, or real estate developers in the decades before the Civil War just as Robert Smith, William Buckland, and Thomas Dawes had done during the colonial and Federal periods. Ithiel Town wrote in 1836 that he could not afford to devote himself solely to architecture. He still traveled widely to promote and install his patented wooden truss, used in bridge construction. James Gallier supervised buildings that he did not design and developed real estate in New Orleans beginning in the 1830s. Their building interests made them wealthy men, allowing Town to indulge his taste for books and prints on trips abroad and Gallier to retire in 1850, devoting himself to travel and writing his autobiography. Yet working as a contractor or developer involved substantial risks, and architects with little personal capital often found financial disaster, not wealth and leisure, in building.[29]

John Stirewalt, an aspiring architect who had studied with Alexander J. Davis in New York, eventually left architecture for building. He wrote to Davis from Louisville, Kentucky, where he was trying to practice in the 1840s: "I have made up my mind that if I continue longer as an architect I shall certainly starve. There was no building worth the attention of an architect erected last season nor do I see any to be built this coming year, so with me there is no alternative but to change professions."[30] Abandoning his Louisville practice, Stirewalt accepted a stonecutter's offer to join him in opening an Ohio River quarry. A practice based only on design and supervision was simply too rarefied for the limited building market in Kentucky during the 1840s. But fifty years later Stirewalt's story was still not uncommon. Although 1893 was the year of the profession's triumph at the Chicago World's Fair, W. W. Carlin, an AIA member from Buffalo, stated that architects still worked as builders "in the smaller towns and in the portions of the community where the professional architect would starve."[31]

Peripatetic Architects   Every major architect in New York, Philadelphia, Boston, and Washington, D.C., traveled far afield to find work before the Civil War. There were simply not enough opportunities in these large cities to sustain a professional practice. Ithiel Town, Alexander Jackson Davis, Thomas U. Walter, Richard Upjohn, William Strickland, Samuel Sloan, John Notman, Isaiah Rogers, and Robert Mills all accepted commissions in the South and Midwest. The southeastern states, where traditionally architects were few and clients wealthy, provided many opportunities. Hiring a prominent architect like Strickland, Davis, Walter, or Upjohn became a point of pride for many southern clients and building committees during the antebellum period.[32]

Strickland's career demonstrates the professional difficulties that even a gifted designer and skilled engineer faced in the United States. Before receiving his first major commission, the Second Bank of the United States in 1818, Strickland worked at a variety of jobs in New York and Philadelphia. He painted scenery and city views and designed ornaments, furniture, and machinery for carpenters and mechanics. Strickland also worked for the Army Corps of Engineers. Although it was a steady position, the low pay caused him to leave. Freelance design and drafting evidently paid better. He later recalled that in Philadelphia "the few acquaintances I had . . . were artists struggling onward like day laborers and paid about as well:—architecture was at a low ebb and Master Carpenters directed the taste of City Edifices— I had no patrons, nor a single opportunity to practice my profession." But he finally had "an opportunity to show my architectural knowledge" when he won the competition for the Second Bank of the United States. After thirteen years of struggle, Strickland was finally working in the "profession of my early study and delight."[33] But this security was short-lived. Beginning in the late 1820s, Strickland had to seek work far beyond Philadelphia, in Rhode Island, Washington, D.C., and North and South Carolina. His practice foundered after the panic of 1837. In 1845 he designed the Tennessee state capitol, a high-profile commission that led to residential and ecclesiastical work in the Nashville area. The Tennessee capitol gave him a second act in his career.[34]

Some northeastern architects permanently resettled in the Southeast during the years before the Civil War. After struggling in New York during the 1830s, both James Dakin and James Gallier relocated to Louisiana, where they became the leading architects in and around New Orleans, Baton Rouge, and Mobile, Alabama.[35] This tradition of relocating continued after the Civil War, when the southwestern and western states drew eastern architects. George Mann, mentioned previously, left New York and established a practice in Saint Joseph and then Saint Louis, Missouri, during the late nineteenth century. When he won the competition for the Arkansas state capitol in 1901, he moved again to Little Rock. Henry Van Brunt, a Harvard graduate and Hunt student, left the refined circles of Cambridge and Boston in 1887, drawn by Union Pacific Railroad commissions in the boom town of Kansas City. A. Page Brown, Willis Polk, Bernard Maybeck, and A. C. Schweinfurth left offices in New York and Boston for San Francisco between 1889 and 1890. All these transplanted easterners brought an academic and professional culture to the South, Southwest, and West Coast, where they gained architectural opportunities and economic rewards that eluded them on the more competitive East Coast.[36]

Regional Practice   Other architects did not relocate but created regional practices from their urban bases. The railroads, telegraph, and new graphic processes like photolithography and halftone made such far-flung practices feasible after 1850. Architects like G. P. Randall of Chicago, who specialized in school and church designs throughout the Midwest, used long-distance travel, improved communications, and

FIGURE 22. Letterhead of J. B. Legg, Saint Louis, 11 November 1887 (The American Institute of Architects Archives).

inexpensive illustrated promotional materials to build thriving regional practices. After training with Asher Benjamin in Boston, Randall moved to Chicago in 1856 in search of opportunity. While he won such prestigious commissions as the original buildings for Northwestern University, Randall aggressively marketed his services to small congregations and school boards throughout the Midwest in a series of brochures. Before Daniel Burnham, Randall's clientele exceeded that of any other midwestern architect.[37]

Like Randall, J. B. Legg of Saint Louis also won important commissions in the smaller cities and towns of the Southwest. After attending college, he studied and worked with a Saint Louis architect and a builder in the late 1860s. Forming his own practice, Legg won the commission to make extensive alterations to the Missouri state capitol in the 1880s. The prominence he gained from this commission secured work for banks, schools, hospitals, theaters, and courthouses throughout southern Illinois, Missouri, Arkansas, Texas, Kansas, and Louisiana. Legg's business grew to such an extent that he established four branch offices in the Southwest. His business stationery was just as promotional as any advertising brochure; he illustrated it with his portrait and listed all his branch offices (Fig. 22).[38]

Architects like Randall and Legg, working out of major cities like Chicago and Saint Louis, robbed local practitioners of the most challenging regional work. They stymied and retarded local professional development, creating a colonizer and colonized relationship between the urban centers and outlying areas. But even prominent midwestern architects, associated primarily with commercial work, found that commissions for prestigious residences, government buildings, and institutions often went to eastern architects. Although there was a well-established professional community in Cincinnati, H. H. Richardson received the commission for the chamber of commerce building in that city. Bryan Lathrop, who commissioned Chicago commercial work from Holabird and Roche, chose McKim, Mead and White to design an elegant classical house for him, but he retained Holabird and Roche to supervise the production and construction of the eastern firm's design. As Robert Bruegmann notes, when Chicagoans wanted "high-style clothes or furniture," they went to the established cultural capitals of London and Paris. When they wanted prestigious architecture, they looked to New York.[39]

While architects like Randall and Legg marketed aggressively, using brochures, souvenir sketchbooks, and letterheads to promote their practices over a broad area, nationally prominent architects usually employed more discreet and refined advertising to build national practices. Davis, Upjohn, and Sloan had published pattern books in the decades before the Civil War. The next generation of professional leaders like Richardson, Burnham, and McKim, Mead and White utilized the emerging professional press and lay journals (the *American Architect and Building News, Inland Architect, Scribner's,* and *Century*) to illustrate and promote their work.[40]

Because professional architects relied on a building market traditionally dominated by builders and artisans, they devised a number of strategies to keep their private practices afloat. Drafting, building, and developing were necessary for many leading architects before the Civil War and continued to be so for less prominent practitioners after the war. But promotion and marketing, whether blatant or restrained, were necessary practices for all American architects.

Women and Minorities   While some architects struggled to create an economically viable practice, others found that ethnicity, gender, and race blocked their very access to the profession. Dennis Francis noted a preponderance of English surnames in his survey of architects practicing in New York City between 1840 and 1900. Irish and Scotch names were also prominent, followed by German, including Austrian and Swiss. Architects with French, Hispanic, Italian, eastern European, and Jewish surnames were decidedly scarce. Given the tradition of architect as gentleman, Francis's findings are not surprising and probably hold true for the American profession as a whole. There were, as noted previously, few women architects during the nineteenth century. The census in 1870 listed only one woman architect, but by the 1890 census there were twenty-two women architects, and the 1900 census showed nearly a fivefold increase, with a hundred women architects listed. In the 1890 census women accounted for just 1.9 percent of all architects, designers, and "draftsmen," but their representation increased to 3.5 percent in the 1900 census. But architecture, as an art, was still more appropriate for women than engineering, where they represented only 0.3 percent in 1890 and then 0.2 percent in the census statistics for 1890 and 1900.[41]

The 1850 census was the first to compile occupations by race; it listed an African American architect as practicing in New Orleans, the first official reference to an architect of color in the United States. Statistics for the 1890 national census include forty-three "colored" architects: twenty-two Chinese, Indian, and Japanese men and twenty-one African American men. There were no women architects of color. In the 1900 census fifty-two African American men were listed as architects, designers or draftsmen, accounting for 0.02 percent of that field.[42]

Although women artisans appear in census records during the late nineteenth century, the first women architects were usually educated either in offices or in academic programs during the last two decades of the nineteenth century. Office training was a more unusual background for women in architecture. Louise Bethune, one of the few women architects trained in an office, studied with a Buffalo practitioner and then became his chief assistant. In the 1880s she practiced with her husband, taking responsibility for commercial and school commissions.[43]

Bethune's acceptance into mainstream practice was exceptional. Although women "draftsmen" and designers appear in census records as early as 1870, they were usually absent, often even as clerical employees, from leading architectural offices in the late nineteenth century. Charles McKim rebuffed overtures made in 1894 for Henrietta Dozier, one of the first women to study architecture at MIT, as a potential draftsperson in his office. Dozier eventually established her own practice in Atlanta, where she specialized in Colonial Revival work and historic preservation. She reportedly listed herself as H. Dozier or Harry Dozier to bring in clients.[44]

More women architects began practicing in the first quarter of the twentieth century, but they typically worked alone or in partnership with other women: Dozier in Atlanta; Anna Schenck and Marcia Mead in New York; Florence Luscombe and Ida Annah Ryan in Waltham, Massachusetts; and Lois Lilley Howe, Eleanor Manning, and Mary Almy in Boston. Julia Morgan was exceptional, a principal architect presiding over a sizable San Francisco office with as many as six draftspersons in 1915.[45]

Almy, Howe, Luscombe, Manning, Mead, Morgan, Ryan, and Schenck came from upper-middle-class families among whom education and serious interests, if not careers, were not unusual for women. Howe's and Manning's families were involved with contracting and real estate. As a group these women were especially well educated, with architectural and engineering training from American universities and the Ecole des Beaux-Arts. They based their practices on residential work, women's clubs and colleges, YWCA buildings, and early public housing. Commissioned by middle- and upper-middle-class women, this work was substantial, but it did not command great respect in a profession fixated on large-scale building. However, Phoebe Hearst, of the powerful and wealthy California Hearst family, did provide Morgan with exceptional opportunities for large-scale public and private commissions.[46]

There was a long tradition of African American artisans in the South, where skilled workers of any race were traditionally in short supply and highly prized. Free African American artisans practiced in southern cities and towns, albeit in limited numbers and under legal restrictions. Hundreds of free and enslaved African Americans made building materials and provided labor for the White House, Capitol, and other early federal buildings in Washington, D.C. After the Civil War, it was estimated that black artisans outnumbered white artisans by five to one in the South. Skilled black artisans, however, were unwelcome in the North, where white immigrants and trade unions barred them from building sites. The census of 1890 listed 22,310 carpenters and 596 builders who were African Americans, accounting for 3.7 percent and 1.3 percent of the total workers in those respective trades.[47]

Like women, African Americans with formal training in architecture were just becoming established in the late nineteenth century. Their practices matured and gained prominence in the early twentieth century as new African American communities grew and prospered. Tuskegee Institute was, as explained previously, the birthplace of African American professional architects, and Booker T. Washington secured commissions for black architects for YMCAs, libraries, schools, and housing funded by white philanthropists like Andrew Carnegie and Julius Rosenwald. Robert Taylor, Wallace Rayfield, William S. Pittman, and John Lankford combined practice with teaching at historically black colleges and universities. Here they came to the attention of a rising middle class of African American ministers, entrepreneurs, and professionals who commissioned churches, schools, clubs, stores, offices, and homes. Lankford, among the first to study at Tuskegee, established the first black architectural practice in 1899 in Jacksonville, Florida. He and Rayfield became particularly renowned for religious work; Rayfield published a book of his church designs in 1916 and carried out architectural commissions for African-Methodist Episcopal congregations throughout the world. The large and prominent African American community in Washington, D.C., employed many of the first black professional architects. Lankford and Pittman built national practices from Washington.[48]

Other Tuskegee graduates like Vertner Woodson Tandy established practices in northeastern cities, where large numbers of African Americans moved in the early twentieth century. Tandy moved to New York and joined George W. Foster, who had attended Cooper Union's architectural program, in a practice on lower Broadway. Many black architects of the next generation trained in their office. Tandy received commissions totaling $350,000 from Madame C. J. Walker, who built a beauty products empire, and other members of an emerging African American elite in Harlem.[49]

Unlike Henrietta Dozier, whom McKim rejected, Julian Abele did overcome the discrimination against women and people of color in major architectural offices. Abele became a designer in the office of Horace Trumbauer, a prominent Philadelphia firm favored by society clients in the early 1900s. Houses for James B. Duke in New York and New Jersey and the Duke University campus in North Carolina were among Abele's most important commissions. When most African American architects were involved with race uplift, designing for vibrant new African American communities, Abele seemed content to create buildings for a racist society. Abele established a practice only after Trumbauer died in 1938 and his office was closed.

Abele's crossover into a leading white firm, however, remained an isolated example until the late twentieth century.[50] Architects from marginalized groups in late nineteenth-century America opened their own offices or formed partnerships with each other. Nevertheless, architecture offered women and minorities an opportunity for challenging and gratifying vocations at a time when careers in government or corporations were closed to them. The professions were a haven for educated women and minorities because they valorized the independent and self-employed practitioner. But architects like Julia Morgan and Julian Abele, who competed and worked with white male professionals, were exceptions. Even today women and people of color are rarities in the upper ranks of prominent architectural practices. American architecture remains an overwhelmingly white and male occupation.

SETTINGS FOR PRACTICE

American architects pursued independent practice in a variety of settings, referring to their workplaces as workshops, ateliers, and offices. New organizational structures arose to cope with the increasing scale and complexity of design and building before and after the Civil War. Architects were no longer just single practitioners.

They organized partnerships and large offices. Although these nineteenth-century settings and structures have persisted into the late twentieth century, they have received virtually no attention from architectural scholars. Thus an extended study of architectural work—its structures and settings—follows.

Ateliers

Studies of the profession today suggest that many architects believe the atelier, presided over by a charismatic designer, is the ideal setting for both education and practice. Belief in the studio as the locus for architectural creativity seems to grow stronger as professional lives diverge further from this ideal. As architects' days are consumed with administrative, marketing, and financial matters, they fantasize about the architectural studio.[51]

The atelier or studio entered the discourse of American practice with architects who returned from studies at the Ecole des Beaux-Arts in Paris beginning in the 1850s. They brought the culture of the Paris atelier into American education and practice. The success and publicity surrounding Richard M. Hunt and H. H. Richardson, prominent architects educated at the Ecole, gave rise to the idea of the studio as the center for architectural creativity. But the realities of American entrepreneurial practice also intruded into the studio. The association of Hunt and Richardson with the art of architecture and Ecole ateliers has obscured their concerns with the business of architecture and the daily routines of their practices.

Richard M. Hunt   Esteemed as the "dean of American architecture" during his lifetime, Hunt was admired for, if not his creativity, his erudition and academic method. The art critic Royal Cortissoz praised him as "an academic artist" who "drilled [his countrymen] in the logic of architecture." His former student Henry Van Brunt wrote: "He did not pretend to be inventive, or desire to be original, and the impulsive personality . . . nearly disappeared behind the historic types which he used in design."[52]

Hunt gave the American architect social standing as well as academic credibility. The son of a Vermont lawyer and congressman, he had lived abroad between the ages of sixteen and twenty-eight. After studying at the Ecole and traveling through Europe and the Middle East, he settled in New York during the 1850s. Hunt married Catharine Howland, the heiress to one of the country's great shipping fortunes, and they became part of New York and Newport society.[53] Despite his wealth, Hunt's practice was a serious matter for him. In a letter of introduction, former president Martin Van Buren wrote that Hunt, "being easy in his circumstances, . . . is induced to practice his profession in the United States more as a mat-

FIGURE 23. New York University Building, Town, Davis, and Dakin, architects, lithograph, published by Henry Hoff, 1850 (New-York Historical Society).

ter of taste, and to reap its Honors, than for immediate pecuniary advantages."[54]

To satisfy his exacting taste and ambition, Hunt subsidized his own early work. According to a stonecutter, Hunt paid for the carving of banded columns on the ground story of the Rossiter House, his first American commission. He "wanted to show something to New York," the mechanic testified in the 1861 lawsuit over the house, and he gave "a hundred and fifty dollars out of his own pocket to have it done."[55]

An artist and a gentleman needed a studio; Hunt did not locate, at first, in the commercial districts of lower Manhattan where architects traditionally worked. Like artists since the 1830s, he rented rooms around 1856 in the New York University Building on Washington Square in the midst of the Greek Revival townhouses of old New York society (Fig. 23). Here Hunt installed his books, prints, drawings, casts, and objets d'art. Theodore Winthrop, Hunt's childhood friend, described the architect's rooms as the Wunderkammer of a European aristocrat, "the Museum of some old virtuoso Tuscan Marquis, the last habitable chamber of his palazzo, the treasury where he has huddled all the heirlooms."[56]

Hunt presided over a loyal and devoted staff like an Ecole patron ruled over his atelier. By the early 1870s his employees included seven assistants and draftsmen.

Two of them, who managed the office, remained with Hunt until his death in 1895. Although retaining any permanent staff was unusual when most architects practiced on their own, Hunt's office was not large by late nineteenth-century standards. Yet it had produced 120 major works at his death.[57]

Realizing the advertising advantages of locating in a building of his own design, Hunt moved in 1858 from the University Building to the Studio Building, his innovative design for artists' living, working, and exhibition space on West Tenth Street. Although Hunt kept a studio and his students there until the 1870s, he also rented office space in lower Manhattan. As his practice grew to include commercial commissions, he needed an office, not just a studio, for business clients. After completing the Delaware and Hudson Canal Company on Cortlandt Street, his first office building, he moved his practice there in 1877. The Tribune Building, an early skyscraper across from City Hall Park and his most important commercial work, became his headquarters in 1882. He remained there until 1892.[58]

Hunt's move from studio to office building also reveals his evolution from a cultivated artist-architect to a tough-minded businessman. Frank Wallis, who worked in Hunt's office for eight years, remembered him as a "pungent cusser" and a crusader for the profession. Van Brunt described Hunt's conduct of affairs and office atmosphere as "exact . . . [and] business-like."[59] When crossed in business, Hunt proved litigious. He not only sued his first client, Dr. Eleazor Parmly, who commissioned the Rossiter House, but also became involved in lawsuits with Mrs. Paran Stevens and Whitelaw Reid, clients, respectively, for the Stevens Apartments and the Tribune Building. Each of these three cases involved a dispute over his fees and services. Hunt won court judgments in the first two cases; the dispute with Reid was settled out of court for an undisclosed amount. Charles McKim believed that Hunt's legal battles established the 5 percent fee as the standard charge clients came to accept. Consequently, he and his partners, McKim wrote, never had to sue a client for their fees.[60]

But Hunt also understood that American architects operated in the marketplace. Cultivating and pleasing clients was as important as knowing when to sue them. As he counseled his son, "Your business is to get the best results you can following their [the clients'] wishes." In 1890 he advised AIA members that "the architect does not select his time or subject, he must be ready at a moment's notice to carry out the schemes of others, . . . to do so even should it at times be necessary to sacrifice some of our artistic preferences."[61] Although he was hard-nosed about financial matters, Hunt proved accommodating about artistic issues. Style was open for discussion, and he willingly presented alternative designs to clients like Mrs. Josephine Schmid for her Fifth Avenue mansion (Fig. 24). His stylistic flexibility recalls César

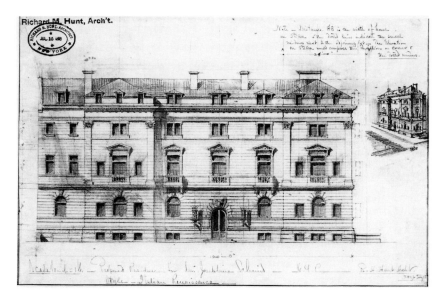

FIGURE 24. Richard M. Hunt, alternative designs for Mrs. Josephine Schmid mansion, New York City, 1893? (Hunt Collection, Prints and Drawings Collection, The American Architectural Foundation).

Daly's disparaging account of *architectes éclectiques* like Hector Martin Lefuel, who was Hunt's Ecole *patron*. The *architecte éclectique* was, Daly wrote, "above all positive and practical. . . . he is enthusiastic about no particular period of the past; he does not plunge into a dream of future architecture. His notion of architecture is . . . above all satisfying the client, the last is nearly all his doctrine." [62] As personified by Hunt, the *architecte éclectique* adapted well to the American architectural marketplace.

Catharine Hunt recalled that her family of "hardheaded businessmen" opposed her marriage to an artist. Hunt ultimately proved to his wife's male relatives that he was not an eccentric ensconced in an atelier. His business practices, litigiousness, and lavish use of profanity projected a resolute masculinity that inspired a younger generation of architects. It was not only his erudition and cosmopolitanism that earned him the title dean of American architecture. [63]

H. H. Richardson   H. H. Richardson was the other prominent American architect who was closely identified with the atelier. Whereas Hunt's contemporaries respected him, they revered Richardson as an artist. When he died at the age of only forty-four in 1886, Richardson was mourned as the architect who had created the eponymous Richardsonian Romanesque. A longtime associate described his practice as "not an office in the present sense, but an atelier where one lived and thought art and the hours did not count." [64]

Richardson began his career in New York, like earlier architects, by working as a draftsman for a builder in the 1860s. He then formed a partnership with Charles Gambrill, a former Hunt student, in 1867. Richardson designed the buildings and superintended construction, and Gambrill saw to the working drawings and office management. Their office was in a commercial building in lower Manhattan. When the firm won the competition for Trinity Church in Boston, Richardson established a field office there in 1874 to supervise their most important work to date. [65] But the partnership frayed during the Boston years, ending in 1878 when Richardson established his own practice. He never took another partner. Mariana Van Rensselaer, the architect's biographer, wrote that "he found it hard enough to bear the checks and limitations which came to him from his clients, and could not have consented to a division of authority in his office. . . . His individual ideas and personal fame had grown dear to him." [66]

Without a partner Richardson now relied on a succession of head draftsmen to produce working drawings and manage the office. Charles McKim and Stanford White were among the more prominent architects who worked as his head draftsman. Young men, especially from MIT, considered it a privilege to work for Richardson and stayed an average of six to seven years. Richardson also accepted students, but

FIGURE 25. H. H. Richardson's assistants in his private office and library, Brookline, Massachusetts, ca. 1886 (Boston Athenaeum).

it does not appear that he was as scrupulous as Hunt about segregating them from the office work. As in an Ecole atelier, a hierarchy of *anciens* and *nouveaux* existed where older assistants trained and helped the newcomers. Staff members later reminisced about late-night sessions with Richardson, hours spent reading in his library, office concerts and dinners, and staff tennis and quoit games (Fig. 25). His office was a studio, Van Rensselaer wrote, "fraternally bound and loyally devoted to their chief."[67]

In Boston Richardson established himself not in the business district but in his suburban home in Brookline. Economy might have influenced his decision, as well as the need to work around the clock on the Trinity Church commission. This melding of home and office, as his assistant Charles Coolidge noted, resembled "the old medieval method of working," when the master craftsman lived next to his workshop.[68] A journalist for the *American Architect and Building News,* however, offered a different reading:

Starting out with the assumption that an architect will produce the best work if he treats his profession as an art to be lived with and known . . . and not as a business to be locked up and left "down-town" each evening and let out again each morning, Mr. Richardson has established his own office at his house, two miles away from the railway station of a small suburban town, without thought or care whether clients may find such an arrangement as convenient for themselves as most usually adopted by the profession.[69]

The divorce between home and work that many Americans were experiencing with suburbanization did not affect Richardson. The inconveniences his clients endured to reach him testified to his achievements and fame. The trip became an architectural pilgrimage. According to the article, architecture was an all-consuming art and did not keep business hours.

At first Richardson and his staff worked in his home. As the practice grew, he constructed a one-story wooden addition to the house. This wing contained an entry vestibule, drafting alcoves (known as the coops), a general drafting room (also used to exhibit renderings and photographs), a business office, a room for special projects like competitions, and Richardson's study, containing his collection of books and prints (Fig. 26). The coops resembled the alcoves where Ecole students toiled away on their initial sketches for a competition project. The study was secluded, with its own entrance and a private piazza; a passageway led to the draftsmen's alcoves and the general office, where visitors entered.[70]

Richardson used these different spaces to great effect. He sat "in state to give audience" to his staff and creditors against a backdrop of expensive drapery and from behind a large table in the general workroom. Prospective clients were ushered into his study, a combination gallery, library, treasury, and curiosity cabinet, where there were Oriental rugs spread across deep blue carpets, bookcases and couches along the walls, a huge fireplace, and a large table covered with rare volumes and choice bric-a-brac. Oriental lamps hung from the cherry beams in the gold ceiling (see Fig. 25).[71]

A clubman since his Harvard days, Richardson thrived in an atmosphere of eating, drinking, smoking, and playing pranks. He became legendary in Cincinnati, where he designed the chamber of commerce building, for the amount of beer he consumed from a loving cup. Work was never far from relaxation, with clubs, dinners, and entertainments providing him with access to potential clients for private and public work. As one state senator said after hearing the Richardsonian sales pitch, he could "charm the bird out of the bush."[72] In his meetings with clients in Brookline, Richardson left little to chance, rehearsing what he would say with an assistant

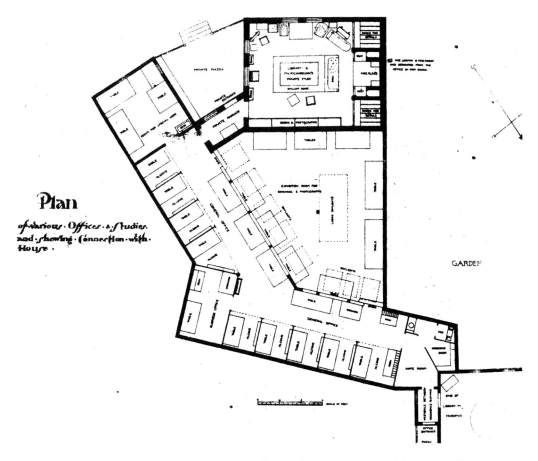

Plan

of various Offices & Studies and showing connection with House

GARDEN

beforehand. To complete the exotic effects of his surroundings, he donned a monk's robe in the colder months and summoned his office boy with an Oriental temple gong. "Who could resist such a man," one former draftsman wrote, "especially in this overpowering environment?"[73]

Richardson did not rely exclusively on old-boy networks for his opportunities. He was remarkably sophisticated in utilizing the new media of journalism and photography to promote his career. He served as editor of the *New York Sketchbook* (1874–76), in which he illustrated his own and his associates' work. He made sure that the *American Architect and Building News* editors had illustrations to reproduce. Recognizing the power of photography, he insisted that photographs of his completed buildings, not sketches or drawings, illustrate his work, and he paid the additional costs associated with such reproductions. His friends Mariana Van Rensselaer and Frederick Law Olmsted wrote about him and his architecture in lay journals like *Scribner's* and *Century*. As the *American Architect and Building News* editors observed, Richardson was the first American architect to become a celebrity.[74]

Commissions for work flooded into the Brookline office. Richardson was responsible for eighty-five buildings and sixty-five projects during his career. At a time when most architects could not collect the AIA standard charge of 5 percent, Richardson got 8 percent. For interior work like mantles, ceilings, and wainscoting, he charged 50 percent of the cost.[75] Although Richardson knew how to cultivate clients and win commissions, he did not know how to manage his money, and he had no partner with financial acumen or administrative skills. When he died in 1886, he owed almost five thousand dollars to his friend Frederick Law Olmsted, his general contractor Norcross Brothers, and his London tailor.[76]

The huge workload took a toll on Richardson's health and on the atelier environment. Although an intimate and artistic atmosphere "was the ideal," one assistant wrote, "it soon proved to be impracticable. . . . Commissions assumed greater magnitude and importance: work was done in less time; we were rushed on and were no longer allowed to seek relief among the treasures of the study."[77] Richardson could no longer spend an entire morning working on a window design with a young assistant and teaching in the process. To develop his ideas and sketches, he now closeted himself with the head draftsman, who assembled a team of junior draftsmen to prepare working drawings and copies for the job superintendent and contractor. Furthermore, he depended heavily on Norcross Brothers, his general contractor since Trinity Church, to function as an extension of his office on the building site.[78] The pressure of work and his declining health made Richardson a more remote figure, but his success, charisma, and memories of the old atmosphere sustained morale and esprit de corps as the studio evolved into a more hierarchical office.

The Legacy of the Studio

The myth of the Richardsonian atelier endured through the writings of Van Rensselaer and the gilded recollections of Richardson's former assistants. Architectural critics and historians have perpetuated it as well, making the studio a powerful symbol for architects. Although Shepley, Rutan and Coolidge—his successor firm— moved the practice to an office building in downtown Boston, Frank Lloyd Wright re-created Richardson's suburban studio as an addition to his own Oak Park, Illinois, home in 1898. Like Richardson, he designed a library as the architectural centerpiece of the studio, explaining in a brochure for prospective clients that this setting was especially conducive to artistic work. Nevertheless, Wright illustrated the plan for his Steinway Building office in this same brochure, announcing that he attended to contracts and superintendence in this downtown Chicago commercial space, not in the studio. Wright, more like Hunt than Richardson in this instance, gave both the art and the business of architecture their due, giving each its own distinctive physical identity.[79]

A provincial architect like Henry S. Moul of Hudson, New York, also preserved, albeit in painfully modest terms, the Richardsonian ideal of the studio. Although he specialized in bread-and-butter commissions like wooden houses and knitting factories in upstate New York, Moul fancied himself an artist. He emphasized his taste with an Ionic column and peacock feather on the cover of an advertising brochure designed and distributed in the early 1900s. Moul illustrated his office, a three-story building where he also lived (Fig. 27), and showed the cramped drafting room where he, a draftsman, and an office boy, all properly dressed, posed stiffly for the photographer (Fig. 28). But a bit of Moul's domestic life, a child framed in the doorway, crept into his solemn world of art and business.

Richardson, Hunt, Wright, and Moul all realized architecture was a business that required marketing of an architectural identity as well as services. The studio was important in constructing this identity. Nevertheless, a greater degree of administration and financial acumen was becoming necessary to create a viable practice even in the hallowed spaces of the studio by the late nineteenth century.

Partnerships

The partnership predated the atelier as a form of architectural practice in nineteenth-century America. It emerged, like other early professional constructs, in the 1820s and 1830s. Although most architects practiced alone, with occasional help from assistants or students, a few leading practitioners found partnerships useful in the expansive and entrepreneurial years before the Civil War. These architects attempted to rationalize and specialize their architectural work as it grew in size and complexity. The early partnerships of Ithiel Town and Alexander Jackson Davis, formed in the late 1820s, and of Dankmar Adler and Louis Sullivan in the 1880s and 1890s demonstrate the evolution of this type of association over the course of the century in the East and Midwest.

FIGURE 27. Office and residence of Henry S. Moul, Hudson, New York, from *Modern Buildings by Henry S. Moul,* 1900 (The Avery Architectural and Fine Arts Library, Columbia University).

Town and Davis   One of the first American architects to form a partnership was Ithiel Town, a successful architect and bridge engineer, who in 1827 formed a year-long partnership with Martin Thompson, a former builder like himself. Thompson saw to the partners' joint building projects in New York, while Town traveled to promote his lattice truss for bridges and accepted architectural commissions on his own. When this arrangement ended, perhaps because the two men's strengths were not complementary, Town asked Alexander Jackson Davis to form an "Association to practice Architecture professionally" in 1829.[80] Town had previously bought drawings, especially perspective views, from Davis, who worked as a freelance draftsman, specializing in what he called architectural composition.

Town, an acknowledged leader of the Greek Revival and Gothic Revival, was nineteen years Davis's senior. According to their arrangement, Town secured commissions for the firm and promoted his truss business throughout the Southeast and Midwest while Davis stayed in New York to design, draft, instruct students, and manage the office. But Town was always present to collaborate with his partner when work on a major design was just beginning. Supervision was often entrusted to a builder because of the size and dispersed nature of their practice.[81]

Town and Davis were partners from 1829 until 1835. James Dakin, Davis's student, briefly joined them as a third partner in New York when Davis set up branch offices in Washington, D.C., and Baltimore between 1832 and 1833. The two founding partners dissolved their association in 1835, when Town decided to concentrate on his bridge engineering, but Davis continued to do some drafting for him, and they collaborated on a few competition projects. In 1842 they formed a new partnership that lasted just one year. After Town's death in 1844, Davis never took another partner.[82]

Town and Davis did not meld as partners; they maintained separate professional identities during the years of their association. An early announcement noted that while Davis "attend[ed] to all kinds of Drawing" and offered instruction in drawing, perspective, and architecture, Town pursued "his profession of Bridge Engineer and Architect in any part of the United States." Davis's diary entries from the partnership years indicate that each man continued to accept his own commissions. The articles of agreement they drew up when they reunited in 1842 point to the underlying tensions in their previous association. Now each partner agreed not to let his individual pursuits "interfere" with their mutual interests. Furthermore, they pledged to limit travel to only what was absolutely necessary for the firm.[83]

Although little is known about their offices in the Wall Street area, Davis left an intriguing comment on the architectural workplace in his undated "Design for an Architect's Office" (Fig. 29). Modifying a Roman temple, he carved out both honorific and practical spaces for the architect. Two rooms lie behind a portico defined by four columns. An office and "p[rint?] cabinet" with a sleeping alcove are placed to either side of a central staircase. Each room has a door to the library, which spans the rear width of the building, opening out to a loggia. While Davis clearly claimed the cabinet as his turf, another hand penciled in "I. Town" over the office space.[84] Since the design is undated, it may represent either Davis's fantasy about grounding his peripatetic partner or an ideal space for his own practice. He segregates business (the office) and art (the cabinet) in spaces that, nevertheless, mirror each other. Given his knowledge and use of Town's extensive collection of architectural books, it is revealing that Davis devotes half of the office space to a library. As the repository of antebellum architectural science, the library connected aesthetics and tectonics figuratively and art and business literally in Davis's plan. While the basic elements of Davis's ideal office reappeared in many settings for later nineteenth-century practice, the compactness, connection, and symmetry his plan offered would be dramatically altered.

Adler and Sullivan   A May-December relationship like that of Town and Davis was difficult to sustain, especially when there was no regular office staff to relieve one partner who wished to design, as did Davis, from the burdens of production and management. But when the older architect had managerial skills and a staff, the younger man might flourish, as Louis Sullivan did when he joined Dankmar Adler. Sullivan joined Adler, his senior by twelve years, in partnership during the early

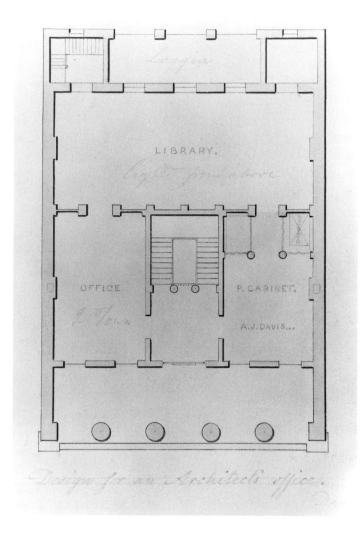

FIGURE 29. Alexander Jackson Davis, "Design for an Architect's Office,"
n.d. (The Avery Fine Arts and Architectural Library, Columbia University).

1880s.[85] Writing of himself in the third person, Sullivan recounted his youthful plan
"to select a middle-aged architect of standing and established practice with the right
sort of clientele, . . . mak[ing] himself indispensable [so] that partnership would
naturally follow."[86] But Adler played a significant role in the firm. The partnership
thrived because the two men had separate spheres of creativity and staffs to support
them. Adler, an established designer, conceded the younger Sullivan's superior

artistry and concentrated on "the study and solution of the engineering problems . . . in the design of modern buildings." The partners employed an office foreman and from twenty to thirty draftsmen by the late 1880s and early 1890s in offices on the sixteenth and seventeenth floors of their Auditorium Building.[87]

Frank Lloyd Wright, hired as Sullivan's principal assistant for the Auditorium commission, remembered Adler as the "big chief" who inspired confidence in contractor and client alike. Although others praised his interpersonal skills, Adler never believed these were his real strengths. He considered himself an architect whose design gifts happened to be in engineering.[88] But the layout of the office confirms Wright's description of Adler as the contact for clients and contractors: whereas Adler's office was near the reception area, Sullivan's was located in a corner far from the entrance (Fig. 30).[89]

Chicago offices with commercial practices like Adler and Sullivan's expanded during the real estate booms of the 1880s and early 1890s. But the high operating costs of maintaining a large staff made them especially vulnerable during the depression of 1893, when Adler and Sullivan had to dismiss most of their assistants. The Adler and Sullivan partnership was not strong enough to weather this financial adversity. After two years of struggle, Adler dissolved the partnership to accept a lucrative consulting contract with an elevator company. After only one year, however, he returned to architectural work. In 1896 he established a bread-and-butter practice of factories, grain elevators, and tanneries with his two sons. Efforts to reconcile the two former partners did not succeed. Sullivan continued on his own with a few loyal draftsmen, but his opportunities for imposing commercial commissions dwindled. His alcoholism and erratic temperament kept away clients whom Adler had attracted and reassured. Separately, the two men were unable to equal the practice that they had created together. Clearly, the process of collaboration had brought out the best in each partner.[90]

Large Offices in New York and Chicago

Partnerships that endured were sometimes family businesses. Although Richard Upjohn's office of seven draftsmen in New York was not large by the late nineteenth-century standards of Adler and Sullivan, it was apparently one of the first sizable practices before the Civil War. Upjohn and his son, Richard Michell, practiced together for over twenty years.[91] At midcentury Upjohn's practice consisted of two junior partners (Upjohn's son and his son-in-law Charles Babcock), seven draftsmen, and a business manager. Upjohn also accepted students in the office. But Richard

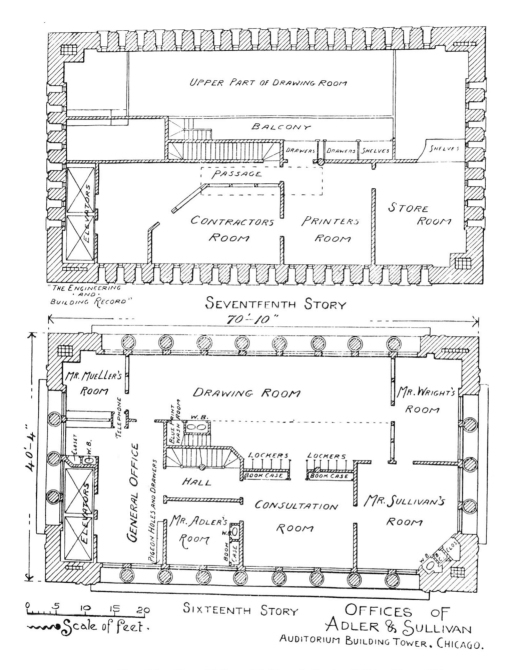

UPPER PART OF DRAWING ROOM

BALCONY

DRAWERS DRAWERS SHELVES SHELVES

PASSAGE

CONTRACTORS ROOM

PRINTERS ROOM

STORE ROOM

ELEVATORS

"THE ENGINEERING · AND · BUILDING RECORD"

SEVENTEENTH STORY

70'-10"

40'-4"

MR. MUELLER'S ROOM

DRAWING ROOM

MR. WRIGHT'S ROOM

TELEPHONE

W.B.

BLUE PRINT WASH ROOM

GENERAL OFFICE

CLOSET W.B.

ELEVATORS

HALL

LOCKERS LOCKERS

BOOK CASE BOOK CASE

CONSULTATION ROOM

MR. SULLIVAN'S ROOM

PIGEON HOLES AND DRAWERS

MR. ADLER'S ROOM

W.B. BOOK CASE

W.B. W.C. CLOS.

0 5 10 15 20
Scale of Feet.

SIXTEENTH STORY

OFFICES OF
ADLER & SULLIVAN
AUDITORIUM BUILDING TOWER. CHICAGO.

FIGURE 30. Plan of the offices of Adler and Sullivan, Auditorium Building Tower, Chicago
(*Engineering and Building Record*, 7 June 1890).

Upjohn and Company, Architects, the name under which Upjohn practiced, clearly indicated that the partnership was not one of equals; Upjohn senior received the lion's share of profits until 1858, when Babcock left. Upjohn *fils* then renegotiated an agreement equally dividing the profits with his father.[92]

Upjohn's two junior partners, however, were involved with design, client contacts, and site supervision. Son and son-in-law worked with Upjohn to develop design sketches that the drafting staff turned into presentation and working drawings. Judith Hull notes that there apparently was some specialization, because no single draftsman worked on all the drawings for one commission.[93] The firm's business manager prepared specifications, ordered materials, supervised builders, and paid the bills. Upjohn's practice expanded from the ecclesiastical commissions that first won him fame to include residential, commercial, and institutional works in the Northeast, South, and Midwest. After Upjohn retired in 1872, his son continued the practice until 1895.[94]

The successive office spaces that Upjohn occupied reveal his own transformation from master artisan to professional architect and businessman. When he first came to New York, he occupied a temporary wooden building on the Trinity churchyard grounds. This office, where he probably worked with only one assistant, was a contemporary version of the medieval mason's building lodge (Fig. 31). After completing the church, he rented space on lower Broadway before moving, around 1854, into the Trinity Building, a five-story office he had designed, next to the Trinity churchyard (Fig. 32). A sign for "Richard Upjohn & Company, Architects," just like the ones for coal companies and lithographers visible in the illustration, was affixed to the facade.

The midcentury Upjohn office of eleven men seems quaint and intimate by comparison with late nineteenth-century practices in Chicago, New York, and other major cities. Specializing in large-scale commercial and institutional work, these offices employed from twenty to over a hundred staff members. A young Daniel Burnham confided to Louis Sullivan that he was not "going to stay satisfied with houses. My idea is to work up a big business, to handle big things, deal with big businessmen, and to build up a big organization." This is exactly what Burnham and other architects did in the last decades of the nineteenth century. A Nevada senator praised these large practices as "not only models as far as art is concerned but . . . models in administration. . . . These great architectural firms in New York and Chicago . . . [have] numerous employees, consisting of architects, artists, engineers, constructors, and draftsmen whose entire work is conducted with the most admirable system."[95] Although today conventional wisdom holds that such large offices are incapable of producing art, the architect John Carrère argued the contrary nearly a

FIGURE 31. Watercolor view of Richard Upjohn's office on grounds of Trinity churchyard, ca. 1846, New York (attributed to Fanny Palmer, Richard Upjohn Collection, The Avery Architectural and Fine Arts Library, Columbia University).

century ago. Architects could devote more staff time and office resources to design, Carrère wrote, because modern business methods of administration and delegation made work more economical and efficient.[96]

George B. Post, Burnham and Root, McKim, Mead and White, and Holabird and Roche were among the first and most prominent large offices in the architectural centers of Chicago and New York. Before the panic of 1893, Post had a drafting staff of 20, Burnham and Root 24, McKim, Mead and White 110, and Holabird and Roche 40. Large offices were not limited to Chicago and New York; they also flourished in regional centers like Cincinnati, where Samuel Hannaford and Sons, a family business, employed up to 24 draftsmen in the 1890s.[97]

These were, of course, not the first large architectural offices. In Europe large architectural staffs were built around a single commission like the new Houses of Parliament. But the American firms were new in that they were private entrepreneurial offices.[98] Since little attention has been given to the phenomenon of large offices that were such a formidable force in late nineteenth-century American practice, I will examine them at some length.

The large architectural office for private practice arose at the same time that commercial and industrial conglomerates developed in late nineteenth-century

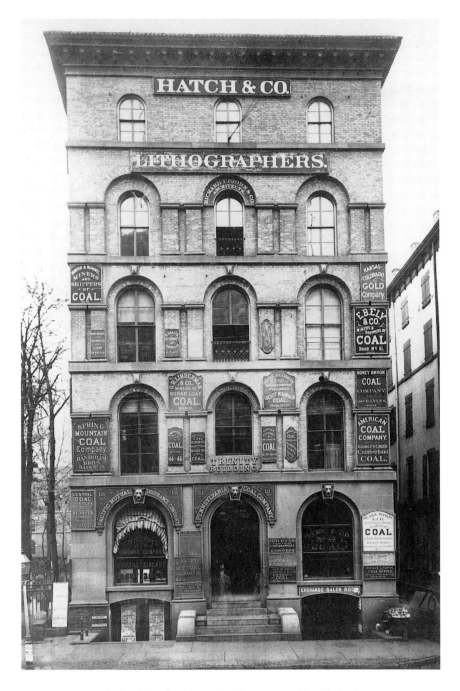

FIGURE 32. Richard Upjohn, Trinity Building, 1851–53, New York, view ca. 1864–68
(New-York Historical Society).

America. These large private practices seem to have been an American invention. McKim observed in 1904 that only a few architects had a sufficiently large practice to maintain "an office force equipped to carry out all branches of building design and construction [for] any considerable period." Although large offices were never numerous in the late nineteenth century, they accounted for some of the most imposing and expensive commissions, just as they do today.[99] Single architects, like George B. Post, presided over a few large offices, but the majority were partnerships. Very few, however, were organized as corporations in the late nineteenth and early twentieth centuries. Despite American architects' praise for modern business methods, the partnership rather than the corporation was the structure deemed suitable for professional practice.[100] Corporations were relatively anonymous bodies designed for maximum profitability; partnerships still focused attention on the individuals who formed the association and performed the services.

Draftsmen accounted for the swelling of staff rosters in these large offices. The number of drawings and copies required for a major building in the 1890s, estimated at between 3,500 and 5,000, drove the formation of these practices. Elaborate written specifications were also necessary, for bidding purposes as well as construction. In 1913 an architect working since the 1850s noted that before the Civil War architects had prepared only "a general plan with a few important dimensions, elevations and sections of a summary character . . . . the rest of the time was spent . . . laying out the work, making templates or drawing profiles on stones. Plumbing, heating, ventilating, refrigerating or electrical installations were unknown."[101] After the Civil War, offices became centers for the production, distribution, cataloging, and archiving of drawings, specifications, and other documents. Drafting rooms were the largest spaces in the office footprint, but specialized areas for clerical staff, job superintendents, and contractors also appeared. Photography and blueprinting facilities, filing cabinets, and fireproof vaults for drawings and specifications were necessary to produce and protect documents (Figs. 33, 34, and 35). Professional magazines like the *American Architect and Building News* and *Inland Architect* published long series advising architects on how to arrange their office spaces to maximize efficiency and productivity.[102]

By systematically organizing their staff and facilities, these large firms took advantage of a robust building economy, producing an unprecedented volume of work. Upjohn's office was responsible for eighty major works around the time of his retirement in the early 1870s. The large offices of the late nineteenth century, especially the partnerships, were even more prolific. While Post accounted for 100 commissions in the thirty-seven years of his practice, Burnham and Root designed more than two hundred buildings in only eighteen years. During their nearly thirty years

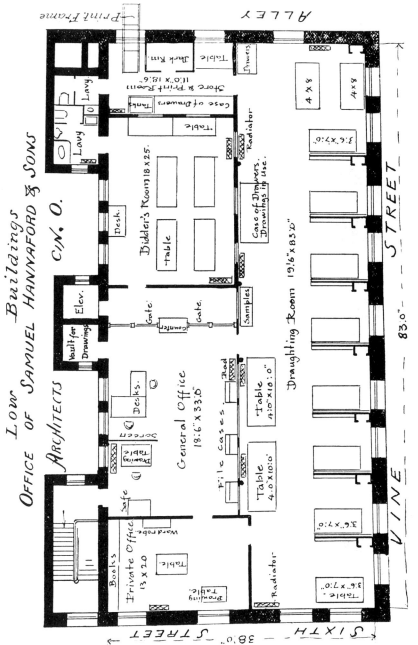

FIGURE 33. Plan of the office of Samuel Hannaford and Sons, Low Building, Cincinnati (*Engineering and Building Record,* 23 August 1890).

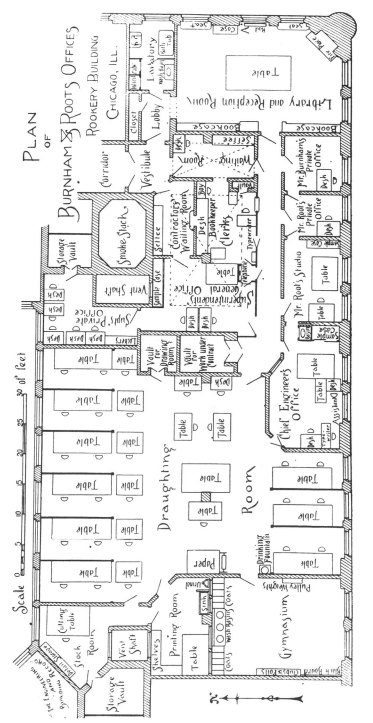

FIGURE 34. Plan of the offices of Burnham and Root, Rookery Building, Chicago (*Engineering and Building Record,* 11 January 1890).

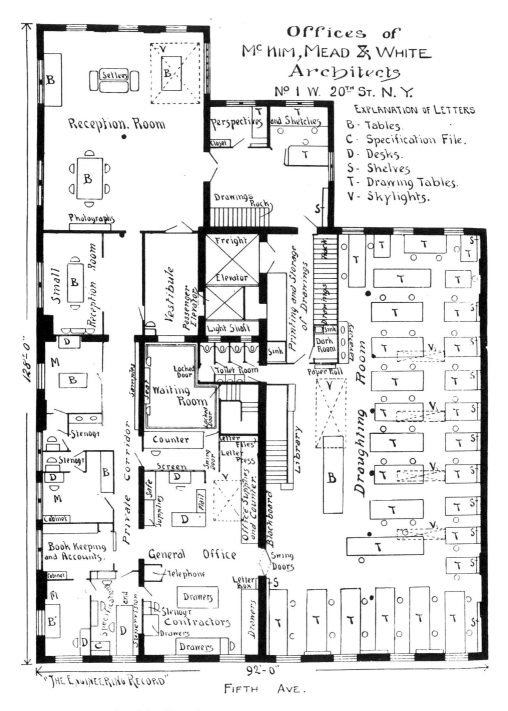

FIGURE 35. Plan of the offices of McKim, Mead and White at 1 West 20th Street, New York (*Engineering and Building Record*, 5 December 1891).

of practice, the triumvirate of McKim, Mead and White worked on over 940 commissions. In dollar amounts, their billings grew from $176,534 in 1880, the first year the three partners practiced together, to $5,110,434 in 1909, the year of McKim's death and three years after White's murder. By 1895 William Holabird and Martin Roche, who formed a partnership in the early 1880s, had executed commissions worth over $2 million.[103]

Administrative and financial skills were essential in a large office. George B. Post worked without partners from 1868 until his two sons entered the practice in 1905. But his engineering and design training and his managerial skills made a partner superfluous. He was known as an architect who could "analyze engineering problems, . . . talk to directors of a financial corporation on the economic and investment aspects, . . . [and] find time even when doing millions of dollars worth of work to render a water color competition drawing with his own hand."[104] According to Diana Balmori, Post transformed a small practice into a modern office with a large and specialized staff when he received the commission for the Western Union Building, an early New York skyscraper, in 1872. Daniel Burnham aimed at building what one former employee called "a highly efficient and well-equipped office to satisfy the needs of rapidly increasing business" when he formed a partnership with John Root in 1873. As another assistant wrote, however, in their commercial work both partners aspired to "pure architecture." The point, as the critic Barr Ferree stated, was to persuade the client for the tall office building to turn a real estate investment into a work of art. *The Economist* eulogized William Holabird in 1923; he was "not only a success in his profession as an architect, but he was a success as a businessman as his buildings . . . were always profitable for their owners. . . . This was the result of talent and clear thinking directed seriously along the lines of beauty and utility."[105]

Partners' talents usually were complementary. While Daniel Burnham, who had some office training, was the acknowledged salesman and administrator, John Root, who had studied engineering and had worked in New York and Chicago offices, was the designer. But Root was as intrigued with the challenge of making tall buildings stand up as he was with their design. The design process began with Burnham's laying out the building footprint and selecting a general style after discussions with the client. Root then developed these ideas further, although he wrote that his facility with a pencil often caused overly complicated designs. Then Burnham was a valued critic and editor, drawing up small sketches for his partner to consider in recasting the design. As one employee noted, Burnham's design function was "consultative and critical . . . but none the less valuable" to Root.[106]

The firm of McKim, Mead and White was unusual for its three partners, two of them principal designers. McKim had studied at the Ecole and then worked as

Richardson's chief draftsman. White entered Richardson's office as an adolescent and rose to become his principal draftsman after McKim had left. Mead had earned an undergraduate degree from Amherst College and had studied at the fine arts academy in Florence.[107] This partnership, unlike those of the Chicago offices, with their concentration on tall office buildings, was known for imposing public and institutional buildings like the Boston Public Library. These were generally McKim's designs, while White took responsibility for the residential and commercial commissions. Mead, whose unfortunate nickname in the firm was Dummy because of his taciturnity, once described his role as preventing his two partners from making damn fools of themselves. According to White's son Lawrence, Mead conceived the heart of some designs and gave timely criticism as projects developed. He dealt with planning and construction, scheduled the work, supervised the office staff, and kept an eye on expenses.[108] But whatever their individual roles, the partners, one critic wrote, were all "moved by the idea that beauty was the prime thing of importance."[109]

Mead's monitoring of time and money was crucial. He spurred on the indecisive McKim, insisting that his partner get on with the design for the Boston Public Library when he seemed to falter. Mead knew that the firm's finances, already stretched in ramping up the office for this first major public building, depended on McKim's moving the library design into the next phase, working drawings and letting contracts, as quickly as possible. Only then would they receive another payment from the library trustees.[110]

White and McKim also served as critics for each other's work. White criticized McKim's sketches brutally, telling his partner on one occasion that his design for a sculpture base looked "like hell." But McKim, too, had an effect on his partner. Leland Roth, a scholar of the firm, attributes the greater simplicity of White's later work to McKim's influence.[111]

William Holabird and Martin Roche built a reputation for solid commercial work ranging from office buildings to electrical generating plants. After studying at West Point, Holabird assisted the army quartermaster and then worked in William LeBaron Jenney's office. He clearly understood hierarchy and logistics after these experiences. Holabird's partner Roche trained originally as a cabinetmaker, a background that was rare for leading architects after the Civil War. They met in Jenney's office, where Roche had become head draftsman after only three years. Although Holabird is traditionally known as the engineer, salesman, and manager and Roche as the sole designer, Robert Bruegmann points out that Roche became increasingly involved with supervision as the practice grew. While Holabird reputedly never made drawings and did little engineering, he did work with building manufacturers to design new products. Edward Renwick, who joined the firm in 1882 and became a partner in 1896, handled specifications, contracts, and supervision. But Holabird and Roche remained the dominant partners, with each of them monitoring projects during all phases of development. Renwick attributed the firm's success to the "well organized office, each having his particular part to do. We each [the three partners] had the part that we were best fitted for."[112]

Of all the large offices surveyed here, the practice of Holabird and Roche seems to have been the least obsessed with creating an architectural aesthetic. The partners prided themselves on an ability to apply new technologies and construction methods. Nevertheless, their attention to ornamental detail was, Robert Bruegmann notes, rare in commercial practices and matched by only a few firms like Adler and Sullivan and Burnham and Root. But the tone of the office was unabashedly pragmatic. Roche frustrated a young draftsman's attempts to engage him in a discussion of what constituted a progressive style. Roche, the young man recalled, spent only a few seconds looking at his drawings and stated that "Holabird will get a new job for the firm, that's progress."[113]

Although partners might follow a project from initial sketches to design drawings to working drawings to final construction, staff members in these large offices usually worked on only one discrete part. Delegation, specialization, and hierarchy became the watchwords in these big firms. A partner usually worked with an assistant or the chief draftsman to develop the initial design after consultation with the client. Many offices had an in-house structural engineer—Burnham and Root added one in 1888 as concerns about liability grew in the wake of a building collapse. Teunis Van der Bent, who joined McKim, Mead and White in 1897 and became a partner in 1909, concentrated on engineering. Holabird and Roche hired an electrical engineer and entered into an agreement with an outside structural engineer in the 1890s. A chief draftsman then supervised the drafting room staff that produced the working drawings from the general studies. Partners like Root might make a daily tour of the drafting room to review the work on the drawing boards. A specifications writer and his staff drafted the written instructions. Designated job superintendents were then responsible for working with the contractors, supervising site work, and writing progress reports. At critical stages the partners also visited the site. A bookkeeper or office manager supervised the clerical staff.[114]

McKim, Mead and White seemed to favor the loosest organizational style among the four large offices surveyed here. Harold van Buren Magonigle, who worked as a McKim, Mead and White draftsman, stated that there was "very little real system or organization in the office, no head draftsman, no division heads, no squad bosses." There was also no chief superintendent for construction until the early 1900s, when the firm designed Pennsylvania Station, a huge commission. McKim and White

FIGURE 36. Reception room of McKim, Mead and White at 160 Fifth Avenue, New York
(*The Brickbuilder,* 22 December 1913).

organized their staff around a given project, as in an Ecole atelier; draftsmen considered themselves either McKim men or White men. Loyalties were fierce, again akin to an Ecole student's for his atelier *patron.* The draftsman in charge of a partner's project followed the building to completion, supervising the working drawings, acting as liaison with contractors, and meeting and corresponding with the client. There were, however, some specialists in the office. George Martin, the bookkeeper from 1888 until 1914, wrote the specifications, drafted the contracts, monitored the costs, and paid the accounts.[115]

All these large practices did have their own office protocol and sense of decorum. Office spaces were arranged to segregate clients from contractors, draftsmen, and staff. Only partners or their chief assistants met with clients, who were received in the partners' private offices or in libraries where renderings, photographs, models, and objets d'art were tastefully displayed (Figs. 36 and 37). Contractors who were bidding on works or meeting with job superintendents were given a separate waiting room and kept away from client reception areas and circulation paths. Drafting rooms were a back-office area of large, well-lit, open spaces akin to factories, a decided contrast to the earlier darkness and clutter of the Upjohn office (Figs. 38 and 39). Some offices even published rule books on hours, overtime, and staff conduct. Post's office, for example, had stringent rules preventing visitors from entering the drafting room without special permission, and draftsmen from conferring with contractors, clients, and building supply agents.[116]

The offices were located downtown in commercial buildings, often designed by the firms. Burnham and Root occupied space in their own Montauk and then Rookery Buildings. Holabird and Roche located in the Monadnock Building, a Burnham and Root building for which they designed an addition in 1891–93. Practices based on residential and institutional work presented a different face to their clients. John Carrère and Thomas Hastings occupied an old brick town house on Bowling Green in lower Manhattan. Harold van Buren Magonigle, who worked there as a draftsman as well as for McKim, Mead and White, remembered that what a client first saw was not a reception area filled with bookkeepers, typewriters, and clerks "supposed to impress the business mind" but a light, airy drafting room filled with renderings, paintings, and ornaments. Carrère and Hasting's move uptown to an elegant town house on Madison Avenue near the site of the New York Public Library, an important firm commission, required some compromises. The reception room maintained the air of a French *hôtel* salon, but the drafting rooms were jerry-built into the upstairs domestic spaces (Figs. 40, 41, and 42).[117]

Keeping these large offices afloat financially involved a delicate balancing act. The Chicago offices serving the commercial real estate market were particularly vulnerable to economic downturns. Adler and Sullivan, as noted previously, did not survive the depression of 1893. Military work, smaller commercial buildings, and lofts provided a steady income for Holabird and Roche during the lean years following the panic of 1893. Burnham, who maintained the office after Root's death in 1891, balanced commercial buildings with such institutional work as libraries, museums, and railroad stations.[118]

McKim, Mead and White faced special challenges because of McKim's commitment to large-scale public works and his indecisiveness as a designer. Fourteen years passed before McKim, Mead and White received final payments for the Boston Public Library. As McKim noted, an office building costing the same amount as a major public building like the library could easily be completed in two years. When the architects' fees were spread out over such a long period, overhead and opportunity costs associated with a project rose and eroded profits. McKim noted in 1895 that the office had the usual problems: "two million dollars' worth of orders and two cents in the bank."[119]

FIGURE 37. Burnham and Root in their office library, Rookery Building,
Chicago, *Inland Architect and News Record,* September 1888,
Ryerson and Burnham Libraries, The Art Institute of Chicago).

FIGURE 38. Drafting room of George B. Post, 33–35 East 17th Street, New York, from *Architectural Record,* 10 July 1900 (Fine Arts Library, Cornell University).

FIGURE 39. Drafting room of Richard (?) or Richard Michell (?) Upjohn's office, n.d. (The American Institute of Architects Archives).

FIGURE 40 (*above*). Carrère and Hastings office at Madison Avenue and
41st Street, New York (*Architectural Record,* October 1900).

FIGURE 41 (*opposite, top of page*). Reception room of Carrère and Hastings
office, New York (*Architectural Record,* October 1900).

FIGURE 42 (*opposite*). Drafting room of Carrère and Hastings office, New
York (*Architectural Record,* October 1900).

FIGURE 43. Erection of trial plaster cornice at the Boston Public Library building site
(Trustees of the Boston Public Library).

McKim's perfectionism exacerbated the financial problems. He kept designs in a "plastic state far beyond the point at which others would have regarded them as finished." The full-size trial cornice erected on site for the Boston library exemplifies his costly practices (Fig. 43). Making changes after the contracts were let was an expensive and contentious process. If the partners could not convince the client to spend more, the firm had to absorb the additional costs associated with design revisions.[120]

Lawrence Grant White astutely distinguished between McKim's work and his father's: "Each building McKim produced was an architectural event. He built in the grand manner. . . . White was exuberant, restless, a skyrocket of vitality. He worked at a terrific pressure and produced a great many buildings which are graceful and charming rather than imposing."[121] White's contribution was vital to the firm's financial well-being because the commercial and residential projects he produced at a feverish pace bought McKim the time, staff, and resources he needed to revise and perfect the public works. Harold van Buren Magonigle reported the office rumor, which circulated during the late 1880s and 1890s, that White had brought ninety commissions into the office, McKim eight, and Mead two.[122] Between 1886 and 1897, for example, Robert and Ogden Goelet commissioned nine commercial projects from White, accounting for over ninety-four thousand dollars in profits. The Boston library, which tied up the office for eight years, ultimately produced a profit of only twenty-two thousand dollars, with the final payment received six years after the building was completed.[123]

White drove himself and his draftsman at a breakneck pace, yelling at Magonigle to push the work along, White told him a bay window for a club "ain't the Parthenon, it's made of tin." White clearly understood that his productivity was essential to the financial health of the partnership.[124] McKim readily acknowledged his partners' importance to him and the firm, and he always insisted that credit for any work go to McKim, Mead and White, not to any particular partner. Although he considered establishing his own practice in Boston after marrying Julia Appleton, he quickly realized he could not practice alone. In a letter to a colleague, McKim stated that he needed "a practical man whose abilities would be of a business kind" to complement his artistic gifts. Even when his wife died, McKim remained with his partners Mead and White, who, each in his own way, provided practical ballast for the firm. The three men were fiercely protective of the partnership. When Stanford White's personal financial debacles threatened the firm in the 1900s, the partners drew up an agreement demoting him to a salaried employee. His creditors could not attach firm assets, and the erstwhile White could not drag the partnership down with him. But White and the work he brought in were still a part of the firm.[125]

The four practices surveyed here all survived their founders into second and third generations of partners. Post's grandson closed the office only in 1980. Burnham built an organization that continued after Root's death in 1891, taking Charles Atwood and then Peirce Anderson as his designers; it survived after Burnham's own death in 1912, with Ernest Graham, his former assistant, reorganizing the firm as Graham, Anderson, Probst and White. Holabird's son John formed an association with Root's son, and the two created Holabird and Root, a firm that still exists today. Lawrence Grant White, Stanford's only son, continued the firm with Mead; they were joined by Burt Fenner and William Kendall, McKim's former assistants. The firm practiced as McKim, Mead and White until 1961.[126]

The successor firms' work was well designed, responsibly executed, and solidly constructed, but the founders' creativity was more difficult to sustain. An unsigned

and undated caricature (probably from after 1909 when both White and McKim
were dead) summarizes the dilemma of the surviving firms (Fig. 44). Mead, in
rompers, plays with a Corinthian column, trying to assemble a design in the tradition of Pennsylvania Station and Low Library at Columbia, models of which sur-
round him. The machine for production survived, if not the creative spark.

When Robert Peabody gave his presidential address at the AIA convention of
1901, he acknowledged that the large office was now a professional fact of life. American architects as diverse as Charles McKim and Dankmar Adler agreed on one fundamental point: a successful professional practice required entrepreneurial initiative
and business acumen. Just what business tactics and procedures were professionally
appropriate remained vague. The AIA sanctioned the large offices' organization,
hierarchy, and bureaucratization as ways to deal with architectural practices driven

by private building markets. The large practices also seemed well equipped to produce the high-profile public and commercial commissions that the profession valued as the most important architectural work. But such offices depended on architects who were employees. Large architectural firms simultaneously celebrated the self-employed architect as head of the design and building team and surrounded him with a bureaucracy of specialized architectural workers. The web of interconnecting relationships needed to construct a design is the final subject of this study.[127]

CHAPTER 5

ASSISTANTS, RIVALS,

AND COLLABORATORS

In our art the productions of the individual have been supplanted.
It now takes several men to make a good architect.
Robert Peabody, Address to the AIA, 1901

Because of new materials and mechanical systems introduced in the late nineteenth and early twentieth centuries, building even a house of moderate cost could involve as many as twenty artisans and mechanics. Drawings, specifications, coordinated supervision, and logistics became critical even at this modest scale of practice.[1] When the commission was for a tall office building, the task became infinitely more complex. As Leopold Eidlitz noted, these structures required millions of bricks, shiploads of cement, lumberyards of floor plank, and miles of water, gas, and steam pipes. Furthermore, investors demanded that their skyscrapers be constructed and opened for tenants as quickly as possible, often within six months to a year.[2]

The market for building services grew increasingly specialized and fragmented in late nineteenth-century America, making it even more difficult for professional architects to direct all aspects of design and construction. Architects with both modest and large practices now had to work with a number of collaborators, who were sometimes their assistants and sometimes their rivals. These collaborators have typically been shunted aside in architectural histories. The account that follows looks behind the usual picture of solitary creation to the reality of architectural work.

THE ARCHITECTURAL EMPLOYEE

A leading Boston architect was supposedly horrified when a local contractor offered him a job on his design staff. The architect turned down the offer, unwilling to sacrifice what he called his self-respect and architectural principles. Only independent practice, the man asserted, could sustain him psychologically and aesthetically.[3] After 1850 the architect as employee became, however, a fact of professional life. Working for architects, builders, interior decorators, landscape architects, stock plan publishers, and engineering companies was an alternative to independent practice. These jobs also involved design, drafting, documentation, and superintendence. Many architects worked full-time, others part-time, and some freelance, often hoping that these arrangements were just way stations to their own practices. Others settled into these positions for the rest of their working lives. Some men and women ultimately left architecture and worked successfully as contractors, interior decorators, landscape designers, and real estate developers.[4]

The Drafting Room

The drafting room was usually the point of entry into the architectural office for aspiring designers. While George Barber employed inexperienced men to copy his mail-order designs, large and prominent firms like McKim, Mead and White, Burnham and Root, and Holabird and Roche attracted ambitious, educated draftsmen. Their employees usually had prior office experience or some academic training. As one McKim, Mead and White alumnus explained, it was a "great privilege to be admitted to the offices." So esteemed was the firm that the partners could ask prospective employees for a trial period of six months to a year during which they received no pay.[5]

Copying drawings was traditionally the first task given to an office novice. Strickland, Latrobe's apprentice, wrote of being promoted from cleaning the office to copying ground plans. More than a century later the entry-level draftsman at firms like Burnham and Root, McKim, Mead and White, and Holabird and Roche was still a tracer, an employee who copied drawings.[6]

The early procedures for copying were laborious. In Upjohn's midcentury office, copies were made from inked drawings by placing two or three sheets underneath the original and then pricking it with a pin. The draftsman used these pinpricks as guides for the copies. Some architects continued to use this method after the Civil War, but tracing on translucent linen or yellow tracing paper placed over the inked drawings eventually became common.[7] Despite the monotony of tracing, many architects claimed the routine produced some superb draftsmen. William Partridge, who worked with McKim on the Boston library, wrote that "this grinding duplication of copies—[and] the elaboration of full-size details"—created an unrivaled "flexibility of fingers and delicacy of touch."[8]

After 1850 new graphic technologies were available to copy drawings. The Supervising Architect's Office in the Treasury Department used photolithography to make as many as nine sets of working drawings. But photolithography was a relatively complicated and costly process. Blueprints, made by placing a translucent trace or linen drawing over photosensitive paper and then exposing it to light, were inexpensive, accurate, and easy to produce. By the late nineteenth century, offices like Samuel Hannaford and Burnham and Root (see Figs. 33 and 34) made their own blueprints in house. Wooden frames were mounted outside the drafting room windows to hold and expose the drawing and blueprint paper.[9]

Tracers were vulnerable to these new technologies. Burnham and Root's chief engineer, who had charge of the drafting room, decided to replace tracers with reproductive processes in the late 1880s. While an individual tracer was inexpensive, he concluded, their collective pay was too great. By eliminating tracers, Burnham and Root shrank its drafting force from sixty to between eighteen and twenty-four men. By the 1890s, tracing drawings cost ten times more than making blueprints.[10]

After working as a tracer, a young man progressed to freehand and mechanical drawing and developing detail studies under the supervision of more experienced draftsmen. These senior men did all kinds of drafting and, in some offices like Richardson's, supervised the production of working drawings, wrote specifications, and represented the office on the building site. These responsibilities, with the exception of specification writing, were also assigned to senior draftsmen at McKim, Mead and White. Other large firms like George B. Post, Burnham and Root, and Holabird and Roche compartmentalized these tasks, apportioning them among chief draftsmen, drafting staff, chief engineers, specification writers, and job superintendents, all with very specific rather than overlapping duties.[11]

Working with a design principal was the mark of a rising man in the office, but it was often frustrating and nerve-racking too. In the early days of his office, Richardson apparently spent hours with a draftsman, rubbing out as the man drew and redrew a design. Frederick Law Olmsted recalled that his friend Richardson believed tracing paper and India rubber were the architect's most valuable tools. McKim's methods were similar to those of his former master. Harold van Buren Magonigle, a self-professed White man, disliked the long hours that McKim spent "dictating" a design, erasing a draftsman's work again and again. While Magonigle had no desire to become one of McKim's "architectural valets," William Boring, a regular McKim assistant, appreciated the partner's time. McKim's lengthy dictation sessions, Boring recalled, made the draftsmen "participants in the creation and [a partner] treated them as equals."[12]

Working for White was a completely different experience. Whereas McKim worked with a draftsman for hours, White spent only a few minutes. Pushing the draftsman off his stool, he intently studied the plan or detail in question and then sketched several variations on tracing paper. Exhorting the draftsman to "do that," White then brought his hand down on perhaps two or three of his sketches. Then, Magonigle recalled, "You had to guess what and which [sketch] he meant. The sketch might have to do with what you were working on, or it might not . . . or it might be something he had forgotten to mention. He almost never explained. It was grand practice in guessing."[13]

John Root, according to his draftsmen, did not give them vague sketches to puzzle over. His ideas were well realized and developed by the time he first put pencil to paper. One man remembered Root as low-key as he conducted his morning rounds of the drafting room. He "simply looked at the drawing, . . . made a few suggestions, perhaps pushing you off the stool." Another draftsman claimed that "no fault was ever found with our work by either Mr. Burnham or Mr. Root. . . . They must have gone into a closet for a private swear now and then." But another draftsman recalled a less easygoing atmosphere. Claiming that he "had to knuckle down," the man recalled doing as he was told when given one of Root's preliminary studies to develop.[14]

Office work was often numbing and the pace frenetic. One man at McKim, Mead and White left, saying it was too much of a "grind-mill," and went to Carrère and Hastings in search of a more atelier-like atmosphere. Magonigle concurred that McKim, Mead and White draftsmen were under intense pressure. Yet Paul Starrett found the Burnham and Root office busy but less formal and constraining than his earlier places of employment in a hardware store and insurance office. The intensity increased as drawings were prepared for reproduction and distribution to contractors submitting bids. A young Holabird and Roche draftsman recalled that his only instruction at such times was to trace as quickly as possible while the staff worked evenings and weekends to make the necessary documents.[15]

Experience and skill determined a draftsman's salary. In the early 1800s Latrobe supposedly paid one hundred dollars a year to each pupil who assisted him with drafting or site supervision. James Dakin gave James Gallier four dollars a day, considered a high salary, for drafting in the early 1830s. A draftsman claiming experience in tracing and copying specifications and drawing ground plans and "plain" elevations asked Upjohn for a weekly salary of five dollars in 1851. Alpheus Morse, who also asked Upjohn for a job, wanted nine dollars a week to work on the drawings for Trinity Church.[16] Upjohn hired Morse, but his salary is unknown. Occasionally tensions arose between draftsmen who had "graduated" from the boards and those with some formal study. Charles Rutan, who had only a high school education when he began working as an office boy for Richardson, supposedly resented Charles McKim, who received fifteen hundred dollars a year because of his Beaux-Arts training.[17]

By the late 1880s an experienced draftsman like James Brite, who joined McKim, Mead and White, earned $8.00 per week. When Brite completed a difficult interior perspective for a competition submission overnight, the partners raised his weekly salary to $20.00. More than a decade later experienced draftsmen, McKim estimated, earned between $25.00 and $60.00 per week.[18] In the late 1880s Burnham promised Paul Starrett a weekly salary of $7.50, which would rise to $12.50 if he stayed three years. After proving himself as a job superintendent over the next two years, Starrett was rewarded with a salary of $25.00 per week.[19] By contrast, Burnham took at least a $100,000 out of the firm in 1891. Mead hoped that the practice would pay each partner $450 per month in 1887 and 1888. This figure climbed to more than $8,000 per month in the first five months of 1905.[20]

Offices were usually open six days a week, five and a half in the summer months. Each draftsman signed the drawings he worked on and recorded his hours on a time ticket (Fig. 45). A draftsman's time was carefully tracked and monitored in these large offices, but it is not clear if and how such record keeping related to remuneration. Office procedures spelled out further staff regimentation. Carrère and Hastings published a rule book in 1900 that prohibited staff from conducting loud conversations or smoking in the drafting room during business hours. Furthermore, no private work was to be done during the firm's time; and library books, photographs, drawing paper, and other supplies were only for office use.[21]

Some firms offered outlets for relaxation and recreation amid the pressure, bureaucracy, and regulation. In a gymnasium located just off the drafting room in the Burnham and Root office, the staff could box, fence, juggle Indian clubs, play handball, and lift weights (see Fig. 34). Burnham occasionally appeared and gave fencing lessons. Yet the gymnasium was part of his plan for greater efficiency and productivity. According to Starrett, Burnham believed that physical exertion sharpened a man's wits.[22] At McKim, Mead and White baseball was the sport of choice. Camaraderie grew as the partners and staff played against other architectural firms. According to a scorecard from a game with the office of R. H. Robertson, White played shortstop, and Mead and McKim were in left field (Fig. 46). W. T. Partridge, an office draftsman, recalled that White slashed wildly at the ball, but McKim, who had played at Harvard, led the office in batting.[23]

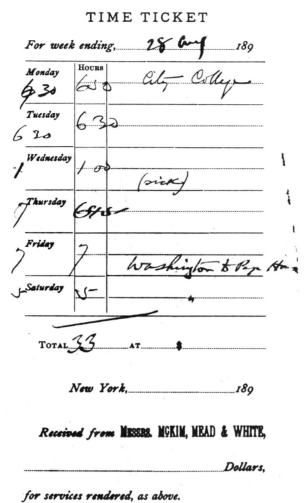

FIGURE 45. Draftsman's time ticket, McKim, Mead and White, 28 August 1891? (Philip Sawyer Papers, The Avery Fine Arts and Architectural Library, Columbia University).

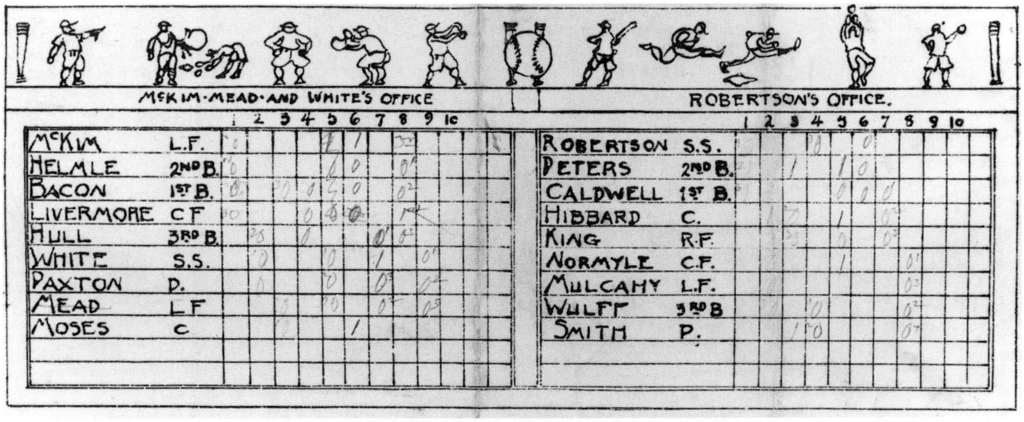

McKIM·MEAD·AND·WHITE'S OFFICE — ROBERTSON'S OFFICE

McKIM MEAD AND WHITE'S OFFICE		ROBERTSON'S OFFICE	
McKIM	L.F.	ROBERTSON	S.S.
HELMLE	2ND B.	PETERS	2ND B.
BACON	1ST B.	CALDWELL	1ST B.
LIVERMORE	CF	HIBBARD	C.
HULL	3RD B.	KING	R.F.
WHITE	S.S.	NORMYLE	C.F.
PAXTON	P.	MULCAHY	L.F.
MEAD	LF	WULFF	3RD B
MOSES	c	SMITH	P.

FIGURE 46. Baseball game roster for McKim, Mead and White office versus R. H. Robertson office, 1894–95? (Philip Sawyer Papers, The Avery Fine Arts and Architectural Library, Columbia University).

Both McKim and White continued the tradition of dinners and parties that was familiar from their years in Richardson's office. These events were important for bonding and morale. After winning the competition for the Rhode Island state capitol, the office celebrated with a costume ball, familiar from McKim's days in the Ecole ateliers (Fig. 47). There were bishops with crucifixes made from T squares and miters constructed out of the models of the capitol. Revelers, carrying placards that read "We Have Fared Capitolly" and "We Have Tempted Providence," chanted these legends and similar doggerel.[24]

Fraternity and Alma Mater

The large architectural office was clearly a fraternity. Its "alumni" grew nostalgic for the enthusiasm and ambition of their first years in the drafting room. Egerton Swartout, who worked for McKim, Mead and White from 1892 to 1900, asserted that the "old" office meant more to his generation of draftsmen than their own practices did later.[25] It is clear why women and minorities were deemed alien presences in such an environment. The baseball games, gymnasium workouts, costume balls, and dinners were decidedly male affairs. Even the partners' demands and the pressure of work became initiation rites affirming masculinity. Magonigle wrote that "White's way was to load us youngsters way beyond our powers and force a result out of us if it could be squeezed out—sometimes it couldn't. But it was

FIGURE 47. Costume ball celebration of McKim, Mead and White staff after winning the competition for the Rhode Island Capitol, January 1892? (Philip Sawyer Papers, The Avery Fine Arts and Architectural Library, Columbia University).

wonderful training if you didn't crack under the strain—it made a man of you—or it didn't."[26]

The architectural office was also an alma mater. Many men had no training apart from office experience. The McKim, Mead and White alumni were especially loyal and fervent. Although there are some accounts from former staff at H. H. Richardson, Burnham and Root, and Holabird and Roche, a remarkable number of former McKim, Mead and White men wrote reminiscences (published and unpublished) about their years in the office. The partners made a point of exposing ambitious staff members to the full range of architectural practice—design, drawing production, supervision, and even client contact. They also treated them like prospective colleagues. Many former employees recalled that McKim, in particular, nurtured and educated them. He loaned them money to travel abroad and singled them out for praise in letters to clients. Mead assured draftsmen departing to form their own practices of the partners' help in finding those crucial first commissions.[27]

An extraordinary number of architects did "graduate" from McKim, Mead and White to open their own practices. By 1919 five hundred men had worked in the office. Many partners, including Carrère and Hastings, York and Sawyer, Boring and Tilton, and Bacon and Brite, first met there. Prominent alumni of McKim, Mead and White also included Cass Gilbert and John Galen Howard. No other single firm, one commentator claimed in 1922, had such a profound impact on shaping young American architects. Large firms like George B. Post and Burnham and Root, with highly specialized job descriptions, do seem not to have created nearly as many independent practitioners as McKim, Mead and White. Nevertheless, McKim, Mead, and White could be hardheaded businessmen about their staff when necessary. During the financial depression of the early 1890s, they ruthlessly slashed their employment rolls from 110 men to 55.[28]

Draftsmen saw themselves as white-collar employees who dressed with decorum (Figs. 25 and 48). Bosworth described Richardson's men as "charming, intelligent, high-bred gentlemen." A draftsman for Burnham and Root remembered that "the men were treated invariably like gentlemen."[29] Furthermore, they felt they were part of important and challenging work, the making of art. The idea of working in a studio like Richardson's was crucial for morale and motivation. But large offices could also nurture architecture as an art. As Magonigle wrote, "McKim, Mead and White was an association of artists working in architecture as our principal medium. . . . when we had to work overtime, we got a dollar for our dinner—nothing for our time—and broke our backs to get the work done." But draftsmen's sense of self-importance was not borne out by their salaries. According to financial records from the 1900s, a senior draftsman at McKim, Mead and White received far less than a job superintendent or specifications writer.[30]

Although an undated petition protests the lack of ventilation in the McKim, Mead and White drafting room at 160 Fifth Avenue, I know of no other organized complaints against working conditions, salaries, or hours of late nineteenth-century large offices. Architectural staff certainly did not identify with unionized workers. Many did not even see themselves as permanent employees. There was always hope that winning an important competition or receiving a first commission would enable a draftsman to open an office and perhaps become an employer himself.[31] But even if they did not, draftsmen at high-profile architectural offices still considered themselves part of a professional elite. Glenn Brown, who studied architecture at MIT, shocked his friends when he took a job with Norcross Brothers rather than going into a prominent practice like Richardson's. But Brown wanted to learn about practical building.

FIGURE 48. McKim, Mead and White staff, n.d. (McKim, Mead and White Collection, The Avery Fine Arts and Architectural Library, Columbia University).

General contractors like Norcross Brothers and George Fuller needed draftsmen when they created in-house drafting services. While McKim, Mead and White draftsmen made several hundred drawings for the New York City Municipal Building, the firm's first skyscraper, in the early 1900s, Norcross Brothers produced the balance of seven to eight thousand working drawings. This meant large architectural offices that worked routinely with contractors like Norcross hired fewer draftsmen, reducing their overhead expenses. Thus the entry-level positions as unpaid tracers at firms like McKim, Mead and White became scarcer and even more coveted.[32] The mystique of art and the prospect of contributing to it made the breakneck pace, nerve-racking pressures, and financial sacrifices palatable for many young draftsmen. The firms depended on more intangible forms of compensation like professional reputation, dedication, and camaraderie to hold on to their staffs.

Freelance Draftsmen

But perspectives, especially those for presentation and publication, were often the work of freelance artists and architects rather than staff draftsmen. Before his association with Ithiel Town, Alexander Jackson Davis had a flourishing career as a draftsman in the 1820s. Builders and architects paid him well for his drawings, especially perspective views. Hammatt Billings, who trained as both an architect and an illustrator, prepared architectural drawings and views in Boston beginning in the 1830s. Billings, like Davis, had a gift for picturesque compositions. Upjohn contracted with the artist Fanny Palmer and her husband for watercolor perspectives of his buildings during the 1840s (see Fig. 31).[33]

During the late nineteenth century, men who specialized in perspectives and moved from office to office were known as journeymen draftsmen or itinerant renderers. Among the more celebrated were E. Eldon Deane and Theodore Langerfeldt, who worked as perspectivists for prominent Boston architects. Hughson Hawley, who began as a scene painter, became a widely published perspectivist for leading New York architects. Harvey Ellis, who practiced architecture intermittently on his own in Rochester, New York, was one of the most renowned of the so-called architects' artists. He worked in midwestern offices from Minneapolis to Saint Louis. A frequent contributor to the architectural press, Ellis set a style for pen-and-ink renderings that was copied in many architectural offices (see Fig. 6).[34]

Unlike photographers, who rarely received a credit line in the architectural press, renderers like Deane, Langerfeldt, Hawley, and Ellis signed their works and received recognition. These architects' artists were yet another indication of the growing specialization of architectural work. Some commentators even hinted that they were their employers' design collaborators as well as hired renderers. If so, they remained unacknowledged for this element of their work. But, unlike anonymous office staff, they did enjoy some measure of fame within the architectural community and the professional press. Despairing of the hustle and connections needed to run an architectural practice, an artistically inclined draftsman at Holabird and Roche left the office and worked as a freelance renderer in the 1900s.[35]

BUILDERS

Just as some antebellum master builders were drawn to architectural professionalism for reasons of status and independence, many other craftsmen tried to rise by becoming builders. James Gallier complained that the New Orleans artisans whom he considered most qualified all left his employ. During the real estate booms before the Civil War, these craftsmen believed they could do better by becoming building contractors responsible for labor, materials, and supervision.[36] Money was also the reason antebellum professionals like Gallier himself; Ithiel Town and Martin Thompson in New York; John Haviland, Thomas U. Walter, Samuel Sloan, and John Notman in Philadelphia; and Alexander Parris and Solomon Willard in

Boston supervised building contracts for works they had not designed.[37]

Many builders expanded their scale of operation to take advantage of new opportunities in the antebellum period. The master craftsman who presided over a small workshop transformed himself into a businessman trying to serve new urban and regional markets beginning in the 1820s and 1830s. But these undercapitalized businesses sometimes foundered. John Holden Greene, the leading designer and builder in Providence, Rhode Island, during the early 1800s, accepted more apprentices when he expanded into real estate development and manufacturing of prefabricated ornaments. But Hiram Hill, one of Greene's apprentices, noted it was all too much for "one man to do," and Greene's overextended and thinly capitalized business empire collapsed in 1824.[38]

Industrialization as well as capitalism began to transform the practice of building well before the Civil War. The balloon frame of the 1830s, an assemblage of precut wooden components joined by commercially manufactured nails, changed traditional construction methods. Although flimsy by comparison with master carpenters' heavy timber frames secured with mortise and tenon, the balloon frame was inexpensive, went up quickly, and required only semiskilled labor to erect it.[39]

After 1860 even child laborers as well as semiskilled workers operated steam-powered machinery to produce building components like doors, window sashes, moldings, and trims. Steam technology also transformed the handicraft process of brickmaking. Large commercial brickworks replaced small, local brickmakers by the 1870s. When architects, builders, and owners simply ordered building components from catalogs and had them delivered to the site, carpenters and masons became assemblers of industrialized parts. They were no longer highly skilled craftsmen who designed building elements, selected materials, and executed the work. Industrialization diminished the role of craft, motivating many building mechanics to take up contracting.[40]

Practical Architects, Builders, and Speculative Developers

Building and architectural journals chastised builders and disparaged so-called practical architects (men trained in a building craft rather than in an architectural office) who allegedly colluded with speculative developers seeking unconscionable profits from their investments. By the 1880s the editors of *Shoppell's,* which sold stock house plans to builders and speculators, decried some developers' profits of 40 to 100 percent wrung, it was charged, from their builders' and practical architects' use of shoddy materials and construction methods.[41] The editors first lectured the developers, who should be content with a respectable 10 to 15 percent profit. Then they excoriated the practical architects who entered into unholy alliances with such developers, endangering public safety and bringing all architects into disrepute.[42]

Accounts of building collapses caused by the shoddy work of unscrupulous builders and speculators filled the pages of the first professional architectural journals. The subtext was the promotion of the architectural profession as the only safeguard against incidents like the collapse of a Massachusetts mill in the 1860s where the builder had used sand rather than mortar. A verse entitled "Death, the Builder" in the *Architects' and Mechanics' Journal* for 1860 attacked speculators and builders who maximized their profits and endangered the public with flimsy construction (Fig. 49). Accompanying the verses was a drawing of a building mason as the grim reaper who serves the "lords of enterprise" by making the wall look strong; the blood and bones of his victims ultimately bind the wall. In the background the speculator, Shylockian with his greasy hair and hooked nose, turns away, clutching his bag of coins.[43] Builders were responsible, the professional press also reported, for illness as well as injury and death. The *American Architect and Building News* published an account of a builder who refused to spend three hundred dollars to connect soil pipes to street drains. As a result, raw sewage discharged into the party walls, spreading illness throughout an entire residential block. Meanwhile, speculative builders who used architects' plans for their residential developments and discountenanced such deadly economics earned praise from the *American Architect* editors.[44]

Ethnic and class distinctions also began to divide builders from architects during the nineteenth century. Builders' guides like Edward Shaw's *Modern Architect: or, Every Carpenter His Own Master* (1854) portrayed a class solidarity between the practical architect, his mechanics, and clients, depicting all as middle-class men properly, if impractically, attired for the building site in the frontispiece to the book. The working mechanics wear long-sleeved shirts, vests, and neckties, as do the architect and his clients, who also wear coats and top hats (Fig. 50). Shaw himself was a practical architect, the descendant of a long line of New England builders who combined design with building work. The male middle-class client could be confident that a practical architect like Shaw shared his outlook and interests.[45]

But the ethnic composition of the building community began to change markedly with new waves of immigration. The Irish were particularly important, dominating the carpentry and bricklaying trades in New York City by the 1880s. Other immigrants found work in the skilled building trades in late nineteenth-century New York: Italians as stonemasons, Englishmen as bricklayers, Germans as truss

DEATH, THE BUILDER.

HERE is a Builder, whose name
is Death,

A fearful one I ween;

He builds the frail walls with a breath,
And blood's the cement between.

FIGURE 49. "Death, the Builder," *Architects' and Mechanics' Journal,*
4 February 1860 (The Avery Fine Arts and Architectural Library,
Columbia University).

framers, and French and Germans as decorative workers. American workers born in this country dominated only one building trade, plumbing.[46]

This rise of immigrant artisans and builders disturbed many in the architectural and building community. The art and architectural press engaged in ethnic stereotyping, characterizing the practical architect and builder not as the familiar

BOSTON,
DAYTON & WENTWORTH,
1854.

FIGURE 50. Frontispiece, Edward Shaw, *The Modern Architect: or, Every Carpenter His Own Master,* 1854 (Fine Arts Library, Cornell University).

middle-class figures of Shaw's frontispiece (see Fig. 50) but as the ignorant and ridiculous Philologus Brown, an Irishman, satirized in a long-running series of the 1850s published in *The Crayon.*[47] A more vicious caricature of an Irish practical architect appeared in the *Architectural Sketchbook,* a journal published by a Boston professional society during the 1870s. Drawn by architects George Tilden and William Preston, it depicts Patrick McFlabby, Brown's landsman (Fig. 51). Disheveled and

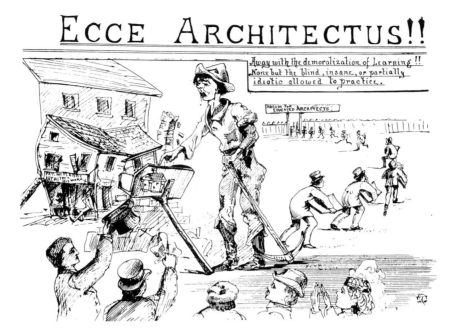

FIGURE 51. George Tilden and William Preston, "Ecce Architectus!!" *Architectural Sketchbook,* March 1875 (The Avery Fine Arts and Architectural Library, Columbia University).

drooling, he presents his latest design, a childish sketch of a house, before an admiring and well-dressed crowd. To the left lies McFlabby's business establishment, a ramshackle building raining down bricks from its chimney. In the background men wearing top hats and frock coats and carrying portfolios slink off to the "asylum for educated architects." All this occurs under the legend: "Ecce Architectus! Away with the demoralization of learning!! None but the blind, insane, or partially idiotic allowed to practice." [48] The American builder, for architects like Tilden and Preston, was now an illiterate, alien, and dangerous figure. "Ecce Architectus" warns middle-class clients not to be deceived. Now only the professional architect was a social peer and trusted adviser who understood their needs and aspirations. [49]

Irishmen did become prominent building contractors, but men like John Crimmins belied the stereotypes of the Philologus Browns and Patrick McFlabbys in the professional press. Trained as a bookkeeper, Crimmins was the son of an Irish builder on Manhattan's East Side. Having expanded his father's business, he built over four hundred residences by 1871, employing some twelve thousand workers directly and hiring several thousand more through subcontractors. In the 1880s and 1890s Crimmins held public and private contracts for city streets, sewers, and the elevated rail-roads. Success gave him the means to collect Irish rare books and manuscripts; his contributions to Catholic charities earned him a papal knighthood. Crimmins demonstrated how builders as well as professional architects could become American gentlemen.[50]

Despite the architectural profession's editorial campaigns against them, practical architects and builders continued to create the residential and small-scale commercial works that were the connective tissue of American cities and towns. In many communities, especially those far from urban centers, they still received commissions for important private and public works. But Montgomery Schuyler, a late nine-teenth-century architectural critic, wrote that builders responding "to the demand of the market" were also responsible for the "bulk of building which gave its character to New York and the country."[51] Furthermore, some builders had impeccable architectural credentials. Clarence True, who had trained in Richard Upjohn's office, designed and developed middle-class residences on Manhattan's Upper West Side, an area of intense real estate speculation after the Civil War. Many practitioners and their clients saw the combination of architectural and building skills as decidedly desirable. A late nineteenth-century guide to New York real estate and building described True favorably as one of the "few architects who builds himself, ensuring the carrying out of his plans to a correct issue."[52] His work as a designer, builder, and developer gave True the kind of comprehensive control that few in the profession ever possessed.

GENERAL CONTRACTORS

Most builders worked on a small scale, usually beginning by overhauling or altering existing buildings and then progressing to new construction. After 1850 large general contracting firms, a new breed of builders, emerged to manage institutional and commercial commissions. Before this owners or architects let contracts individually, and the work was carried out under the architect or the client's supervisor. The client now made a single contract with the general contractor, who in turn negotiated with all the building laborers and suppliers. Norcross Brothers, George Fuller, and Marc Eidlitz—the three general contractors surveyed here—were leading firms in late nineteenth-century America.[53]

Although early general contractors like O. W. Norcross and Marc Eidlitz had backgrounds in the building trades, later men—like George Fuller and Paul Star-rett—had worked in large architectural offices as job superintendents. Paul Starrett, who worked for Fuller and then established his own general contracting firm, found the Burnham and Root office where he worked a place of "quiet, secure artistic leisure compared to the hazardous, hurly-burly of building." He preferred the latter because there was "more money in building." At a time when prominent architects received 5 percent of the building cost for their fee, general contractors collected from 5 to 15 percent. These high fees demonstrated general contractors' ability to put up sound buildings efficiently and quickly.[54]

While some general contractors provided only labor (skilled and unskilled) on the construction site, others supplied materials from their own lumberyards, brickworks, and stone quarries. A few maintained design and engineering staffs and began developing real estate. All, however, offered managerial and administrative expertise. General contractors prepared estimates of materials and labor; coordinated the bids and awards of contracts; handled scheduling, logistics, and site superintendence; and certified payments for materials and work.[55] They challenged the architect's control over supervision, his leadership of the design and building team, and his advisory role with the client.

The influence of general contractors over all aspects of building, some late nineteenth-century observers argued, grew with the rise of speculative office buildings. Real estate developers, especially those involved with skyscrapers, found that general contractors provided them with sound and rapid construction, ensuring better returns on their investments. The general contractors wielded clout in negotiating terms for material and labor because of the number and scale of their operations. Contractors like George Fuller and Paul Starrett became financial advisers, suggesting changes in design, structure, or construction to save money. It was Fuller who reputedly suggested using rivets to construct Holabird and Roche's Tacoma Building, thereby expediting work. Developers sometimes asked Paul Starrett to recommend architects for their projects.[56]

Large architectural firms like George B. Post, Burnham and Root, and McKim, Mead and White continued to employ their own job superintendents. While these men dealt with building mechanics and tradesmen during the bidding process, their principal job was to ensure that the executed work conformed to the architect's drawings and specifications. The job superintendents also suggested certain changes to the architect in charge as the work progressed, but they did not provide the kind of service a general contractor offered a client. Job superintendents inspected only periodically, not daily. Nor did they advise clients, with whom they rarely interacted, on structural, logistical, and financial matters.[57]

The general contractor supplied full-time administration for a building process that had become exceedingly complex. During the building of a skyscraper, the general contractor dealt with and managed as many as thirty separate building trades. In masonry alone there were now specialists who dealt exclusively with foundations, face brick, fireproofing material, and stonework.[58] General contractors also negotiated with trade unions, a crucial responsibility as labor and management relations grew increasingly bitter during the late nineteenth century. Clients wanted a general contractor who could ensure labor peace on the building site. But because of their size and importance, general contractors became favored targets for labor action; contracts with them established wage and hour standards for the entire industry. When O. W. Norcross locked out workers and hired scabs on one project in 1891, the unions retaliated by shutting down his building sites in Boston, Chicago, New York, and Omaha. Whereas Norcross was adversarial, George Fuller was conciliatory, reputedly buying labor peace by bribing union leaders.[59]

Norcross Brothers was a family contracting business that survived until the 1920s. O. W. Norcross was the heart of the firm. Trained as a carpenter, he gained experience on large-scale projects, building bridges and roads, for the Union army. He was responsible for the firm's estimates and supervision. Continuing the tradition of ingenious mechanics, he obtained patents for his invention of new fireproofing materials and reinforced concrete slabs. His brother James managed the office and financial affairs.[60]

The operations of Norcross Brothers was vertically integrated. Beginning with the stone contract for Trinity Church in Boston, they provided materials as well as skilled and unskilled labor. Eventually the brothers acquired brickworks, timber mills, iron foundries, and quarries in holdings that stretched from Maine to Georgia. Such a degree of integration was highly unusual when less than 5 percent of all carpentry and brick contractors manufactured their own materials in 1890.[61]

O. W. Norcross counseled architects like H. H. Richardson and McKim, Mead and White on materials, structure, finances, and construction methods. McKim found his advice on steel-frame construction invaluable. Glenn Brown, who worked for Norcross on such commissions as Richardson's Cheney Building, considered the contractor "a working branch of the architect's [Richardson's] office." Although Brown came away from his Norcross experience with great admiration for the contractor's integrity, craftsmanship, and supervision, he found that Richardson "ignored practical considerations to obtain artistic effects." Norcross reconciled these inconsistencies and dealt with design changes often made on the building site. Norcross Brothers, Brown maintained, translated Richardson's ideas into reality, acting as the architect's true collaborator.[62]

Marc Eidlitz and Company was another family contracting business whose operations predated Norcross. Marc Eidlitz, the brother of architect Leopold, trained with a New York builder. In the 1850s Eidlitz received his first contracts, earning a reputation with his work on the Broadway Tabernacle, one of the largest Manhattan churches, in 1854. He sent his sons to study architecture and engineering at Cornell and then brought them into the family business, ensuring a full range of services in design, structure, and materials. The partners and staff prepared drawings and estimates, dealt with materials and labor, and supervised work on the site. But Eidlitz did not own quarries, mills, or foundries like the Norcross Brothers. His business involved contracts for large institutional, commercial, and residential commissions: Astor Library, Metropolitan Opera, Steinway Hall, the Harper Brothers Building, and houses for J. P. Morgan and Ogden Goelet.[63] His geographic focus was also more circumscribed than Norcross's, with works concentrated in New York City and Long Island for architects like McKim, Mead and White, George B. Post, Carrère and Hastings, H. J. Hardenbergh, Shepley, Rutan and Coolidge, his brother Leopold Eiditz, and his nephew Cyrus.[64]

George Fuller built an institution that still survives, nearly a hundred years after his death in 1900. Fuller studied architecture at MIT before working as a draftsman for Peabody and Stearns in Boston. He gained building experience when they made him job superintendent for their New York commissions in the early 1880s. By 1882 Fuller had set up his own contracting business, and eighteen years later he had a national practice, with offices in Chicago and New York.[65] His firm was the general contractor for such prominent skyscrapers as Burnham and Root's Rookery Building, Holabird and Roche's Tacoma Building, and Burnham's Flatiron Building, Fuller's own New York headquarters. Fuller, like Norcross, was an industry innovator. He developed electrical hoists and steel fasteners in his construction of tall office buildings and developed a delivery system for materials that brought them to the site only as they were needed. Fuller had a reputation for saving his clients time and money.[66]

Fuller had an important edge over his competitor Norcross: peace on the construction site. A reputation for completing buildings on schedule because of no labor actions brought him clients. Although he owned no quarries or mills, Fuller maintained a large staff of building mechanics and laborers. Consequently, he subcontracted out very little work on his building sites. His employees, unlike Norcross's, were content; they received their wages promptly and regularly. Fuller was an enlightened employer, insuring his workers against injury and loss of life.[67]

Both large architectural offices and general contracting firms were responses to the increased scale and complexity of American construction after the Civil War. They also indicated the higher financial stakes surrounding building, especially commercial works, and the consequent pressures to expedite design and construction. Although many architectural leaders applauded the large professional office, they were more ambivalent about the rise of general contractors even as they, too, grew dependent on them. Whereas Richardson and McKim acknowledged Norcross's contributions and valued his advice, other architects were wary of general contractors' power, especially over contracts and other financial matters. Cass Gilbert complained that general contractors compromised the architect's design and usurped his supervisory role by awarding contracts only on the basis of the lowest bid. But architects, even the professional journals chided, willingly relied on contractors for information, working drawings, and specifications; doing so saved them on time, drafting costs, and supervisory staff. But architects paid a price for this convenience. Such arrangements further reduced their involvement in the building process and again raised the question of who directed and ensured the execution of architectural designs. The erosion of architects' supervisory responsibilities could have profound financial repercussions. Architects with large offices, like Charles McKim and George B. Post, estimated that they began to earn a profit only during the supervisory phase of building.[68] While it was desirable for architects to outsource costly drafting services to contractors, supervision was where they traditionally made their profits. Furthermore, an architect who was not involved in supervision risked becoming a picture maker and facade designer whose ideas were easily altered in the construction process because of structural or financial considerations.

Equally serious, however, was the general contractor's undermining of the privileged position the professional architect sought to maintain with the client. O. W. Norcross, Marc Eidlitz, and George Fuller were not Philologus Brown or Patrick McFlabby. They offered expert advice based on training and experience. Eidlitz's sons were formally educated in architecture and engineering. Norcross and Fuller were innovators in materials and construction methods. They, not the architect, defended the client's financial interests. The business methods, specialized service, and efficient organization that large architectural firms proudly offered clients also characterized the general contractors' operations. Furthermore, contractors did not struggle to resolve the professional conflicts of serving self, the client, public welfare, and the art of architecture. Striving to serve the client, they were a better fit for a high-stakes building economy driven by speculative real estate development.

Civil Engineers

Only a few American civil engineers—often architects like Latrobe, Mills, Strickland, and Town—had independent practices during the nineteenth century. Engineers were typically employees of private railroad, canal, or mining companies. As Daniel Calhoun has written, the American corporation "supported and sustained the engineer, and quite early defined his career." The model of independent practice that characterized the architectural profession was rare for engineers in the nineteenth century.[69]

Before 1850 civil engineers dealt primarily with wooden or masonry structures, relying on a working knowledge of materials and construction. Antebellum builders' guides and manuals provided some additional information; few men had any formal training in engineering. There were over 4,000 engineers in 1870, but only 75 had an engineering degree, and 130 had less than two years of academic training. Furthermore, the nineteenth-century curriculum for civil engineers remained rather general in contrast to the specialized courses of study for mechanical, mining, and chemical engineers.[70]

The growing use of iron and then steel for bridges and buildings did not necessarily create opportunities for independent engineering practice. The first metallic structures were hardly examples of precise engineering. They were simply overbuilt in the absence of theoretical knowledge, controlled laboratory testing, and proven formulas for calculating loads and stress. Owners, builders, and architects relied not on engineers but on early ironwork manufacturers like James Bogardus and Daniel Badger to provide them with drawings and specifications. As manufacturers like Andrew Carnegie sought new markets for steel in the wake of railroad overexpansion during the late nineteenth century, they also supplied architects with handbooks to figure the size of different building members. As a result, Paul Starrett claimed, there was a "lot of amateurish engineering" in architectural offices.[71]

Firms like George B. Post, Burnham and Root, and McKim, Mead and White hired engineers as staff members beginning in the 1880s and 1890s. Burnham and Root retained a chief engineer, who had charge of the drafting room. They also hired engineers as job superintendents. These men, the firm maintained, were "able to make their own calculations and meet their own emergencies" on the building site. Root, his brother later recalled, now "had no time to learn and keep up the many branches of construction. He was rusty in his calculus and trigonometry and ditto much of the applied mathematics. I do not believe he would have cared to trust himself to calculate an important truss; it was not necessary nor desirable that he should."[72] Engineers were architects' employees. Accustomed to working in bureaucratic organizations, they were ideal additions to large architectural offices. They were socialized into the business culture of hierarchy, bureaucracy, and specialization.

Nevertheless, architects like Daniel Burnham seemed to have a certain disdain for engineers. He advised a young Paul Starrett to study the business side of architecture, since "any engineer could be hired to do the routine calculations." But Burnham soon needed engineering expertise beyond routine calculations. He hired E. C. Shankland, an experienced designer of steel bridges, after the collapse of Burnham and Root's Midland Hotel in Kansas City.[73] Not all the engineers working in architectural offices, however, had Shankland's Missouri experience or credentials. One professional commentator observed that many of the so-called engineers working in architects' offices were wholly unqualified, like the man who had formerly tended a machine presented as the "civil engineer" of one firm.[74]

Unlike Daniel Burnham, Dankmar Adler respected engineers' contributions to architecture. He argued, in fact, that the architect must be an engineer as well as an artist and businessman. Structural solutions for tall office buildings in Adler's office were not cribbed from manufacturers' handbooks or drawings. Adler asserted that architects like himself who solved these structural problems were just as gifted as canal, bridge, and railroad engineers. Nevertheless, for him his engineering staff were "the same as other draughtsmen" hired to carry out his "conception and ideas as to the design of the building."[75]

Adler's remarks underscore engineers' status as employees in architects' offices. Men like George B. Post, John Root, William LeBaron Jenney, William Holabird, and Adler himself all had backgrounds in engineering (through either formal training or army experience), but they chose to practice as architects. Practitioners who had studied at American schools of engineering accounted for 13 percent of all AIA members in 1870 and 11 percent in 1891. During the nineteenth century engineers did not necessarily compete with architects; they became architects.[76]

Architecture, not engineering, was the basis for the independent practice of engineers like Wilson Brothers of Philadelphia. After studying engineering at Rensselaer Polytechnic Institute, John A. and Joseph M. Wilson first followed the usual engineering career path: employment with a railroad, in their case the Pennsylvania Railroad. Their professional lives were transformed when the architects designing the main building for the Centennial Exposition in Philadelphia failed to reduce building costs and lost the commission.[77] The Wilson brothers stepped in and designed a building, essentially a huge train shed, that did not exceed the construction budget.

After establishing their reputation with the 1876 exposition, they opened an independent practice in Philadelphia, hiring architects because they could not survive on engineering contracts alone—too many large companies had their own in-house engineering staffs. Wilson Brothers designed and supervised the construction of bridges, docks, viaducts, trestles, and wharfs. But architectural commissions for banks, offices, houses, and educational buildings provided an important stream of revenue. The firm prided itself on providing complete service; a client always dealt with a partner, not an assistant, and had no need to hire any outside specialists.[78]

Wilson Brothers was an early model for architectural and architectural engineering practices that today position and market themselves as full-service firms.

The tall office building, surprisingly, did not immediately create opportunities for private civil engineering practice during the late nineteenth century. C. T. Purdy, an engineer who had worked on steel-frame structures in Chicago and New York, was warned not to establish an independent practice in New York during the 1890s. He persisted, but by 1904 there were only twenty-five independent engineering practices like his in the entire United States, with New York alone accounting for seventeen of them.[79]

Other Engineering Specialists

During the late nineteenth century, architects began to consult sanitary, mechanical, and electrical engineers, whose work, unlike that of structural engineers, was seen as too specialized and arcane for architects to master. Professionals like George B. Post, who was trained as an engineer, willingly ceded the control of sanitation, heating, and ventilation to engineering experts who worked as freelance consultants for a number of architectural offices.[80] There was simply not enough work for architectural firms to hire them as full-time staff members. McKim, however, believed that he had to carefully monitor these outside consultants; otherwise their mechanical systems absorbed more and more building space, destroying his design. For this reason McKim, Mead and White assessed the client an additional 2.5 percent supervisory fee on the sanitary or mechanical engineer's charges. Although this practice was highly controversial in the building community, the AIA ultimately incorporated it into the schedule of charges. It was an attempt, usually unsuccessful except for prominent firms like McKim, Mead and White, to maintain the architect's position as head of the building team amid the growing number of specialists. Only the architect, some in the profession argued, could understand and coordinate all these disparate efforts.[81] This was an increasingly difficult argument to sustain as the ranks of general contractors and independent engineering consultants grew in late nineteenth-century America.

CLIENTS

Early American settlers actively participated in the construction of their buildings. Members of a community, whether or not they were craftsmen, helped to raise timber frames for houses and churches. As building grew more complex in design, structure, and mechanical systems during the nineteenth century, this kind of involvement ceased for most Americans. In this new environment, professional architects tried to structure a hierarchical relationship with their clients just as they attempted to with their assistants and engineers.[82]

Although Latrobe expected his clients to defer to him as an expert and a gentleman, he also knew that powerful men like Jefferson had to be handled with the tact that only the true gentleman possessed. Nevertheless, his diplomacy masked a condescension, revealed in comments to his clerk about Jefferson's ideas for designing executive department offices: "I am sorry that I am cramped in this design by his [Jefferson's] prejudices in favor of the architecture of the old French books, out of which he fishes everything,—but it is a small sacrifice to my personal attachment to him to humor him."[83] It was Jefferson, however, who prevailed in their debate over another federal design problem, how to illuminate the House of Representatives chamber.

Less imposing clients than a president elicited different responses from the professional architect. Richard Upjohn adopted the tone and manner of a stern schoolmaster when clients pressed their own ideas. F. K. Hunt of Lexington, Kentucky, provoked this reaction when he commissioned a country house from Upjohn in 1849. Hunt knew what he wanted: a house in the Gothic style for an elevated site, costing between ten and twelve thousand dollars. In his reply to Hunt, Upjohn did not rule out the Gothic, provided it "was adapted to the particular locality, site, and climate." However, he praised the Italianate style as especially well suited to clients with either limited budgets or unsophisticated workmen. The latter was a valid concern when Upjohn would be absent from the site and would communicate only through drawings and specifications.[84]

Hunt did not take Upjohn's hint. Further correspondence ensued about the plan, but Hunt refused to proceed until he saw the design for the exterior. Upjohn sent drawings for an Italianate house along with arguments for its adoption on grounds of economy and ease of execution. Hunt politely rejected the design. He then asked Upjohn to send him a bill and forward his requirements to Alexander Jackson Davis, renowned for his Gothic Revival residential designs.[85] Upjohn was not pleased and sent a stern lecture to the obdurate Hunt:

> I do not wish to be understood as opposed to pointed architecture when it
> is properly treated . . . but I am most decidedly opposed to Mimic Castles,
> abbeys and other absurd buildings of the present age. . . . My decision may be
> against me in a pecuniary point of view, but as there is much good yet to be
> done by a right development of the Arts, I for one will make it my study so
> far as I am capable, to design in the most *truthful* manner, such work as may
> be confided to my care.[86]

Asking Hunt to return his designs and letters, Upjohn refused all compensation. His actions and emotions seem those of a jilted suitor, or at least a spurned mentor. Yet Hunt saw the relationship as a strictly business one. He wanted a Gothic house, not an education in design and architectural truth. If Upjohn could not accommodate him, he was willing to pay the architect for what he had done before he went on to a more obliging designer.[87] Upjohn saw the dispute as a classic test of his professional authority.

A client questionnaire prepared in the Upjohn office appears to date after the contretemps with Hunt. Perhaps Upjohn felt such a document would improve communication with clients and avoid misunderstandings like those with Hunt. Prospective clients answered twenty-three queries on such issues as materials, structure, water closets, servant rooms, and budget. One item was more a directive than a question: "We suppose you want a house of good proportions, but not richly ornamented. We wish to have it evidently *wooden* in design, not an imitation of stone or brick. The Italian Style is best."[88] With this question Upjohn tried to finesse any arguments over the proper residential style. This client's response must have gratified Upjohn: "Manifestly *wooden*. Great aversion to imitation of any-thing. Greatly prefer Italian style." Now Upjohn knew from the outset that this client was no Hunt who would dispute his professional advice on style.

Male architects frequently adopted paternal and pedagogical roles with their female clients. Alva Smith Vanderbilt, wife of W. K. Vanderbilt, commissioned many works from Richard M. Hunt, including a château on Fifth Avenue in New York and the Marble House in Newport, and clearly enjoyed this tutelage. She wrote that the architect "was my instructor and dear friend and the work we did together was for me always an endless delight and great resource." Draftsmen were put at her disposal as the design evolved, and she spent many hours in Hunt's office approving the work.[89] During these sessions with Hunt, she internalized lessons about architecture, family, and prestige that the architect believed were important for his clients. She later wrote: "These houses were not merely beautiful private residences, they were the means of expression in outward and visible terms of the importance of the Vanderbilt family. They represented not only wealth, but knowledge and culture. . . . So I felt about the Vanderbilt fortune, and I preached this doctrine at home."[90] Through these lessons Alva Smith Vanderbilt became Hunt's best ally in the Vanderbilt family councils on building.

Architects like John Root, with largely commercial and institutional practices, found female clients alien, usually encountering them only for the rare residential commission. In a toast at a banquet of architects, Root poked fun at "Madame," who broke the office monotony with her "frou frou of silk, the odor of patchouli . . . and a little plan on scented note paper she had studied at home." But suggestions from male clients about residences, he claimed, were welcome because the architect's "technical and professional point of view in art is not always the truest." As long as architect and client were both men, the architect, Root felt, needed "to see as an intelligent layman may see."[91]

In commercial work, Robert Bruegmann notes, firms like Burnham and Root and Holabird and Roche often had to defer to the "intelligent layman" whom Root had praised in his toast. These commissions dealt with constraints imposed by construction, financing, real estate, and building law. Clients and their general contractors possessed this knowledge, and many architects had to defer to their expertise.[92] Whereas architects like Root valued businessmen's financial, legal, and technical experiences, they discounted women's knowledge, associating it with private and domestic spheres.

One wonders how Root would have fared with a client like Theodate Pope, an heiress to the United States Steel fortune. After travel abroad and work in the settlement house movement, Pope decided to design a home for her parents. Although she retained McKim, Mead and White, Pope clearly understood business negotiation and dictated the employment terms at the very outset: "As it is my plan, I expect to decide on all the details as well as all the more important questions of plan that may arise. . . . In other words, it will be a Pope house instead of a McKim, Mead and White. . . . I am not nearly as difficult to deal with as this would seem, for I am very tolerant of advice and always open to suggestions and good reasoning."[93] After vetoing the office job captain assigned to her, Pope took part in supervising construction. McKim, Mead and White supposedly reduced their charges because of her work on the house.[94]

But Pope was also a worldly client seasoned by travel abroad and settlement house work. The partners may have conceded her a degree of involvement usually not allowed to clients, especially women, because of her prominence and the prospects for future work she represented. However, she commissioned no more work from the firm, instead establishing her own office, where she practiced for the next thirty years.[95]

Pope's experience contradicted the popular view of the client-architect relationship. William Dean Howells, Mead's brother-in-law and a client of the firm, explored the architect as Pied Piper in his 1885 novel, *The Rise of Silas Lapham*. A Boston Back Bay house with an ever-increasing budget causes the downfall of the protagonist, Lapham. The architect, Howells wrote, was "skillful, as nearly all architects are in playing" upon this self-made yet unworldly Lapham who now wanted taste and social acceptance.[96]

During the nineteenth century, however, the businessmen whom many architects encountered were more often shrewd speculators rather than naive and malleable Laphams. Dr. Eleazor Parmly, who commissioned the Rossiter House from Richard M. Hunt, is a good example of the breed. Although Parmly was a dentist, he speculated in the lucrative market of Manhattan residential and commercial properties during the antebellum years. He purchased plans from practical architects and builders like Martin Thompson and William Thomas; Parmly's mechanics then erected buildings from these drawings. If any additional details were necessary, the dentist selected them from a book, and his mechanics copied them.[97] Given Parmly's past practices and Hunt's inexperience in the American building market, it is not surprising that the two became embroiled in a lawsuit over fees. Parmly believed he was purchasing a commodity—architectural drawings—and paid Hunt a lump sum. Hunt, however, assumed he was providing professional service, design, and supervision charged as a percentage of the building budget.[98]

Architects seasoned in the building market, like John Van Osdel of Chicago, accepted clients and prevailing practices for what they were. Also Van Osdel was not, like Richard Upjohn or Richard M. Hunt, a proselytizer for truth and art. When Chicago businessmen balked at his charges for design, he did not sue but "worked with men as they were, using the means and materials at hand, always doing a little better than he had promised and alertly seeking better ways to do what had to be done. The most building for the money [he understood] had to be the rule . . . in those formative years [of Chicago]."[99]

By the late nineteenth century, some real estate developers became convinced that design was a good investment if they wished to attract high-paying tenants. Louis Sullivan, however, admitted that the architect spent much time educating developers about the tangible rewards of increased rents from the "tall office building artistically considered."[100] But a client like the publisher Frank Munsey wanted to build a monument to himself in his eponymous headquarters in Washington, D.C. His general contractor warned him that an architect like Stanford White would "just put a lot of embellishment into it that will cost much more money." But money was not the object here, and Munsey hired McKim, Mead and White for his Washington, D.C., building. When White persuaded him to spend an additional $150,000 dollars for better foundations and a more elaborate cornice, Munsey saw the expense as simply another affirmation of his own success and achievements. The architect was now a status symbol for the commercial client, just as Hunt had been for Alva Smith Vanderbilt.[101]

Most American architects only dreamed about a client like Frank Munsey. They did not have large offices with draftsmen, job superintendents, freelance artists, and engineering consultants. Their competitors were plan book merchandisers like Benjamin Price and George Barber and builders like Clarence True who combined design with construction and development. But as the nineteenth century drew to a close, many architects did not even have this measure of independence. They were employees of other architects, contractors, and developers. The goal of independent practice was just as unrealistic for them as the myth of architect as solitary creator was for their employers.

Capitalism, urbanization, and industrialization stimulated the development of the American architectural profession in the early nineteenth century. But these forces also created opportunities for other experts and specialists like general contractors and mechanical and sanitary engineers. Civil engineers posed less of a threat to architects, but they were beginning to emerge from the cocoon of corporate employment as the nineteenth century ended. Builders and practical architects, who had traditionally controlled the housing market at the professional architect's expense, adapted to new market conditions. House pattern books and stock plans helped them to maintain a hold over middle-class housing. Despite professional and educational advances during the nineteenth century, professional architects still found authority and control in the competitive American building market elusive and fragmentary.

CONCLUSION

The architect, indeed the ideal man, is an artist, gentleman, and man of business.
John Carrère, "Making a Choice of a Profession," Cosmopolitan *(July 1903)*

After more than a century of effort, American architects of John Carrère's generation could write confidently for a general audience about architecture as a man's profession. But Carrère himself was a novelty in American professional circles, a practitioner with academic training in architecture as a fine art. Office experience was still the most common preparation for American architects who practiced in the late nineteenth and early twentieth centuries. Although he had studied at the Ecole des Beaux-Arts, Carrère, too, spent time "on the boards" in the McKim, Mead and White office before establishing his own practice. Office training, with its roots in the artisanal world of apprenticeship, became the common bond, uniting star performers with lesser lights, and antebellum architects with Gilded Age Beaux-Arts designers.

The acceptance of professionalism in the United States depended on this linkage between the artisanal and architectural worlds through the office. Learning in an office grounded the architect in workplace realities. The office bridged construction site and art studio, building yard and drafting room; it educated the citizen-architect, who joined art with craft and reconciled private gain with public responsibilities.[1] Furthermore, the office gave readier access to the profession than the academy or university, at least for white males. When women and African Americans with university degrees established their own architectural offices in the late nineteenth century, they seemed only to validate the American ideology of opportunity and egalitarianism. During the nineteenth century, the office mediated between professional architects' ambitions for honor and authority and American society's ingrained suspicion of rank and privilege.

But the office had to be about private practice; only then was professionalism palatable in America. Capitalism, not the state or public institutions, was the milieu of American architectural practice. Architects and other professionals offered expertise and service for a fee. They were entrepreneurs, go-getters, who earned their livelihoods in the free market. Moreover, some American artists and architects celebrated entrepreneurial practice, believing it freed them from the constraints of private and state patronage. For them the marketplace was not an imposition but an opportunity. The entrepreneurship of antebellum artisans continued to shape American architectural practice, surviving the transformation of architecture from a craft to a profession.

Although select practitioners received commissions for large-scale public and private works, most architects designed prosaic buildings: modest houses, churches, and stores. An architectural pecking order evolved comparable to that in medicine and law; each profession had its generalists and specialists, its corporate and storefront practitioners. Nineteenth-century America accepted such stratification in the professions as long as it seemed the inevitable outcome of marketplace competition. Art and architects must prove themselves in the marketplace.

In ascribing artistry and gentility to architects, Carrère, in his *Cosmopolitan* article, gave a European cast to professional identity. But his reference to the professional architect as a businessman would have dumbfounded Continental architects. After training at state institutions, French, German, and Italian architects aspired to public positions, state appointments that on the Continent conferred honor and authority; employment in the private sector was not the path to an illustrious career.[2] British architects would have found Carrère's idea of the architect as businessman insulting and outrageous. Although they, like Americans, were independent practitioners, not state functionaries, British professionals shared the upper-class aversion to "trade." Businessmen in Great Britain were exhorted to become disinterested professionals. Advising merchants and manufacturers to abandon capitalism, John Ruskin urged them to unselfishly "provide for the nation." Moreover, some leading British architects even disdained professionalism, believing that general standards and certification fostered mediocrity and undermined artistic freedom and expression.[3]

The architect as "man of business" was, as I have demonstrated, a uniquely American contribution, one that united diverse practitioners: the George Barbers and the Daniel Burnhams, the John Carrères and the Dankmar Adlers of the profession. Yet architectural historians do not recognize this common bond among nineteenth-century American architects. In a recent account of Holabird and Roche's practice, Robert Bruegmann concludes that Chicago and New York architects differed more about the business of architecture than about the art of architecture. While New York architects, Bruegmann writes, thought of themselves as artists and created in ateliers, Chicago architects were businessmen running modern offices.[4] Eastern architects like Richard M. Hunt and H. H. Richardson may have called their practices ateliers, but they were just as concerned about the business of architecture as any midwestern architect working in a high-rise office. Hunt, in particular, was a hard-nosed and, if necessary, litigious businessman. Richardson assiduously cultivated business, and as his practice grew in size, the studio atmosphere waned. George B. Post and McKim, Mead and White organized large offices like those created by Burnham and Root and Holabird and Roche. These firms emulated the specialization and bureaucratization of American business conglomerates. It was the commissions the architects came to be known for—public work versus private work or commercial buildings versus institutional buildings—that distinguished major practitioners in New York and Chicago. Eastern architects may have been more savvy, successfully marketing themselves as both artists and businessmen, than many of their Chicago colleagues. McKim, Mead and White sold themselves as artists to a Holabird and Roche client for an imposing town house, but they also convinced New York real estate developers to commission them for speculative office buildings.

Defining the architect as a businessman became especially important in American professional circles during the late nineteenth century. Although many American architects worked as building contractors or real estate developers, few constructed any part of the buildings they designed. The marketplace now required greater administrative skill and business acumen rather than manual labor. Such credentials proved that architecture, despite architects' attenuated ties to the building crafts and construction, was still a vital, masculine vocation.[5]

The forms of practice also changed in response to the business of architecture. Before the Civil War partnerships evolved to deal with the growing entrepreneurial demands on architects as well as the increasing complexity of art and tectonics. House pattern books and mail-order designs were new techniques for cultivating a larger audience in a free market. To survive on design and supervisory work, architects developed practices that spread over states and regions. The architectural office reinvented itself when large private offices developed in the late nineteenth century. The specialized, integrated services such large firms offered reassured businessmen and public officials who presided over large bureaucracies.

Still, the architect, committed by profession to art and public service, could never be a pure businessman, fixated on profits; a residue of the English professional ideal of the disinterested gentleman remained. Yet some American architects honored this idea more than they actually observed it. Leading architects like Stanford White, Daniel Burnham, William Holabird, and Martin Roche quietly acquired real estate and took equity positions in buildings they designed. Such conflicts of interest were rigorously policed only among the rank and file, not the leaders, of American architecture, just as in the other professions.[6]

The skyscrapers and public buildings of the late nineteenth century seemed to confirm American architects' faith in the marketplace. Private practitioners coaxed Chicago and New York real estate developers to transform their speculative office buildings into works of art. They also persuaded businessmen and government officials to involve private architects in planning and designing the public realm, the City Beautiful. But artistic and professional success dependent on the private market exacted a high price. While financial booms periodically buoyed the profession, economic busts also routinely devastated it. A firm like Holabird and Roche slashed its staff roster from forty to three employees within a few years of the 1893 financial panic.[7] Architects with large offices had to concentrate on complex and costly new building programs to meet their high overhead as well as to challenge their abilities. Housing for the poorest and most vulnerable Americans and preservation of historic buildings and urban fabric were never priorities in the nineteenth-century economy. Because the state (apart from commissioning large public buildings) refused to play a role, profits, expansion, and personal aggrandizement essentially drove a profession dependent on the private building market.

But private enterprise shaped the entire building industry, not just the architectural profession, in nineteenth-century America. The national aversion to taxation and state ownership meant that capital for turnpikes, canals, and railroads came from the private sector. The government was always a reluctant and hesitant patron of engineering projects as well as architecture.[8] Furthermore, the promotion of taste and aesthetics was essentially a private, not a state, concern; it was never a national value. Most American museums, libraries, theaters, and educational institutions were local or individual undertakings. In such a climate, architecture was a commodity that entrepreneurial professionals offered for private and public consumption.

All the professions grew in stature as American work became increasingly specialized, bureaucratized, and routinized in industrial and corporate conglomerates after 1850. Whether railroads, steelworks, sugar refineries, or insurance companies, these huge organizations aroused ambivalent feelings, Olivier Zunz writes, about "bigness and smallness, hierarchy and independence, and homogeneity and diversity" in American life.[9] Large industries and corporations exposed the growing gap between contemporary life and traditional values in the United States. If nineteenth-century Americans found reassuring the possibility of an independent professional practice seemingly open to all, the private practices of architects like Henrietta Dozier, opened because mainstream offices refused to hire them, cloaked and denied the systemic economic, sexual, and racial inequities of American life.[10]

But the large architectural offices of the late nineteenth century affirmed the same culture of big business that the professions supposedly denied. Although architectural historians and critics routinely suppress this irony by emphasizing individual agency and celebrity designers, the architect as salaried employee became a commonplace of professional life beginning in the late nineteenth century. The center of activity for nineteenth-century architects, whether they were employers or employees, was the private office. It educated and socialized architects into the culture of professionalism; it was both alma mater and fraternity; it united work and education, practice and theory. No other institution—professional society, school, or the press—matched the office's influence in shaping nineteenth-century professional practice in the United States.

The most enduring legacy of nineteenth-century American professionalism was this belief in the private office. It weathered the economic shocks and dislocations of the nineteenth century but also those of the twentieth century. This was not true elsewhere. During the worldwide depression of the 1930s British practitioners became either salaried government employees or subcontractors. Their dependency on public-sector employment continued into the postwar welfare state. Architects headed and staffed the planning and housing departments of every major city in Great Britain, developing public housing and new town plans.[11] American private practice, however, remained intact through the depression. The federal government encouraged it by casting depression relief efforts as only temporary stimuli for the private sector. Thus Public Works Administration (PWA) housing commissions—the first significant federal intervention into low-cost housing—were awarded to private practitioners. Individual architects formed new offices to satisfy government requirements for maximizing employment. Thus Richmond H. Shreve, William Lescaze, Arthur Holden, and seven other New York architects formed a new partnership expressly to work on a Brooklyn PWA housing project in the 1930s. They never became government employees, and they received a standard professional percentage fee while maintaining their own individual practices.[12]

American private practice rebounded in the 1950s, 1960s, and early 1970s. Large offices experienced unprecedented growth, causing Gordon Bunshaft, design principal of Skidmore, Ownings and Merrill (SOM), to call these decades the "golden age" of architecture.[13] Like nineteenth-century American entrepreneurs and big businessmen, American corporations commissioned a stream of buildings from large firms like SOM, which operated four offices employing thousands by 1958. Modernism, which had expressed European social engineering, became in postwar American society the style of corporatism.[14] Such an evolution was inevitable given the historical dependency of American architectural practice on the free market.

But the 1970s proved to be a turbulent decade for modernism and the architectural profession. Historians, critics, and even practitioners generally attribute this sea change to male architects and postmodernism. Stanley Tigerman, the Chicago architect and educator, claimed that the architect and theorist Robert Venturi "was to [modern] architecture what Vietnam was to America: . . . They both made the subject fall from grace."[15] But I would argue that modern architecture's Vietnam was not so much Robert Venturi and postmodernist theory as the grassroots preservation movement of the 1960s and 1970s and the failure of public housing projects like the notoriously dysfunctional Pruitt-Igoe in Saint Louis, demolished in 1972. Outraged architectural "consumers" (middle- and upper-middle-class white and African American community activists) did more to discredit modernism than either Robert Venturi or postmodernist theory.[16]

The profession, too, came under scrutiny. The Justice Department forced the AIA to suspend its fee schedule and prohibitions against architects' advertising and financial involvement with contracting and real estate. And like physicians and lawyers, architects were held legally liable. Lawsuits proliferated, and malpractice premiums soared. To limit personal liability, firms abandoned traditional partnership structures and reorganized themselves as corporations.[17] Individual practitioners soon followed the large firms' example. Government agencies and the courts regarded the architectural profession as just another way to earn a living. Grassroots community action and the consumer movement of the 1970s discredited not only modernism but also traditional professionalism. The civil rights movement inspired women, consumers, and other minorities to find their own voices in the 1970s. In such an atmosphere, architecture and the other professions, associated with the power and authority of white males, came under attack.

In another sense, however, Stanley Tigerman was right to call attention to Venturi's role. Venturi's prominence signaled the ascendancy of the university as much as a critical reappraisal of modernism. Venturi, Michael Graves, Charles Moore, and Robert A. M. Stern were all university professors or part-time teachers when they launched postmodernism. The university, rather than the architectural office or studio, was now the incubator for innovative ideas. Accustomed to combining practice with teaching at the Bauhaus, Walter Gropius and Mies van der Rohe first gave prominence to the professor-architect during the American postwar building boom. Louis Kahn also developed his reputation and career while teaching at Yale and the University of Pennsylvania. First postmodern architects, then deconstructivists like Bernard Tschumi, and now cyberarchitects like Hani Rashid and Marcos Novak continue this tradition into late-twentieth-century America.

Invented by American architects in the decades after the Civil War, university programs were initially weak vehicles for training professionals.[18] In the 1890s there were only nine architectural schools, which enrolled fewer than four hundred students. Graduating classes were even smaller. But the programs grew in influence and stature as middle-class Americans came to regard university degrees as prerequisites for social status and economic success in twentieth-century America.[19] The passage of state accreditation laws also enhanced the schools' reputations. Their curricula promised better preparation for the proliferating licensing examinations than haphazard office training.

By 1912 there were thirty-two architectural programs, with enrollments triple those of the 1890s. That same year architectural schools formed their own organization, the Association of Collegiate Schools of Architecture (ACSA), to establish uniform standards and to ensure quality. By the 1930s fifty-two American universities offered an architectural degree. The National Architectural Accrediting Board (NAAB) was created in 1940 to examine and accredit these schools. By 1994–95 the NAAB had evaluated and accredited 103 architectural programs enrolling 35,527 full- and part-time students.[20]

Today architectural schools are relatively stable institutions, better insulated from economic shocks than private offices. As Robert Gutman notes, school enrollments, budgets, and faculty lines have remained steady over the past decade, a period when the architectural market has often been severely depressed. In fact, the schools experienced a surge in graduate enrollments when architects, sitting out the depression of the early 1990s, returned to school, earning postprofessional degrees with the help of tuition loans and fellowships.[21]

Architectural schools have their own agendas, values, and culture. The academic culture, Dana Cuff observes, privileges design above all.[22] The structure of the Beaux-Arts curriculum (studio, theory, juries, individual competition, and historical precedent), remarkably, remains intact today. Collaborative projects, technological studies, administrative skills, business knowledge, interdisciplinary work, and history as anything except formal precedent and design analysis are generally marginalized in architectural schools today. Obligatory professional practice courses usually stress only a familiarity with standard AIA contracts. Arranging office internships is generally left to students and individual practitioners. As a result the content and effectiveness of these office experiences vary wildly.[23]

While the schools slight nondesign courses and office internships, programs at major research institutions evidence a fascination with architectural theory derived from literary, philosophical, and cultural studies. Young faculty who research and publish on theoretical issues—which generally require only modest research outlays—are rewarded with promotion and tenure.[24] Moreover, many academic gatekeepers find architectural practice difficult to evaluate, considering it neither research nor creative work. Some universities even unwittingly discourage it with stringent restrictions on faculty consulting, constraints that do not apply to publications, speaking engagements, and art sales.[25] All this conveys the message that professional practice does not really foster intellectual or artistic discoveries.

The "star" designers on university faculties are not advocates for the profession or for practice. Although they accept awards and speaking engagements from professional organizations, they rarely involve themselves with professional issues. Unlike nineteenth-century leaders, their principal allegiance is to the university, not the profession. It is no wonder that many practitioners feel estranged from the schools, finding the theoretical discourse baffling and complaining that graduates lack the technical, production, and managerial skills that account for 90 percent of a firm's time.[26]

Architectural enrollments also create a serious separation between the schools and profession. Today the production of graduates far exceeds the profession's ability to absorb them into private practice. The number of architects grew by 253 percent—the greatest increase for any professional group—between 1960 and 1980. But the amount of construction in real dollars remained flat or depressed until the late 1990s.[27] Conditions were exploitative, with young architects willing to work for very low wages or even nothing if the employer was a star architect. In the late nineties, the market is improving, judging by my Cornell students' prospects, but starting salaries—averaging $23,000 in 1997—are still painfully low. Meanwhile, the schools create increasingly sophisticated and seductive marketing campaigns involving Web sites and videos, and the NAAB continues to accredit new programs. The media are also complicit with their celebration of "signature," invariably male, architects like Richard Meier, Frank Gehry, Rem Koolhaas, and Bernard Tschumi in newspapers, magazines, books, television, and museum exhibitions. Architecture is now a chic vocation for characters in films, television series, and advertising campaigns.[28]

Compounding the problem is the continuing emphasis on independent practice as the career goal for young architects. But most jobs in the architecture market today are for employees—as Robert Gutman writes, those whom "supervisors tell what to do and how to do it." Furthermore, these jobs are increasingly outside of private practice. In 1994 it was estimated that nearly one in five AIA members and one in three American architects were employees of corporations, schools, hospitals, universities, or government.[29]

These employment trends are profoundly disturbing in a profession where private practice has traditionally been valorized. When Robert Gutman reported them at a 1992 conference on architectural practice, they "grabbed nearly everyone's attention," according to one observer, and "really upset some participants."[30] In the midnineties the Harvard Graduate School of Design organized a yearlong symposium on architectural practice, responding to what Dean Peter Rowe called the "sense of crisis" in the profession. Although the participants produced a publication ostensibly exploring multiple "practices," they essentially reaffirmed traditional beliefs in independent practice. That, they generally concluded, would continue if architects educated the public, developed global markets, and mastered the new media of cyberspace and virtual reality. They paid no attention to architects as middle-class salaried employees at the Harvard symposium. Education, entrepreneurship, and technology—familiar from nineteenth-century discussions of professionalism in this country—were again enshrined.[31]

But architects trained in offices during the nineteenth and early twentieth centuries found it difficult to sustain illusions about practice. The pressures and frustrations of work were soon apparent to even an entry-level tracer. The importance of the business of architecture was also obvious. Furthermore, a glance around the drafting room made it clear that not everyone graduated "from the boards" to become a partner or to open a firm.

Today architectural students bring a sense of accomplishment and entitlement into the workplace. They have spent time and money to acquire university degrees, enduring the hazing rituals of all-night *charettes* (the intensive and frantic final efforts to complete a project) and presentations before demanding design jurors. Their studio critics, history teachers, and the media teach them to idolize "star" designers and to understand design as a solitary activity. As one of my Cornell students told me, "We need our design heroes to get through the pressures of studio." The profession they hope to join still celebrates private practice. Architectural graduates expect to become firm principals in their own or a group practice—not to remain employees.

Women, whom the schools have heavily recruited in recent years to sustain their high enrollments,[32] may become especially disappointed and alienated after graduation. Just when they are entering the profession in significant numbers, their career paths may begin and end working at monitors producing computer drawings. Unlike nineteenth-century draftsmen, who identified with firm principals, women may find little consolation in the achievements of an overwhelmingly white male professional culture. Minority students, although they still account for a small percentage of architectural school enrollments, may be similarly disillusioned. The professions, especially with the advent of university degrees and state accreditation, promised autonomy, economic success, and social status. These promises ring increasingly hollow for many young architects at the end of the twentieth century.

In the world outside the university and profession, architecture remains marginal. In 1996 the Carnegie Foundation for the Advancement of Teaching published a study of architectural education and practice. Architecture, the study concluded, despite its "vast potential," fails "to connect itself firmly to the larger concerns confronting families, businesses, schools, communities, and society." Although architects can "bestow beauty or inflict damage too permanent and profound," they still "remain in the shadows."[33] Robert Gutman has stated this more succinctly, calling architecture "a strong art but a weak profession." Echoing Latrobe's early complaint, American society's relative indifference to art supposedly explains the profession's modest economic rewards and everyday irrelevance.[34]

There is no dearth of solutions for architecture's problems. Fifteen years ago computer-aided design (CAD) was supposed to revolutionize architectural practice, allowing architects to produce better designs, not only faster but cheaper. Current claims for cyberarchitecture go even further, recalling the utopianism of early modern architects. Young cyberarchitects, radicalized by poststructuralist theory and empowered with sophisticated animation software, now proclaim nothing less than a social and spatial revolution where interactive buildings will allow each person to explore and shape his or her world. Amid the hype Garry Stevens, one computer guru, offered a more sobering assessment of computers and architecture. Claiming that computer software and hardware generally become obsolete after ten years, he wrote that only large firms and corporations could afford to reinvest in new programs, machines, and staff training. He also argued while there is little evidence that computer-aided design has enhanced productivity, it has maximized management's control over the drafting staff, creating a new underclass of cyber inkers and tracers.[35]

Despite his gloom, the computer has profoundly changed the ways in which some architects practice. A husband-and-wife partnership in Boulder, Colorado, can design large-scale projects like shopping centers and housing from their dining room because of commercially available drafting programs. Using software created by a French aerospace manufacturer, Frank Gehry showed how titanium steel could be shaped into fantastic yet structurally feasible forms for his Bilbao Museum in Spain. Resolving structural problems on the computer, rather than on site, saved time and money. At the Bilbao Museum, cyberarchitect Stephen Perrella notes, Gehry proved that he could "build a complex building and build it on time and on budget." The computer gave Gehry, long acknowledged as an artist, a professional credibility that had previously eluded him.[36]

But computers can also empower other players in the design and building process. At one end of the market, house pattern book designs are now available as software. A prospective home owner can not only choose a design but also manipulate it on his or her personal computer. Prominent architects have also run afoul of computers in high-profile commissions. While designing the Getty Center in Los Angeles, Richard Meier agreed to work with Bill Jepson, head of UCLA's Urban Simulation Laboratory. Jepson used an advanced software program to create images with near-photographic quality from Meier's drawings. At first, Jepson recalls, Meier "really liked what we were doing. He completely changed the art history building because we were able to show him that he was not getting the views and perspectives from the lobby that he wanted." But then the Getty trustees, who were unhappy with Meier's design for a staircase inside the center's main entrance, asked to see it on Jepson's computer. Consequently, the staircase was redesigned, but Meier then refused to work with Jepson. "I don't hold that against Richard," Jepson reflected. "It was difficult for him to have this third party between him and his client. He needed to control the information that was flowing back to the trustees, so we were removed from the process."[37]

During the late nineteenth century, technologies associated with the skyscraper created opportunities for general contractors, engineering consultants, and financial advisers, diminishing architects' authority and privileged relationship with clients. Today the computer can also bite the architectural hand that tries to use it, empowering both the computer expert and the client. Computer programs are not simply tools for architects; they are pathways into the design process for both architects and nonarchitects.

Revising school curricula is another remedy proposed for the current professional malaise. Current recommendations include less time in school and more time learning in offices for students; fusing design studios with history, theory, and technology projects as interdisciplinary collaborations for design students, faculty, and jurors; encouraging design programs dealing with prosaic buildings and urban design problems as well as the trophy commissions of villas, museums, and skyscrapers. Historians are urged to move beyond the Howard Roarks of architecture, stressing vernacular buildings and the interactions of users, clients, technology, economics, culture, and politics with architecture. Universities are advised to encourage faculty to practice with research grants and flexible sabbaticals and to reward practitioners with promotion and tenure.[38]

As a teacher of architects, I am fundamentally sympathetic to ideas for improving architects and architecture by revising educational content and structure. I should be, since they privilege my role as educator. But we are in danger of endowing education, regardless of how and where it is practiced, with the sole power to redeem architecture. I am pessimistic because we fixate only on where architecture is taught. We still pay little attention to where and how it is practiced.

The private sector, essentially unmediated and uncurbed by the state, plays a dominant role in American society. When the professions conflict with it, they come under intense pressure.[39] The current condition of the American medical profession is a case in point. American doctors, like lawyers and architects, were traditionally self-employed practitioners, selling their expertise in the free market for a fee. Beginning in the postwar period, they became the most respected and powerful of all American professionals. Paul Starr subtitled his 1982 history of American medicine "The Rise of a Sovereign Profession and the Making of a Vast Industry."[40] Today, only seventeen years after the publication of Starr's book, the medical profession is in crisis and disarray.

By the early 1990s half of all American physicians were salaried employees in the private and public sectors. Now practically all current medical students can expect to begin their careers as employees and to remain employees. The fear today is not that physicians have too much power; it is that they do not have enough. Physicians are becoming medical functionaries in either profit-driven businesses or cost-cutting public institutions. Financial rather than therapeutic concerns increasingly drive professional decisions.[41]

Beginning in the 1950s, physicians flourished as health care, funded by private or public employers, became a right for middle-class Americans. Then government provided Medicare health insurance for elderly Americans. But there were limits on health care when private, unfettered physicians ordered too many tests, consultations, and hospitalizations. In the late 1960s corporate employers and large insurance companies, their profits eroded by escalating health care claims, began to cut costs by scrutinizing reimbursements and establishing so-called reasonable and customary charges for medical fees and services. Government insurance programs enacted similar restrictions on their medical reimbursements. Because physicians depended on insurance reimbursements to pay their patients' bills, the private market essentially curbed their professional power and autonomy. The private sector, not the medical profession, set the standards for professional fees. Then private investors, having created successful for-profit nursing homes based on Medicare benefits, established for-profit hospitals and health maintenance organizations employing physicians in the 1980s. Public funds for hospitals dwindled. More and more doctors are now employees, answerable to either corporate executives or public bureaucrats for the financial implications of treatment recommendations.[42] Private practice, the cornerstone of American professionalism, is in jeopardy.

If physicians can fall so precipitously, a weak profession historically tied to the marketplace like American architecture has little chance. Ever since the decline of the master artisans amid the pressures of early nineteenth-century capitalism, American building has been an increasingly competitive and fragmented market. Even as large architectural offices emerged in late-nineteenth-century America, general contracting and real estate companies also developed, challenging architects' expertise and leadership. Today the situation has not improved; in fact, one expert calls the building industry "the most fragmented sector of the United States production economy."[43] Mastering such a fragmented market seems impossible given architects' stock-in-trade, whether aesthetics or social engineering, has never been a priority of either capitalism or the state in America.

It is true that entrepreneurs are now looking beyond hospitals and nursing homes to such unlikely prospects for privatization as prison facilities and state welfare systems. They are converting governmental, professional, and nonprofit organizations into for-profit businesses.[44] In such a climate, surely architecture must seem a tame and sound investment. Celebration, Florida, a suburban community outside Orlando, seemed so to Walt Disney executives. A Disney subsidiary retained Robert A. M. Stern and Jaquelin Robertson to design the Celebration town plan and commissioned buildings from Charles Moore, Cesar Pelli, Denise Scott Brown, Robert Venturi, Philip Johnson, and Michael Graves. Describing itself in promotional materials as "a committed patron of architecture," Disney hinted that it might develop Celebration-like communities across the country. The company seemed ready to fulfill nineteenth-century American architects' faith in the private market as the ultimate source of professional enrichment and empowerment. But creating and managing a new community proved far more difficult and controversial than Disney executives ever imagined. Disputes over school curricula and community governance—and the concomitant negative publicity—have apparently soured Disney on developing any more new towns like Celebration.[45]

Engineers, historically middle-class employees, have been the weakest of all the American professionals.[46] But they may become the model for professional life in late-twentieth-century America. Doctors, lawyers, and architects are already well on their way to becoming salarymen and salarywomen. Fewer and fewer American architects will juggle the multiple roles of artist, gentleman, and businessman that John Carrère saw for them in the early 1900s.

Latrobe identified the architectural profession with aesthetic and structural excellence in large-scale building. Grounding professional practice in the private sector, antebellum architects tried to reconcile Latrobe's legacy with American egalitarianism. Both the academy and the profession honored the private office as the touchstone of nineteenth-century professional identity. But as Barr Ferree wrote in 1893, business, practicing in the free market, was both the glory and the curse of American architecture.[47]

Architecture, with the allure of art and promises of professional prestige and security, is a burgeoning field in late-twentieth-century America. The question is
whether it can continue to attract new recruits when the realities of the architectural
workplace counter the ideal of private practice. Can expensive and lengthy university programs continue to thrive if their graduates become permanent employees?
Can we let go of the antebellum dream of combining professionalism with social
and economic mobility? Will the satisfactions of contributing to their employers'
artistic achievements be enough to sustain the highly educated and ambitious young
architects turned out each year? At least part of the answer depends on whether the
artistry and professionalism of architecture can be made meaningful outside the
American tropes of independent practice and the private office.

NOTES

The following abbreviations are used in the notes:

AMJ   *Architects and Mechanics' Journal*
JAIA   *Journal of the American Institute of Architects*
JSAH   *Journal of the Society of Architectural Historians*

INTRODUCTION

1. Alice Friedman. "Feminist Practice in History?" *Design Book Review* 25 (summer 1992): 16 –18; Robert Gutman, "Emerging Problems of Practice," and Dana Cuff, "Divisive Tactics: Design-Production Practices in Architecture," both in *Journal of Architectural Education* 45 (July 1992): 198 –199 and 208; and Robert Bruegmann, *The Architects and the City: Holabird and Roche of Chicago, 1880 –1918* (Chicago: University of Chicago Press, 1997), xv–xvi.

2. James O'Gorman, *H. H. Richardson and His Office* (Cambridge, Mass.: Harvard University Press, 1974); Diana Balmori, "George B. Post," *JSAH* 46 (December 1987): 342–355; Judith Hull, "The School of Upjohn," *JSAH* 52 (September 1993): 281–306; Ross Miller, *Here's the Deal: The Buying and Selling of a Great American City* (New York:Knopf, 1996); Jerome Tuccille, *Trump* (New York: D. I. Fine, 1987); Carol Willis, *Form Follows Finance* (New York: Princeton Architectural Press, 1995); Louise Hall, "Artificer to Architect in America," typescript (AIA Archives, Washington, D.C., 1954); Ian Quimby, *Apprenticeship in Colonial Philadelphia* (New York: Garland Press, 1985); Mark Erlich, *Working with Our Hands: The Story of Carpenters in Massachusetts* (Philadelphia: Temple University Press, 1986); Gwendolyn Wright, *Moralism and the Model Home* (Chicago: University of Chicago Press, 1980); Sibel Dostoglu, "Toward Professional Legitimacy and Power" (Ph.D. diss., University of Pennsylvania, 1982); Catherine Bishir, Carl Lounsbury, Charlotte Brown, and Ernest Wood, *Architects and Builders in North Carolina* (Chapel Hill: University of North Carolina Press, 1990); Martin Briggs, *The Architect in History* (Oxford: Clarendon Press,

1927); Spiro Kostof, ed., *The Architect* (New York: Oxford University Press, 1977); and Andrew Saint, *The Image of the Architect* (New Haven, Conn.: Yale University Press, 1983).

3. Robert Montgomery, "Commentary on the Center for the Study of the Practice of Architecture Symposium," *Journal of Architectural Education* 45 (July 1992): 230.

4. Robert Gutman, *Architectural Practice* (New York: Princeton Architectural Press, 1988); Magali Larson, *The Rise of Professionalism* (Berkeley and Los Angeles: University of California Press, 1977), and *Behind the Postmodern Facade* (Berkeley and Los Angeles: University of California Press, 1993); Dana Cuff, *Architecture: The Story of Practice* (Cambridge, Mass.: MIT Press, 1991); Judith Blau, *Architects and Society* (Cambridge, Mass.: MIT Press, 1984); Daniel Calhoun, *Professional Lives in America* (Cambridge, Mass.: Harvard University Press, 1965); Samuel Haber, *The Quest for Honor and Authority in the Professions* (Chicago: University of Chicago Press, 1991); and Elliott Krause, *Death of the Guilds: Professions, States, and the Advance of Capitalism, 1930 to the Present* (New Haven, Conn.: Yale University Press, 1996).

5. Michael Crosbie, "The Schools: How They Are Failing the Profession," *Progressive Architecture* 76 (September 1995): 47–53, 94, 96; Ernest Boyer and Lee Mitgang, *Building Community: A New Future for Architectural Education and Practice* (Princeton, N.J.: Carnegie Foundation for the Advancement of Teaching, 1996); Robert Gutman, "Two Discourses on Architectural Education," *Practices* 3/4 (spring 1995): 11–19; The Harvard symposium proceedings were published as William S. Saunders, ed., *Reflections on Architectural Practices in the Nineties* (New York: Princeton Architectural Press, 1995); and Lisa Foderaro, *New York Times,* 21 April 1996, sec. 2, 39.

6. While Andrew Saint and Margaret Floyd Henderson were the two historians at the Harvard symposium, Mina Marefat was the Carnegie consultant. Arthur Weatherhead, *Collegiate Education in Architecture in the United States* (Los Angeles: Hennessey and Ingalls, 1941); and Turpin Bannister, *The Architect at Midcentury,* 2 vols. (New York: Reinhold Corporation, 1954), were the two histories cited in the Carnegie report.

7. Henry H. Saylor, *The A.I.A.'s First Hundred Years* (Washington, D.C.: The Octagon, 1957), 1–9; James M. Fitch, "The Profession of Architecture," in *The Professions in America,* ed. Kenneth Lynn (Boston: Houghton Mifflin, 1965), 239; Larson, *The Rise of Professionalism,* 105; Joan Draper, "The Ecole des Beaux-Arts and the Architectural Profession in the United States," and Bernard M. Boyle, "Architectural Practice in America," both in Kostof, *The Architect,* 209–237, 309–344; Samuel Haber, *Quest for Honor and Authority,* 199–200; and Cuff, *Architecture,* 22–28.

8. Briggs, *The Architect in History,* 12–14, 35; Spiro Kostof, "Architecture in the Ancient World: Egypt and Greece," and William McDonald, "Roman Architects," both in Kostof, *The Architect,* 11–16, 20–22, and 33–37.

9. James Ackerman, "History of Design and the Design of History," *Via* 4 (1980): 13; and Richard Goldthwaite, *The Building of Renaissance Florence* (Baltimore: Johns Hopkins University Press, 1980), 352, 365–366.

10. James Ackerman, "Architectural Practice in the Italian Renaissance," *JSAH* 13 (October 1954): 3; Leopold Ettlinger, "The Emergence of the Italian Architect during the Fif-

teenth Century," and Catherine Wilkinson, "The New Profession in the Renaissance," both in Kostof, *The Architect*, 98, 111–113, 130–136.

11. See Ackerman, "Architectural Practice," 3; Ettlinger, "Emergence of the Italian Architect," 98; Wilkinson, "New Profession in the Renaissance," 134–136; and John Wilton-Ely, "Rise of the Professional Architect in England," in Kostof, *The Architect*, 180.

12. Carl Lounsbury, *An Illustrated Glossary of Early Southern Architecture* (New York: Oxford University Press, 1994), s.v. "architect."

13. Samuel Haber, *Quest for Honor and Authority*, ix–xiii, 5–6.

14. Ibid., 6–7. I use masculine pronouns for architects before the late nineteenth century because I have found no evidence of women architects prior to this period.

15. Ibid.

16. Ibid., 8–9.

17. Louisa Tuthill, preface to *A History of Architecture from the Earliest Times* (1848; reprint, New York: Garland Press, 1988), ix.

CHAPTER I

1. Letter of 12 July 1806 to Robert Mills, in John Van Horne, ed., *Correspondence and Miscellaneous Papers of Benjamin Henry Latrobe* (New Haven, Conn.: Yale University Press, 1986), vol. 2, 239.

2. Letter of 29 March 1804 to Jefferson, in John Van Horne and Lee Formwalt, eds., *Correspondence and Miscellaneous Papers of Benjamin Henry Latrobe* (New Haven, Conn.: Yale University Press, 1984), vol. 1, 472.

3. Letter to Henry Ormond of 20 November 1808, *Correspondence of Latrobe*, 2:680.

4. Letter of 25 May 1817 to Richard Caton in John Van Horne, ed., *Correspondence and Miscellaneous Papers of Benjamin Henry Latrobe* (New Haven, Conn.: Yale University Press, 1988), vol. 3, 882.

5. Howard Rock, *Artisans of the New Republic* (New York: New York University Press, 1984), 15 n. 5; and Roger W. Moss Jr., "Origins of the Carpenters' Company," in *Building Early America*, ed. Charles Peterson (Radnor, Pa.: Chilton Book Company, 1976), 36–37.

6. W. J. Rorabaugh, *The Craft Apprentice* (New York: Oxford University Press, 1986), 6; Hannah Benner Roach, "Thomas Nevell," *JSAH* 24 (May 1965): 153; and Louise Hall, "Artificer to Architect in America," typescript, The American Institute of Architects Archives, Washington, D.C., 1954, 12.

7. Rorabaugh, *The Craft Apprentice*, 6; and Mark Erlich, *Working with Our Hands: The Story of Carpenters in Massachusetts* (Philadelphia: Temple University Press, 1986), 21.

8. The earliest surviving records of the Carpenters' Company are from the 1760s. When the Pennsylvania state legislature incorporated the company in 1740, the date of organization given was 1724. Benjamin Loxley, an early member, noted that the company began in the winter of 1726 or 1727. See Charles Peterson, "Benjamin Loxley and Carpenters' Hall," *JSAH* 15 (December 1956): 24–25, 26–27; and Moss, "Origins of the Carpenters' Company," 43–45.

For the Capitol, see Letter of 17 July 1793 from Jefferson to George Washington, in Saul K. Padover, ed., *Thomas Jefferson and the National Capitol* (Washington, D.C.: Government Printing Office, 1946), 186.

9. Rita S. Gottesman, *Arts and Crafts in New York, 1726–1776* (New York: New-York Historical Society, 1938), 50, 53, 193; *Constitution of the Associated Mechanics of Boston* (1795), in Charles Evans, ed., *The Early American Imprint Series No. 1*, ed. Charles Evans, no. 28315; and Joseph T. Buckingham, comp., *Annals of the Massachusetts Charitable Mechanics Association* (Boston: Press of Crocker and Brewster, 1853), 3–5; title page to *Charter, Articles, Supplement and By-Laws of the Bricklayers' Company* (Philadelphia, 1888); and Catherine Bishir, "A Proper Good Nice and Workmanlike Manner," in Catherine Bishir, Carl Lounsbury, Charlotte Brown, and Ernest Wood, *Architects and Builders in North Carolina* (Chapel Hill: University of North Carolina Press, 1990), 95, 99–100.

10. Gary Kornblith, "From Artisan to Businessman: Master Mechanics in New England, 1789–1850" (Ph.D. diss., Princeton University, 1983), 87, 96–97; and Charles Peterson, introduction to *The Rules of Work of the Carpenters' Company of the City and County of Philadelphia* (1786; reprint, Princeton, N.J.: Pyne Press, 1971), xvi–xvii.

11. Carl Lounsbury, *An Illustrated Glossary of Early Southern Architecture,* (New York: Oxford University Press, 1994). s.v. "architect," "contractor," "master," and "undertaker."

12. Roger Moss and Sandra Tatman, *Biographical Dictionary of Philadelphia Architects* (Boston: G. K. Hall, 1985), s.v. "Robert Smith." and Charles Peterson, "Carpenters' Hall," *Transactions of the American Philosophical Society* 43 (March 1953): 121–123.

13. Moss and Tatman, *Biographical Dictionary of Philadelphia Architects,* s.v. "Robert Smith."

14. Frederic Detwiller, "Thomas Dawes: Boston's Patriot Architect," *Old-Time New England* 68 (summer–fall 1977): 1–18.

15. Bishir, *Architects and Builders in North Carolina,* 43–44.

16. Rosamund Beirne and John Scarff, *William Buckland, 1734–1774: Architect of Virginia and Maryland* (Baltimore: Maryland Historical Society, 1958), 6–16, 34–48, 67.

17. Quotation from the *The Diary of William Bentley* (1905–1914) in Wayne Andrews, *Architecture, Ambition, and Americans* (New York: Free Press, 1964), 96.

18. Moss and Tatman, *Biographical Dictionary of Philadelphia Architects,* s.v. "Samuel Rhoads," "Samuel Powell," and "Robert Smith." Rhoads and Powell, like Smith, were master carpenters and builders prominent in Philadelphia's political, cultural, and economic life.

19. Lounsbury, *Illustrated Glossary of Early Southern Architecture,* s.v. "architect," "builder," and "contractor." The term "contractor" did not come into general use until the late eighteenth century in America.

20. Carl Bridenbaugh, *Peter Harrison* (Chapel Hill: University of North Carolina Press, 1949); Fiske Kimball, *Thomas Jefferson, Architect* (1916; reprint, New York: Da Capo Press, 1968); Elinor Stearns and David N. Yerkes, *William Thornton: A Renaissance Man in the Federal City* (Washington, D.C.: American Institute of Architects Foundation, 1976); and Harold Kirker, *Architecture of Charles Bulfinch* (Cambridge, Mass.: Harvard University Press, 1969).

21. Christopher Misner, "Management: Architect-Developers," *Progressive Architecture* 69 (January 1988): 61–62.

22. H. Paul Caemmerer, *The Life of Pierre Charles L'Enfant* (Washington, D.C.: National Republic, 1950), 1–9, 43, 95; Robert Alexander, *The Architecture of Maximilian Godefroy* (Baltimore: Johns Hopkins University Press, 1974); Pamela Scott, "Stephen Hallet's Designs for the United States Capitol," *Winterthur Portfolio* 27 (summer/autumn 1992): 146–147; Michael Richman, "George Hadfield," *JSAH* 33 (October 1974): 234–235; and for the Trumbull quotation, see Andrews, *Architecture, Ambition, and Americans,* 73.

23. Letter of 8 April 1798 to Henry Antes, in Edward C. Carter II, ed., *The Virginia Journals of Benjamin Henry Latrobe, 1795–1798* (New Haven, Conn.: Yale University Press, 1977), vol. 2, 367–368; and Letter of 14 February 1798 to James Wood, *Correspondence of Latrobe,* 1:40, 78.

24. Editorial Note, *Correspondence of Latrobe,* 1:6; and Letter of 31 December 1814 to Henry Latrobe, *Correspondence of Latrobe,* 3:608.

25. Frank Jenkins, *Architect and Patron* (London: Oxford University Press, 1961), 108–109, 112–115; and Adolf K. Placzek, ed., *Macmillan Encyclopedia of Architects* (New York: Free Press, 1982), s.vv. "Samuel Cockerell" and "John Smeaton."

26. John Soane, *Plans, Elevations, and Sections of Buildings* (London: I. Taylor, 1788), 7. See Talbot Hamlin, *Benjamin Henry Latrobe* (New York: Oxford University Press, 1955), 36–40, for a discussion of Soane's architectural influence on Latrobe.

27. Letter of 21 May 1807 from Latrobe to Jefferson; 18 August 1807 Letter from Latrobe to Jefferson; and Letter of 27 April 1807 from Jefferson to Latrobe, all in Padover, *Thomas Jefferson and the National Capitol,* 390, 394–396, 386–387.

Paul Norton, who described the contretemps as the first serious rift between Latrobe and Jefferson, studied it in "Latrobe's Ceiling for the Hall of Representatives," *JSAH* 10 (May 1951): 5–10.

28. Letter of 16 January 1809 to Isaac Hazelhurst, *Correspondence of Latrobe,* 2:693.

29. For Latrobe's private and public references to the architect as an artist, see the following: Letter of 29 March 1804 to Jefferson, *Correspondence of Latrobe,* 1:472; and Anniversary Oration, Society of Artists of the United States, 8 May 1811, *Correspondence of Latrobe,* 3:65–69. Latrobe, an early member of this society of professional and amateur artists, served as vice president from 1811 until 1814. See William Dunlap, *A History of the Rise and Progress of the Arts of Design in the United States* (1834; reprint, Boston: C. E. Goodspeed, 1918), vol. 2, 234, for the remark about Latrobe's sketchbook.

30. Latrobe made this statement in the context of a lawsuit against Thornton for defamation of character. See "Memoranda of Facts Relating to the Causes of Difference between Dr. William Thornton and B. Henry Latrobe" to Walter Jones and John Law, 26 June 1808?, in *The Papers of Benjamin Henry Latrobe,* microfiche edition, ed. Edward Carter II (Clifton, N.J.: James T. White, 1976).

31. Letter of 26 March 1806 from Latrobe to Bishop John Carroll, *Correspondence of Latrobe,* 2:210–214, 214 n. 1.

32. Ibid.

33. Darwin Stapleton, "Engineering Practice of Latrobe," in *The Engineering Drawings of Benjamin Henry Latrobe,* ed. Darwin Stapleton (New Haven, Conn.: Yale University Press, 1988), 67.

34. Editorial Note and Letter of 13 December 1806 from Latrobe to Bishop Carroll, *Correspondence of Latrobe,* 2:51–52, 324–325.

35. Letter of 14 January 1820 from the Trustees of the Baltimore cathedral to Latrobe, *Correspondence of Latrobe,* 3:1040.

36. Letter of 31 August 1797 to Governor James Wood and the Council of the State of Virginia, *Correspondence of Latrobe,* 1:61–63; Letter of 12 July 1806 to Mills, *Correspondence of Latrobe,* 2:243; and Jeffrey Cohen and Charles Brownell, "Virginia State Penitentiary," in *The Architectural Drawings of Benjamin Henry Latrobe,* ed. Jeffrey Cohen and Charles Brownell (New Haven, Conn.: Yale University Press, 1994), part 1, 101.

37. Editorial Note and "Agreement for Executing the Marble Work of the Bank of Pennsylvania," 26 February 1799, *Correspondence of Latrobe,* 1:128–129, 129–136.

See Letter of 23 February 1799 from Latrobe to Wood, *Correspondence of Latrobe,* 1:125, 129, 136 n. 4, for references to the bank as his masterpiece.

38. Letter of 22 January 1807 to William Waln, *Correspondence of Latrobe,* 2:368–369.

39. Subsequent letters detailing Latrobe's inspection of work and joint reports that he and Thomas Callis, the building superintendent, issued indicate that the dispute was resolved by 1798. See, for example, Letter of 9 July 1798 from Latrobe to Governor Wood, a report on the architect's inspection of a stone arch in the penitentiary cellar, *Correspondence of Latrobe,* 1:87–89; and Letter of 23 February 1799 to Governor Wood, *Correspondence of Latrobe,* 1:125–128.

40. Stapleton, "Engineering Practice of Latrobe," 28.

41. The Spanish missions in the Southwest and California, like San José y San Miguel de Aguayo (1768–77) in San Antonio, Texas; San Xavier del Bac (1784–97) near Tucson, Arizona; and San Carlos Borromeo (1793–97) in Carmel, California, were domed and vaulted structures.

42. Letter of 23 February 1799, *Correspondence of Latrobe;* and Stapleton, "Engineering Practice of Latrobe," 28–30.

43. Letter of 1812, quoted in Cohen and Brownell, "Virginia State Penitentiary," 180.

44. Letter of 11 October 1803 to Isaac Hazelhurst, *Correspondence of Latrobe,* 1:341.

45. Letter of 30 May 1801, Jefferson Papers, Massachusetts Historical Society, Boston, Massachusetts.

46. Editorial Note, *Correspondence of Latrobe,* 2:128–129; Cohen and Brownell, in *Architectural Drawings of Latrobe,* part 1, 199; Stapleton, "Engineering Practice of Latrobe," 70; Letter of 22 January 1807 from Latrobe to William Waln, *Correspondence of Latrobe,* 2:368.

47. *Annals of the Tenth Congress, Second Session* (1808), 1870, 1973–76. Representative Richard Stanton, chair of the investigating committee, made the comment about artists and money. See Letter of 8 April 1808 from Latrobe to Stanton, *Correspondence of Latrobe,* 2:584–591, and 590 n. 2.

48. Letter of 26 April 1808 from Jefferson to Latrobe, *Correspondence of Latrobe,* 2:612–613.

49. Lee Formwalt, *Benjamin Henry Latrobe and the Development of Internal Improvements in the New Republic, 1796–1820* (New York: Arno Press, 1982), 123–124.

50. Letter of 11 October 1803 to Hazelhurst, *Correspondence of Latrobe,* 1:341.

51. Letter of 18 May 1803 from Latrobe to Hugh Brackenbridge, *Correspondence of Latrobe,* 1:300. See Padover, *Thomas Jefferson and the National Capitol,* 520 for a summary of Lenthall's duties at the Capitol.

52. While he worked on the Capitol, Latrobe had commissions for the Delaware canal, Nassau Hall at Princeton University, and Dickinson College in Carlisle, Pennsylvania. See Letter of 11 October 1803 to Hazelhurst.

53. Latrobe, "Report on the Public Buildings" (18 November 1808), *Correspondence of Latrobe,* 2:671; and Letter of 20 November 1808 from Latrobe to Samuel Smith, editor of *National Intelligencer, Correspondence of Latrobe,* 2:662–664.

54. Letter of 23 September 1808 from Latrobe to Jefferson quoted in Padover, *Thomas Jefferson and the National Capitol,* 436–439.

55. Cohen and Brownell, *Architectural Drawings of Latrobe,* 184; and Stapleton, "Engineering Practice of Latrobe," 30. Some were Latrobe's pupils as well as his assistants. I will discuss their training further in chapter 3.

56. Jeffrey Cohen, "Early American Architectural Drawing in Philadelphia," in *Drawing toward Building,* ed. James O'Gorman (Philadelphia: University of Pennsylvania Press, 1986), 15–16; Stapleton, "Engineering Practice of Latrobe," 63; and Letter of 4 November 1804, *Papers of Latrobe,* microfiche edition.

57. Letter of 5 September 1807 from Latrobe to Jefferson; Letter of 25 April 1807 to John Spear Smith; Letter of 25 May 1807 to President and Directors of Bank of Philadelphia; and Letter of 3 May 1807 to William Waln. All in Pamela Scott, ed., *The Papers of Robert Mills* (Wilmington, Del.: Scholarly Film Resources, 1990).

58. Cohen and Brownell, *Architectural Drawings of Latrobe,* 184.

59. Letter of 22 January 1807 to William Waln, *Correspondence of Latrobe,* 2:367–369.

60. Letter of 14 February 1798 from Latrobe to Governor Wood, *Correspondence of Latrobe,* 1:77–78; Letter of 4 November 1804 from Latrobe to Christian Latrobe, *Papers of Latrobe,* microfiche edition.

61. Letter of 21 July 1806 to Isaac Hazelhurst and Letter of 22 October 1807 to Lewis DeMun, *Correspondence of Latrobe,* 2:265, 359.

62. Dunlap, *Rise and Progress of the Arts of Design,* 2:233–234; Hamlin, *Benjamin Henry Latrobe,* 562–565; and Edward Carter, introduction to *Papers of Latrobe.*

For references to Latrobe as father of the profession, see also Leland Roth, *A Concise History of American Architecture* (New York: Harper and Row, 1979), 67; and Bishir, "Traditional Building Practice," in Bishir et al., *Architects and Builders in North Carolina,* 125.

J. Meredith Neil was the first exception to architectural writers' chorus of praise for Latrobe. See Neil, "Benjamin H. Latrobe's Precarious Professionalism," *Journal of the AIA* 53 (May 1970): 67–71.

63. Letters of 21 May 1807 and 28 August 1809 from Latrobe to Jefferson, quoted in Padover, *Thomas Jefferson and the National Capitol,* 392, 462.

64. Letter of 27 April 1807 from Jefferson to Latrobe quoted in Padover, *Thomas Jefferson and the National Capitol,* 386; and Letter of 21 April 1813 from Latrobe to William Jones, Secretary of the Navy quoted in Formwalt, *Latrobe and Internal Improvements,* 184.

65. For Latrobe's reference to being a "man of business," see Letter of 13 April 1803 to John Randolph, *Correspondence of Latrobe,* 2:591. See Letter of 20 January 1812 to Dewitt Clinton, quoted in Stapleton, "Engineering Practice of Latrobe," 68, on building for posterity.

66. Formwalt, *Latrobe and Internal Improvements,* 117–124, 291.

It was not unusual for engineers in early America to be compensated with stock. Far from being seen as a conflict of interest, such an arrangement supposedly guaranteed that an engineer did his best. See Daniel Calhoun, *The American Engineer: Origins and Conflict* (Cambridge, Mass.: MIT Press, 1960), 16.

67. Formwalt makes this point with regard to Latrobe's engineering practice, but it applies, I believe, to his architectural career as well. See Formwalt, *Latrobe and Internal Improvements,* vi, 123–124, 290–294.

68. Letter of 4 November 1804 to Christian Latrobe, *Correspondence of Latrobe,* 1:563.

CHAPTER 2

1. Letter of 28 July 1811 from Latrobe to Constantin Volney, in John Van Horne, ed., *Correspondence and Miscellaneous Papers of Benjamin Henry Latrobe* (New Haven, Conn.: Yale University Press, 1986), vol. 2, 121; Dell Upton, "Pattern Books and Professionalism," *Winterthur Portfolio* 19 (autumn 1984): 113; and Alexander M. Carr-Saunders and P. A. Wilson, *The Professions* (1933; reprint, London: Frank Cass, 1964), 1–5.

2. Carr-Saunders and Wilson, *The Professions,* 1–10; Daniel Calhoun, *Professional Lives in America* (Cambridge, Mass.: Harvard University Press, 1965), 180–192; and Magali Larson, *The Rise of Professionalism* (Berkeley and Los Angeles: University of California Press, 1977), 1–20.

3. Richard Hofstadter, *Anti-Intellectualism in American Life* (New York: Vintage, 1963), 146–155; and Samuel Haber, *The Quest for Honor and Authority in the Professions* (Chicago: University of Chicago Press, 1991), 91–99.

4. Haber, *Quest for Honor and Authority,* 9, 103–105.

5. Ibid., 93–99.

6. Endorsement of 2 November 1836 and Circular Letter of 23 March 1837 from T. U. Walter, Alexander J. Davis, and William Strickland, T. U. Walter Papers, Philadelphia Athenaeum, Philadelphia, Pennsylvania; *Constitution and By-laws of the American Institution of Architects* (Philadelphia: Lydia Bailey, 1837), A. J. Bloor Papers, New-York Historical Society, New York, New York. Louise Hall also reprints the constitution in her "Artificer to Architect in America," typescript (AIA Archives, Washington, D.C., 1954), B-256.

According to the November 1836 endorsement in the Walter Papers, the following architects agreed to meet in New York to form the association: Walter, William Strickland, John Haviland, and John Trautwine of Philadelphia; Alexander J. Davis, Isaiah Rogers, C. [Charles or Karl] F. Reichardt, Edward I. Webb, F. Schmidt, Minard Lafever, Mr. Thomson [name scratched through, Thomas Thomas or Martin Thompson?], and Ithiel Town of New York; Asher Benjamin, Alexander Parris, William [*sic*, Richard] Bond, William Sparrell, and Ammi B. Young of Boston; Robert Cary Long of Baltimore; Robert Mills and Mr. Elliot [William P. Elliot Jr.] of Washington, D.C.; James H. Dakin of New Orleans; then a Kemp [William Cramp or Kramp of New York?] and Mr. Tomason [again Thomas Thomas or his son Thomas Thomas Jr.?]. Walter later recalled that he, Davis, Rogers, Reichardt, Kramp, Schmidt, Thomas, Thomas Jr., Strickland, Haviland, and Bond attended the New York meeting. Walter received letters of support from Town, Lafever, Benjamin, Parris, Sparrell, Young, Trautwine, Long, and Dakin. See Walter, Address, *Proceedings of the AIA* (1870), 207. A Letter of 6 November 1836 from Long to Walter is in the Archives of the AIA. I am grateful to Tony Wrenn, the AIA archivist, for sharing this letter with me.

7. *Constitution,* and Walter Letters of 1836 and 1837. Alexander J. Davis, another charter member, credited Walter with originating the idea for the organization. See Letter of 1841, Davis's Letterbook, New York Public Library, 363.

8. Walter was the son of a bricklayer and first followed his father's trade. Asher Benjamin, Richard Bond, James H. Dakin, Minard Lafever, Alexander Parris, Isaiah Rogers, William Sparrell, Thomas Thomas, Thomas Thomas Jr., Ithiel Town, and Ammi B. Young were all former carpenters' or builders' apprentices. Alexander Jackson Davis, a gifted draftsman and designer, was a former typesetter. See Adolf K. Placzek, ed., *Macmillan Encyclopedia of Architects* (New York: Free Press, 1982), s.v. "Benjamin," "Dakin," "Lafever," "Parris," "Rogers," "Thomas," "Town," and "Young"; see *Biographical Dictionary of Architects in Maine,* vol. 5 (Augusta, Maine: Maine Historic Preservation Commission, 1988), s.v. "Bond." For Sparrell, see Joseph T. Buckingham, comp., *Annals of the Massachusetts Charitable Mechanics Association* (Boston: Press of Crocker and Brewster, 1853), 255. For the reference to Davis, see William Dunlap, *A History of the Rise and Progress of the Arts of Design in the United States* (1834; reprint, Boston: C. E. Goodspeed, 1918), 1:210.

Latrobe would surely have approved of John Haviland, an Englishman who studied with the London architect James Elmes, of William P. Elliot, a student of George Hadfield, and of Karl Reichardt, a Schinkel student at the Bauakademie in Berlin, as acceptable professionals. Yet Robert Cary Long, who had studied with the master builder and architect Martin Thompson in New York, and James Dakin, a student of Alexander J. Davis, might not have met his exacting professional standards. See *Macmillan Encyclopedia of Architects,* s.v. "Haviland" and "Long"; for Elliot, see Pamela Scott and Antoinette Lee, *The Buildings of the District of Columbia* (New York: Oxford University Press, 1993), 190; *Thieme-Becker Allgemeines Lexikon der Bildenden Künstler* (Leipzig: E. A. Seemann, 1934) s.v. "Reichardt." I am grateful to Professor Michael Lewis of Williams College for his help with information on Reichardt.

9. The following American Institution architects also belonged to Bricklayer's Company (T. U. Walter); Associated Housewrights of Boston (Asher Benjamin and William Sparrell); and Massachusetts Charitable Mechanics Association (Richard Bond, Charles or

Karl Reichardt, Isaiah Rogers, Alexander Parris, William Sparrell, Ithiel Town, and Ammi Young). Although Alexander J. Davis was not trained in the building trades, he did join the New York Mechanics' Institute.

10. Haber, *Quest for Honor and Authority,* 91–96; and Howard Rock, *Artisans of the New Republic* (New York: New York University Press, 1984), 239–255.

11. Asher Benjamin, preface to *The Practice of Architecture* (1833; reprint, New York: Da Capo Press, 1972), iii. On Benjamin's titles, see Jack Quinan, "Some Aspects of the Development of the Architectural Profession in Boston between 1800 and 1830," *Old-Time New England* 68 (summer–fall 1977): 32–33. Upton notes the change in Benjamin's attitude toward his readers after 1830. See his "Pattern Books," 118.

12. Rock, *Artisans of the New Republic,* 239–255; Gary Kornblith, "From Artisan to Businessman: Master Mechanics in New England, 1789–1850" (Ph.D. diss., Princeton University, 1983), 502–518; and Mark Erlich, *Working with Our Hands: The Story of Carpenters in Massachusetts* (Philadelphia: Temple University Press, 1986), 23.

13. Kornblith, "From Artisan to Businessman," 518; and David Saposs, "Colonial and Federal Beginnings," in *History of Labor in the United States,* ed. John R. Commons (New York: Macmillan, 1918), vol. 1, 69–71.

14. Dunlap, *Rise and Progress of the Arts of Design,* III, 119–120; Paul Staiti, *Samuel F. B. Morse* (New York: Cambridge University Press, 1989), 151–156, 235–236; Eliot Clark, *History of the National Academy of Design, 1825–1953* (New York: Columbia University Press, 1954), 9–15, 252, 258, 272. Martin E. Thompson was also a founder of the National Academy. It is unclear if he is the Thomson or Tomason(?) on the November 1836 list of architects endorsing the American institution.

15. Daniel Calhoun, *American Civil Engineer: Origins and Conflict* (Cambridge, Mass.: MIT Press, 1960), 164–165, 183–186.

16. On architectural science, see Letter of 2 November 1836 and Article I, *Constitution.* See Haber, *Quest for Honor and Authority,* 7–8 on Hamilton and the professional's science.

17. Article VII, *Constitution,* 5. John Soane had written that the architect mediated between client and mechanic in his *Plans, Elevations, and Sections of Buildings* (London: I. Taylor, 1788), 7. Davis, Haviland, and Walter—the three authors of the constitution—were aware of Soane. Davis owned some unidentified books by the English architect. Haviland worked in a London office from 1811 until 1815, and Walter traveled to London in the early 1830s. See May 1901 catalog of Davis's library, Avery Library; and Roger Moss and Sandra Tatman, *Biographical Dictionary of Philadelphia Architects* (Boston: G. K. Hall, 1985), s.v. "Haviland" and "Walter."

18. Bruce Sinclair, *Philadelphia's Philosopher Mechanics: A History of the Franklin Institute* (Baltimore: Johns Hopkins University Press, 1974), 2–25; Thomas Bender, *New York Intellect* (Baltimore: Johns Hopkins University Press, 1987), 83–87; Mechanics' institutes will be discussed further in chapter 3.

19. Davis joined the New York Mechanics Institute in 1835. See Letter of 1 August [1835] from Owen Warren to Davis, Davis Collection, Avery Library; see chapter 3 for Strickland's, Walter's, and Haviland's involvement with the Franklin Institute.

20. Organized in 1834, the Institute of British Architects was a cozy and select London gentlemen's club. Its president for over twenty years was an aristocrat who was not an architect. The members made no real effort to establish rigorous credentials or standards of practice for half a century. In 1866 Queen Victoria granted the organization a royal charter. Thereafter it was the Royal Institute of British Architects. See Charles Eastlake, "An Historical Sketch of the Institute," *Sessional Papers of the RIBA* (1875–76): 258–272; J. A. Gotch, "R.I.B.A.," in *The Growth and Work of the R.I.B.A.*, ed. J. A. Gotch (London: Simson and Company, 1934), 10–23, 38–40; and Barrington Kaye, *The Development of the Architectural Profession in Britain* (London: George Allen and Unwin, 1960), 82 n. 42.

21. "Articles III and IV," 3 and 4. The circular letter of 23 March 1837 from Walter, Haviland, and Davis identifies them as the committee members who drafted the constitution. The examination areas were familiar from Vitruvius's description of the architect's education. See his *Ten Books of Architecture*, trans. Morris Hickey Morgan (New York: Dover, 1960), 5–13. The RIBA, by contrast, did not create an examination for its prospective junior members until 1862. It was, however, voluntary and did not become mandatory until 1882. See Gotch, "R.I.B.A.," 21.

22. There was a third category, honorary members. They had "taste in architecture" and required nomination by the professors. "Articles III, IV, V," *Constitution* (1837), 3–5.

Minard Lafever recognized defining professional education was a particularly troublesome issue for the fledgling society: "I have my doubts of success, under the constitution now before me. What do you conceive to be professional education, for if, the word professional, should take its full meaning; I fancy that the institution in its infant state [will be] very feeble." See Letter of 30 March 1837, AIA Archives.

23. Letter of 12 July 1806 to Mills, *Correspondence of Latrobe*, 2:242.

24. *Constitution.*

25. Samuel Haber, *Quest for Honor and Authority*, 96; and *Constitution.*

26. Letter of 1841 to Walter, Davis Letterbook 1829–1890, Davis Collection, New York Public Library.

27. Minutes of the 23 February 1857 Meeting, *Proceedings of the AIA* (1857–1871) (unpublished), AIA Archives. Some members suggested the name New York Society of Architects, but Walter proposed the American Institute of Architects. See minutes for 10 March and 15 April 1857 meetings.

28. Van Brunt, "Richard Morris Hunt," *Proceedings of the AIA* (1895), 72.

29. Address of 22 February 1858, AIA, published in *The Crayon* 5 (April 1858): 111; Everard Upjohn, *Richard Upjohn: Architect and Churchman* (1938; reprint, New York: Columbia University Press, 1968), 30–31, 48–50 for biographical information on Upjohn.

30. Address, AIA meeting of 5 May 1857, published in *The Crayon* 4 (June 1857): 182.

31. In 1835 Upjohn worked as a draftsman for Alexander Parris, a Boston architect and founding member of the American Institution. H. W. Cleaveland, Edward Gardiner, and J. W. Priest, who had studied or worked with Upjohn, were also charter members as were the medieval revivalists Henry Dudley, John Wells, and John Welch. For information on the charter members, see *Macmillan Encyclopedia of Architects*, s.v. "Babcock," "Dudley,"

"Eidlitz," "Hunt," "Mould," and "Richard Michell Upjohn." For Welch, see Phoebe Stanton, *The Gothic Revival in America* (Baltimore: Johns Hopkins University Press, 1968), 187. For Gardiner, Priest, and Wells, see Judith Hull, Appendix 1, "The School of Upjohn," *JSAH* 52 (September 1993): 304–305; William Wisely, *The American Civil Engineer* (New York: American Society of Civil Engineers, 1974) 21; Henry Withey and Elsie Withey, *Biographical Dictionary of American Architects* (Los Angeles: New Age Press, 1956), s.v. "Wells."

32. Hobart Upjohn, "The Early Years of the A.I.A.," typescript, (1940?), Avery Fine Arts and Architecture Library, 29; Article 6, *Constitution of the American Institute of Architects* (New York: John W. Amerman, 1858), Upjohn Collection, New York Public Library, 6–7. The constitution also provided for a category for honorary membership.

33. Meeting of 15 April 1857, n.p. The institute rented rooms in the University Building, where Davis and Hunt had studios. See Leroy Kimball, "Old University Building and the Society Years on Washington Square," *New-York Historical Society Quarterly Bulletin* 32 (July 1948): 177–178.

The AIA's love of ceremony persisted. There were soon AIA buttons, watch chains, charms, and pins. In 1923 Henry Bacon, dressed in a medieval cloak, received the AIA Gold Medal while floating in a barge launched on the reflecting pool of the Lincoln Memorial in Washington, D.C. Flying a yellow sail with the AIA seal in black, the barge was pulled by architectural students. See Henry H. Saylor, *The A.I.A.'s First Hundred Years* (Washington, D.C.: The Octagon, 1957), 32, 145–146. In 1992 the AIA College of Fellows held the convocation of new fellows at Trinity Church in Boston.

34. Meeting of 15 April 1857.

35. Entitled "The T-Squares," the articles were unsigned. Eidlitz, however, composed and recited a poem with the same characters at an AIA banquet in 1860. See *AMJ* 1 (3 March 1860): 171. For the articles, see *The Crayon* 5 (February–December 1858): 48–50, 346–351.

36. *Proceedings of the AIA* (1869), 172–175; 22 November 1866 Minutes, AIA Archives; and "What Is an Architect?" *AMJ* 1 (October 1859): 2.

37. Article III, *Constitution,* 6; and "The A.I.A.," *AMJ* 1 (18 February 1860): 150.

38. See minutes for AIA meetings of 23 February and 20 March 1857 on new members. For the 1870 statistics, see Robert Gutman, *Architectural Practice* (New York: Princeton Architectural Press, 1988), 120; and Richard Levy, *Professionalization of American Architects and Civil Engineers, 1865–1917* (Ann Arbor, Mich.: University Microfilms, 1983), Table A-20, 387. See A. J. Bloor, "Sketch of the History and Status of the A.I.A.," *Proceedings of the AIA* (1890), 91, for institute chapters.

39. Levy, ibid., 175; and Turpin Bannister, *The Architect at Midcentury* (New York: Reinhold Corporation, 1954), vol. 1, 100.

40. 22 February 1869 Circular Letter from Upjohn, pasted in Board of Trustees Minutes, AIA Archives.

Fee standards were particularly important to Upjohn, who sued the building committee for the Taunton, Massachusetts, town hall for his design fee and won. When Richard M. Hunt sued his first client over a fee dispute, Upjohn and other AIA members testified for him. See Letters of 7 December 1848, 3 and 24 April 1850, and 29 January 1851 from Morton and Bennett, lawyers, to Upjohn, Upjohn Collection, New York Public Library, and Everard Upjohn, *Richard Upjohn,* 145. See "Important Trial," *AMJ* 3 (16 March 1861): 222–224, for the Hunt lawsuit.

41. The 5 percent fee seems to have originated in the late eighteenth century. See Walter, *Proceedings of the AIA* (1870), 206; and John Van Horne and Lee Formwalt, eds., *The Correspondence and Miscellaneous Papers of Benjamin Henry Latrobe* (New Haven, Conn.: Yale University Press, 1984), vol. 1, 259. Latrobe wrote that he felt degraded when he was paid a daily wage like a common laborer. See Lee Formwalt, *Benjamin Henry Latrobe and the Development of Internal Improvements in the New Republic, 1796–1820* (New York: Arno Press, 1982), 36.

42. Minutes of 1 December 1857 and 2 May 1866 Meetings and "Schedule of Charges, American Institute of Architects" (1866), AIA Archives. See *Proceedings of the AIA* (1869), 132, for Upjohn's comment. For opposition to a mandatory schedule, see Minutes for 1 December 1857 and 5 March 1859 meetings, AIA Archives.

43. On Davis's billing practices, see 15 January 1833 entries for the R. Gilmour House, Davis Letterbook, New York Public Library, 147. He reduced his fee for the Edwin Litchfield House from 5 to 3 percent when his estimates proved too low. See Bill of January 1856 for Litchfield House, Davis Collection, Avery Library.

Upjohn charged a rate of six dollars for an eight-hour day for the Edward Gardiner House executed in the 1830s. See Everard Upjohn, *Richard Upjohn,* 41–43. His fee for the Trinity Building was 2.5 percent. See 15 March 1852 Letter from Berkeley and Claflin to Upjohn, Upjohn Collection, New York Public Library and Everard Upjohn, *Richard Upjohn,* 42, 58–59, 103. On Baltimore architects, see Letter of 13 February 1897 from Edmund Lent to Alfred Stone, AIA Secretary's Incoming Correspondence, AIA Archives.

44. *Proceedings of the AIA* (1869 and 1870), 134 and 206.

45. The professional advantages and disadvantages of competitions were debated at an 1857 AIA meeting. See *The Crayon* 4 (November 1857): 339. See also Hobart Upjohn, "The Early Years of the AIA," typescript (Avery Library, 1940?), 140–141, 146–148.

46. *Proceedings of the AIA* (1870), 233–240; Lois Craig, *The Federal Presence* (Cambridge, Mass.: MIT Press, 1978), 149, 202–203; and "The Bureau Bill," *American Architect and Building News* 1 (26 February 1876): 1, 67–68.

47. Haber, *Quest for Honor and Authority,* xiii, 195–199, 360–361; and Bender, *New York Intellect,* 181–191.

48. *Proceedings of AIA* (1888), 80; and Robert Prestiano, *The Inland Architect* (Ann Arbor, Mich.: University Microfilms, 1985), 208 n. 10.

49. Letter of 22 September 1885 from Illsley to Henry Lord Gay, WAA (Western Association of Architects) Papers, AIA Archives.

50. *By-Laws of the Western Association of Architects* (1884), WAA Papers. Bethune was admitted to the AIA in 1886, but only as an associate member. See Saylor, *The A.I.A.'s First One Hundred Years,* 31. She was apparently nervous about her WAA application. Writing to Root,

the WAA secretary, Bethune expressed relief that her election had occurred with no "taint of ridicule or notoriety." See Letter of 7 December 1885, WAA Papers.

51. The WAA wanted associations in the following states: Indiana, Missouri, Iowa, Minnesota, Kentucky, Ohio, Wisconsin, Nebraska, Tennessee, Louisiana, Michigan, Kansas, Texas, and New York. In 1885 there were organizations in Minnesota, Illinois, Iowa, Nebraska, Kansas, and Missouri. See "Proceedings of W.A.A." (1885). By 1886 all but Louisiana, Kentucky, and Tennessee had associations. See "Committee Reports," WAA Convention (1886).

52. "Proceedings of the W.A.A." (1885), p. 73; and Letter of 12 January 1885 from J. McDonnell to Henry Lord Gay, WAA Secretary, WAA Papers.

53. This was an amendment to the WAA Constitution. See *Inland Architect* 6 and 8 (November 1885 and December 1886): 69–72, 77.

54. "Proceedings of W.A.A." (1885) and "Application for Membership," Treasurer's Papers, WAA Papers. In 1901 the AIA finally adopted an 1897 recommendation that its prospective members either pass an examination or present evidence of a degree from an acceptable school of architecture. This turned out to mean only eastern schools. See *Proceedings of the AIA* (1901), 11.

55. "Committee on Building Laws" *Proceedings of the WAA* (1885), 2–4.

56. See "Licensing of Architects," and "Architect's Registration," *American Architect and Building News* 11 and 87 (12 March 1887 and 4 March 1905): 121 and 75; and Bannister, *The Architect at Midcentury,* 1:353–355. Shaw and other prominent British architects published an entire book about their opposition to professional regulation. See Richard Norman Shaw and T. G. Jackson, comps., *Architecture: A Profession or an Art?* (London: John Murray, 1892). A more limited certification was the diploma awarded by the Ecole des Beaux-Arts for its students beginning in 1862. Adler may have learned about the central European examinations when he traveled abroad to study European opera houses while working on the Auditorium Building in the 1880s.

57. *Inland Architect* 6 (January 1886): 127–129.

58. E. L. Godkin, editor of *The Nation,* addressed the institute members in 1869, urging them to adopt objective standards for professional practice. In the wake of several building collapses during the 1870s, the *American Architect and Building News,* the AIA's organ for publication, advocated architectural examination and licensing. See E. L. Godkin, "Professional Guilds," *Proceedings of the AIA* (1869), 186–194; Bender, *New York Intellect,* 181–191; and *American Architect and Building News* 2 (July 1877): 215–216. The AIA was not persuaded.

59. *Inland Architect* 7 (March 1886): 75. For the WAA position on competitions, see Resolution on Competitions (1884), WAA Papers, AIA Archives.

60. I base these conclusions on my examination of the WAA Papers and the *Inland Architect*'s reports.

61. Daniel Burnham, "Suggestions toward the Best and Speediest Methods for Harmonizing and Utilizing All the Architectural Societies in the United States," *Proceedings of the AIA* (1887), 114–119; Bloor, "Sketch of the History and Status of the A.I.A.," 99–101.

It was an uneasy marriage. The old AIA board insisted that the 1889 convention, the first after the merger, be held in Cincinnati so neither organization's members could dominate. Furthermore, the AIA proposed admitting WAA members only as associates. The WAA leadership threatened to veto the merger. The compromise was to make all members fellows and eliminate the associate category of membership. See 31 July 1889 Minutes, AIA Board of Trustees, AIA Archives.

62. Van Brunt, "Architecture at the World's Columbian Exposition," (1892) and "Historic Styles, Modern Architecture," (1892–1893) both in *Architecture and Society: Selected Essays of Henry Van Brunt,* ed. William Coles (Cambridge, Mass.: Belknap Press of Harvard University, 1969), 234, 300.

63. Van Brunt, architect of the Electricity Building at the fair, drafted the Tarsney Bill. See Minutes of 20 October 1892 Meeting, AIA Board of Trustees, and Letter of 6 February 1893 from Senator Pasco to Van Brunt, AIA Secretary's Correspondence. For the Tarsney Act, see Glenn Brown, "Washington Letter," *American Architect and Building News* 39 (21 January 1893): 44–45; Glenn Brown, "The Tarsney Act," *Brickbuilder* 15 (May 1906): 95–98; and R. H. Thayer, *History, Organization, and Functions of the Office of the Supervising Architect of the Treasury Department* (Washington, D.C.: Government Printing Office, 1886), 5–8. The AIA lobbied to eliminate the Supervising Architect's Office completely, but many congressmen saw the office as a source of patronage jobs and refused.

64. Brown, "The Tarsney Act," 95–98; and *Proceedings of the A.I.A.* (1897 and 1898), 12 and 90–91.

65. Circular of 11 December 1894 from John Carrère, AIA Scrapbook, AIA Archives; and Craig, *The Federal Presence,* 149, 202–203.

66. Post, *Proceedings of the AIA* (1897), 38; and Yost, *Proceedings of the AIA* (1889), 74–77.

67. *Proceedings of the AIA* (1900), 113–114, 150. John Reps, *Monumental Washington* (Princeton, N.J.: Princeton University Press, 1967), 94–154. Frederick Law Olmsted Jr. and Augustus Saint-Gaudens, who worked on the 1893 fair, were also appointed to the McMillan Commission. For the 1904 planning commissions, see Frank Miles Day's report, *Proceedings of the A.I.A.* (1904), 138.

68. Richard H. Collin, *Roosevelt, Culture, Diplomacy, and Expansion* (Baton Rouge: Louisiana State University Press, 1985), 50–54; and Letter of 11 February 1904 from Roosevelt to McKim, McKim Papers, Manuscript Division, Library of Congress, Washington, D.C.

69. Haber, *Quest for Honor and Authority,* 198–199.

70. *Proceedings of the AIA* (1897), 67; and Dankmar Adler, "Influence of Steel and Plate Glass upon Style," *American Architect and Building News* 54 (31 October 1896): 37–39. The editors of the *American Architect and Building News* shared Adler's view; see their earlier "Chicago Architects and Chicago High Building," *American Architect and Building News* 24 (26 December 1891): 189.

71. N. Clifford Ricker, "Results of the Illinois Licensing Law," *Brickbuilder* 10 (February 1901): 28–31.

72. Ibid., 28.

73. Ibid.

74. Ibid., 29–30

75. Ibid.; and *Proceedings of the AIA* (1897 and 1907), 53 and 67–69; and Bannister, *The Architect at Midcentury,* 1:356–357.

76. These states were Arkansas and California (1901); New Jersey (1902); and Colorado (1909). New Jersey architects believed that licensing would give them a competitive edge over New York and Philadelphia architects. See Bannister, *The Architect at Midcentury,* 2:357. On building codes, see Gutman, *Architectural Practice,* 61–62; see *Proceedings of the AIA* (1904 and 1906), 188 and 125–126, on AIA votes. For Wright's remark, see Gwendolyn Wright, "Architectural Practice and Social Vision in Wright's Early Designs," in *The Nature of Frank Lloyd Wright,* ed. Carol Bolon, Robert S. Nelson, and Linda Seidel (Chicago: University of Chicago Press, 1988), 100.

77. The last state registration law for architects was passed in 1951. "Model Form of Law for the Registration of Architects," *Journal of the AIA* 7 (July 1919): 335–338; and Harry G. Robinson III, "Registration and Conduct Rules: Some Common Questions," in *The Architect's Handbook of Professional Practice,* ed. David Haviland (Washington, D.C.: AIA Press, 1994), vol. 1, sec. 1.4, 89.

78. *Proceedings of the AIA* (1869 and 1894), 134–135 and 8, 62–63. When the WAA and AIA merged in 1889, Sullivan reconstituted his committee on ethics codes. A year later, however, he reported consensus was impossible. See *Proceedings of the AIA* (1890), 17–18.

79. Paul Starrett, *Changing the Skyline* (New York: McGraw-Hill, 1938), 53–55. Builders also complained that Burnham and other Chicago architects blackballed builders who used the uniform building contract, adopted by the National Association of Builders (NAB) and the AIA, mandating arbitration when controversies over responsibility for cost overruns arose. See *Convention of the National Association of Builders* (1894), 118. For the full text of the contract, see "Appendix," *Convention of NAB* (1896), 110–112. Boston architects also opposed the uniform contract. See *Convention of NAB* (1893), 28–29.

80. Letter of 6 December 1900 from Baumann to Glenn Brown, AIA Secretary's Incoming Correspondence, AIA Archives. See Harriet Monroe, *John Wellborn Root* (1896; reprint, Park Forest, Ill.: Prairie School Press, 1966), 122; Robert Bruegmann, *The Architects and the City: Holabird and Roche of Chicago, 1880–1918* (Chicago: University of Chicago Press, 1997), 30; and Paul Baker, *Stanny: The Gilded Life of Stanford White* (New York: Free Press, 1989), 150–151, for architects' investments in their buildings.

81. The National Chemigraph Company in Saint Louis and the Architectural Catalogue Company in New York specialized in these publications during the 1890s and 1900s. Avery Library has a particularly fine collection of souvenir sketchbooks. I am grateful to Herbert Mitchell, former Avery librarian of rare books, for his help with these materials. On Mann and Ellis, see George R. Mann, *Selections from an Architect's Portfolio: George R. Mann* (Saint Louis, Mo.: National Chemigraph Company, 1893), n.p.; and "Death of Harvey Ellis," *American Architect and Building News* 83 (23 January 1904): 25–26.

82. "The Advertising Fake," *Real Estate Record and Guide* 57 (25 April 1896): 696. See also "A Scandal to the Profession," and "The Advertising Fake Scandal Again," *American Architect and Building News* 52 and 53 (2 May 1896 and 1 August 1896): 47–48 and 39–40.

83. *Proceedings of the AIA* (1895), 13.

84. "Professional Ethics," *American Architect and Building News* 48 (16 February 1895): 78.

85. "A Circular of Advice Relative to the Principles of Professional Practice and a Canon of Ethics," *Proceedings of the AIA* (1909), 106–110. The code also prohibited members from publishing souvenir sketchbooks and monographs underwritten by building contractors and suppliers. Over the years the AIA has vacillated on making the code mandatory. It was finally withdrawn in 1979 after a Supreme Court antitrust ruling attacked professional codes as limiting competition. In 1997 the AIA drafted a new code with three tiers of compliance: canons (broad principles of conduct), ethical standards (goals members should aspire to), and rules of conduct (mandatory and grounds for disciplinary action). See "1997 Code of Ethics and Professional Conduct," *AIArchitect* 4 (May 1997): 11–12. See James Hurst, *The Growth of American Law* (Boston: Little, Brown, 1950), 329–330, for the lawyers' code.

86. Draftsmen and young architects created their own associations for education like the Architectural League of New York, established in 1881. Similar organizations were formed in Boston, Philadelphia, Pittsburgh, and Chicago. The Architectural League of America, a national organization, was created in 1900. See *Proceedings of the Architectural League* (1881–1889), 64–73; *Proceedings of the AIA* (1904 and 1909), 62 and 38–39; and Gwendolyn Wright, *Moralism and the Model Home* (Chicago: University of Chicago Press, 1980), 227.

87. *Proceedings of the AIA* (1896), 42–49; and Letter of 4 October 1898 from Adler to Alfred Stone, A.I.A. Secretary's Incoming Correspondence, AIA Archives.

The AIA abandoned the schedule in the early 1970s under pressure from the Justice Department, which ruled that fee schedules constituted restraint of trade. Fees are now a matter of negotiation with individual clients. See Douglas E. Gordon, "The Evolution of Architectural Practice," *Architecture* 76 (December 1987): 125–126.

CHAPTER 3

1. See the following: W. J. Rorabaugh, *The Craft Apprentice* (New York: Oxford University Press, 1986), 7–11; Ian Quimby, *Apprenticeship in Colonial Philadelphia* (New York: Garland Press, 1985), 7; Stella Kramer, *English Craft Guilds and the Government* (New York: AMS, 1968), 99–101; and Margaret Gay Davies, *The Enforcement of English Apprenticeship, 1563–1642* (Cambridge, Mass.: Harvard University Press, 1956), 5.

2. Jack McLaughlin, *Jefferson and Monticello* (New York: Henry Holt, 1988), 102–103; Robert L. Harris Jr., "Minorities and Work," *Encyclopedia of American Social History*, ed. Mary Cayton, Elliott Gorn, and Peter Williams (New York: Scribner's, 1993), vol. 2, 1559; and Richard Dozier, "The Black Architectural Experience in America," *Journal of the American Institute of Architects* 65 (July 1976): 162–163. Booker T. Washington's interviews with former slaves were the source for much of the information on antebellum schools for slave artisans.

3. Nancy Gabin, "Women and Work," *Encyclopedia of American Social History,* 2:1542. Rorabaugh, *The Craft Apprentice,* 4–5, 50–51. *Special Reports, Occupations: The Twelfth Census* (Washington, D.C.: Government Printing Office, 1904), li, 14.

4. Joseph T. Buckingham, comp., *Annals of the Massachusetts Charitable Mechanics Association* (Boston: Press of Crocker and Brewster, 1853), 34.

5. Rorabaugh, *The Craft Apprentice,* 69, 207–208. By 1845 it was reported that Massachusetts masters no longer drew up indenture agreements with their apprentices. See Frederick Lincoln's address of 2 October 1845 to the Massachusetts Charitable Mechanics Association quoted in Gary Kornblith "From Artisan to Businessman: Master Mechanics in New England, 1789–1850" (Ph.D. diss., Princeton University, 1983), 533–534.

6. For the 1888 report, see "Report of the Legislative Committee on Apprenticeship," *National Association of Builders Proceedings* (1888), 142.

7. *Pennsylvania Gazette,* 31 October 1771, reproduced in Hannah Benner Roach, "Thomas Nevell," *JSAH* 24 (May 1965): 156–157. Jeffrey Cohen, "Early American Architectural Drawings, 1730–1860," in *Drawing toward Building,* ed. James O'Gorman (Philadelphia: University of Pennsylvania Press, 1986), 22.

8. Jack Quinan, "Some Aspects of the Development of the Architectural Profession in Boston between 1800 and 1830," *Old Time New England* 68 (summer–fall 1977): 32–33.

9. Louise Hall, "The First Architectural Schools? No But . . . ," *Journal of the AIA* 14 (August 1950): 79.

10. Williams's announcement, one of the earliest references to the Adam style in Philadelphia, appeared in the *Pennsylvania Packet* of 4 January 1773, reproduced in Roger Moss and Sandra Tatman, *Biographical Dictionary of Philadelphia Architects* (Boston: G. K. Hall, 1985), s.v. "Williams."

11. Jeffrey Cohen, "Early American Drawings," 15–17, 22–23. See also Jeffrey Cohen, "Building a Discipline: Early Institutional Settings for Architectural Education in Philadelphia, 1804–1890," *JSAH* 53 (June 1994): 139–183.

12. Burr was quoted in the *Annals of the Massachusetts Charitable Mechanics Association, 1795–1892* (Boston, 1892), 73.

13. Frank D. Hurdis Jr., "Architecture of John Holden Greene" (master's thesis, Cornell University, 1973), 19, 35; and Hiram Hill, "Incidents in the Life of Hill," entries for 14 April 1851, 2 December 1824, and 31 July 1826, reproduced as an appendix in Hurdis, "Architecture of John Holden Greene," 233–240.

14. William W. Boyington, "Differences between the Methods of Architectural Practice Prevalent Now and Those of Fifty Years Ago," *Proceedings of the AIA* (1887), 102.

15. Dell Upton, "Pattern Books and Professionalism," *Winterthur Portfolio* 19 (autumn 1984): 107–150. See also my article "The First American Architectural Journals," *JSAH* 48 (June 1989): 117–121; and Charles B. Wood III, "A Survey and Bibliography of Writings on English and American Architectural Books Published before 1895," *Winterthur Portfolio* 2 (1965): 131–137.

The origins of the American builders' guides are the popular architectural handbooks published to disseminate English Palladianism during the early eighteenth century. Benjamin and the authors of the other early builders' guides were familiar with these publications by William Salmon, Batty Langley, Peter Nicholson, and William Pain. These handbooks were all in circulation in pre-Revolutionary America. See Rudolf Wittkower, "English Literature on Architecture," in his *Palladio and Palladianism* (New York: George Braziller, 1974), 95–112; and Helen Park, *A List of Architectural Books Available in America before the Revolution* (Los Angeles: Hennessey and Ingalls, 1973).

16. Asher Benjamin, preface to *The Rudiments of Architecture* (1814; reprint, New York: Da Capo Press, 1972); and Benjamin, preface to *The Elements of Architecture* (1843; reprint, New York: Da Capo Press, 1974), iii.

17. Edward Shaw, preface to *The Modern Architect or Every Carpenter His Own Master* (Boston: Dayton and Wentworth, 1855), n.p.

18. Rorabaugh, *The Craft Apprentice,* 32–35, 220 n. 2, n. 3.

19. "Retrospect," *American Architect and Building News* 18 (16 December 1885): 303 and my "First American Architectural Journals," 133, 135.

20. *Architecture,* vol. 1 (Scranton, Pa: International Correspondence School, 1899). Ware reputedly wanted to give credit for International Correspondence School courses to students accepted by Columbia. The university trustees vetoed his proposal because they felt such courses were not up to Columbia standards. See W. T. Partridge, "Reminiscences of William Robert Ware," typescript, Ware Papers, Avery Library, 3.

21. "Mechanics' Institute of New York," *Mechanics' Magazine* 4 (September 1834): 180; Bruce Sinclair, *Philadelphia's Philosopher Mechanics: A History of the Franklin Institute* (Baltimore: Johns Hopkins University Press, 1974), 2–25; and Thomas Bender, *New York Intellect* (Baltimore: Johns Hopkins University Press, 1987), 83–87.

22. "Mechanics' Institute," 183; and Bender, *New York Intellect,* 83–87.

23. Preface to *Mechanics' Magazine* 1 (30 June 1833), iv; and Charles Quill, *The American Mechanic* (Philadelphia: Henry Perkins, 1838), 27, 54. I am very grateful to Michael Radow for giving me a copy of Quill's book.

24. Quill, *The American Mechanic,* 174–178.

25. Sinclair, *Philadelphia's Philosopher Mechanics,* 109–110, 120–121; and Cohen, "Early American Drawings," 25.

26. *Centennial Celebration of the General Society of Mechanics and Tradesmen* (New York, 1885), 10, 43.

27. Preface to *Mechanics' Magazine* and "Importance of Education for the Artizan [*sic*]," *Mechanics' Magazine* 1 (30 June 1833): v, 285–286.

28. "Mechanics' Institutes," Letter to the Editor from A, *Mechanics' Magazine* 4 (September 1834): 180; and Quill, *The American Mechanic,* 135, 139. For similar references, see "To Mechanics from the Temperance Recorder," *Mechanics' Magazine* 3 (April 1833): 166–167; and "Apprentices: The Mechanic Arts," *Mechanics' Magazine* 8 (December 1838): 287–288. The latter was reprinted from the *New York Evening Star.*

Dell Upton discusses antebellum education and social control in his "Lancasterian Schools, Republican Citizenship, and the Spacial Imagination in Early Nineteenth-Century America," *JSAH* 55 (September 1996): 238–253.

29. Sinclair, *Philadelphia's Philosopher Mechanics,* 119–125; Education Committee Report, *Proceedings of the AIA* (1909), 29–31; and Charles A. Bennett, *A History of Manual and Industrial Education, 1870 to 1917* (Peoria, Ill.: Manual Arts Press, 1937).

30. W. J. Reader, *Professional Men: The Rise of the Professional Classes in Nineteenth-Century England* (London: Weidenfeld and Nicolson, 1966), 118–122; and Harold van Buren Magonigle, "Half a Century of Architecture—1," *Pencil Points* 1 (November 1933): 477.

31. Letter of 20 November 1808 from Latrobe to Henry Ormond, in John Van Horne, ed., *The Correspondence and Miscellaneous Papers of Benjamin Henry Latrobe* (New Haven, Conn.: Yale University Press, 1986), vol. 2, 680–681. Ormond inquired about study for his son, who, however, did not enter the office. See also Cohen, "Early American Architectural Drawings," 24, 31 n. 46.

32. Frederick Graff, Adam Traquair, Lewis DeMun, John Barber, Robert Mills, William Strickland, and Thomas Breillat all studied with Latrobe. Latrobe's son Henry assisted his father with the Capitol and the New Orleans waterworks. Graff became an important engineer. DeMun was Latrobe's draftsman and received some engineering work on his own. He later joined his brothers in Cuba. Traquair worked as Latrobe's draftsman and then joined his father's marble works, where they manufactured sculptures and mantelpieces, which Latrobe used at the Capitol and the White House. Before they absconded with office funds, Breillat and Barber worked as draftsman and clerk, respectively, on the Philadelphia waterworks. See Talbot Hamlin, *Benjamin Henry Latrobe* (New York: Oxford University Press, 1955), 134–135, 214–215.

There is some dispute over precisely when Strickland entered the office. Latrobe wrote that the boy became his student in 1801, when he would have been thirteen. In an autobiographical account, however, Strickland wrote that he was fifteen. Both agree that he stayed four years in the office. See Letter of 11 August 1805 from Latrobe to John Strickland, William's father, in Edward Carter II, ed., *The Papers of Benjamin Henry Latrobe* (Clifton, N.J.: James T. White, 1976), microfiche edition; and Strickland, Autobiographical fragment, ca. 1825, J. K. Kane Papers, American Philosophical Society Library, Philadelphia. Both Talbot Hamlin and Agnes Gilchrist state that Strickland left the office when he was seventeen. See Hamlin, *Latrobe,* 216; and Agnes Gilchrist, *William Strickland, Architect and Engineer, 1788–1854* (Philadelphia: University of Pennsylvania Press, 1950), 216.

33. Letter of 3 November 1804 from Latrobe to Mills, in Pamela Scott, ed., *The Papers of Robert Mills* (Wilmington, Del.: Scholarly Film Resources, 1990), no. 0042.

34. Strickland, Autobiographical fragment, Kane Papers; and John Van Horne and Lee Formwalt, eds., *Correspondence and Miscellaneous Papers of Benjamin Henry Latrobe* (New Haven, Conn.: Yale University Press, 1984), vol. 1, 535 n. 1, for a description of the more tedious chores. Letter of 25 May 1807 from Latrobe to the President and Directors of the Bank of Philadelphia, *Papers of Mills,* no. 0117 for Mills's job as clerk of the works. For information on Latrobe's design and professional advice to Mills, see Letter of 12 July 1806 from Latrobe to Mills, *Correspondence of Latrobe,* 2:239, 245.

Latrobe, however, grew less magnanimous after Mills and Strickland became rivals for projects that he coveted. He accused Mills of stealing the commission for the Monumental Church in Richmond, Virginia, from him and charged Strickland with plagiarizing his design for the Second Bank of the United States in Philadelphia after the younger man won the competition. See Letter of 26 May 1812 from Latrobe to Mills, *Papers of Mills,* no. 0333 on the Richmond church; and Letter of 23 September 1818 to John Meany, in John Van Horne, ed., *Correspondence and Miscellaneous Papers of Benjamin Henry Latrobe* (New Haven, Conn.: Yale University Press, 1988), vol. 3, 996, for the imbroglio over the bank competition.

35. Letter of 25 May 1807, *Papers of Mills,* no. 0117; and Letter of 30 May 1814 from Latrobe to Colonel Samuel Lane, Commissioner of United States Public Buildings, *Papers of Mills,* no. 0458.

36. Letter of 3 October 1806 from Mills to Jefferson, *Papers of Mills,* no. 0088. Latrobe agreed, writing that Mills's previous study under James Hoban had been "much misdirected." Letter of 2 October 1803 from Latrobe to Jefferson, *Mills Papers,* no. 0025.

37. Letter of 19 November 1805 from Latrobe to John Lenthall, *Correspondence of Latrobe,* 2:163.

38. Strickland, Autobiographical fragment, ca. 1825. Stuart refers to Stuart and Revett's *Antiquities of Athens* (1762, 1789). Batty Langley was the author of several eighteenth-century builders' guides with examples of English Palladianism and Gothic Revival designs. Abraham Swan's *The British Architect* (1745) illustrated designs influenced by Renaissance and Baroque architecture.

39. Strickland, Autobiographical fragment.

40. Ibid. Taylor first published his treatise on perspective in 1719. Other editions appeared throughout the eighteenth and early nineteenth centuries.

41. Ibid. and Letter of 10 June 1812 from Latrobe to Secretary of War, *Papers of Latrobe,* microfiche edition.

42. Undated announcement from Letterbook, 1827–1835, Alexander Jackson Davis Papers, Rare Books and Manuscripts Collection, Astor, Tilden and Lenox Foundation, New York Public Library, New York. Given the wording, I would date this advertisement from 1829, the first year of Town and Davis's partnership. For Davis's list of his pupils, see "Pupils in Architecture," in Alexander Jackson Davis Diary, I, 18, Davis Collection, Metropolitan Museum of Art, New York. Davis lists seventeen pupils in his diary. Roger Hale Newton gives the names of three additional students but does not cite the source for his information. See his *Town and Davis, Architects* (New York: Columbia University Press, 1942), 60–61.

43. Letter to author from Professor Patrick Snadon, Mississippi State University, 12 January 1991. The Stirewalt drawings are in the Davis Collection, Avery Architecture and Fine Arts Library, Columbia University, New York.

44. Agreement of 1 May 1842, Davis Collection, Box 8, New York Public Library. In the early announcement of their practice, Town was described as "Bridge Engineer and Architect." Davis Letterbook, New York Public Library, 18. See also Jane B. Davies, "Alexander J. Davis, Creative American Architect," in Amelia Peck, ed., *Alexander Jackson Davis, American Architect, 1803–1892* (New York: Rizzoli, 1992), 18–19.

45. The indentures were for Henry Bayliss, a nephew of the painter Thomas Cole, and Robert Barry. Bayliss was Town's apprentice for a term of five years; according to Barry's indenture agreement, he was to remain with Davis for five and a half years when he turned twenty-one. See folder N-10, Davis Collection, Avery Library, for the Bayliss indentures

dated 1835. The information on Barry's apprenticeship contract is from a 23 May 1836 entry in the Davis Letterbook, New York Public Library.

46. Catharine Hunt, "Biography of Richard Morris Hunt," n.d., Richard M. Hunt Collection, Prints and Drawings Collection, American Architectural Foundation, Washington, D.C., 110, 110b, 110d; Paul Baker, *Richard Morris Hunt* (Cambridge, Mass.: MIT Press, 1980), 100–105; and William Coles, "Life and Career," in *Architecture and Society: Selected Essays of Henry Van Brunt,* ed. William Coles (Cambridge, Mass.: Belknap Press of Harvard University, 1969), 10–12.

Catharine Hunt, the architect's wife, also listed Edward Quincy and E. L. Hyde as her husband's students. They never practiced architecture. Quincy became a painter and Hyde a minister. Baker states that George Bradbury, whom Hunt hired as a draftsman in 1857, was also a student.

47. *Proceedings of the A.I.A.* (1869), n.p., AIA Archives.

48. Catharine Hunt, "Biography," 110b–110c, 112–113. Catharine Hunt collected reminiscences from Furness and Hunt's other pupils for her biography.

49. Ibid., 110b–110c.

50. Henry Van Brunt, "Richard Morris Hunt," *Proceedings of the AIA* (1895), 76–77; and Catharine Hunt, "Biography," 122, for Ware's remarks. See William Coles, "Richard Morris Hunt and His Library," *Art Quarterly* 30 (fall–winter 1967): 224–238, for Hunt's library.

51. "Autobiography of William LeBaron Jenney," *Western Architect* 10 (June 1907): 66, 74–75; and Theodore Turak, *William LeBaron Jenney* (Ann Arbor, Mich.: University Microfilms, 1986), 114.

52. Jenney, "Autobiography," 66, 64–75; and his "An Old Atelier in Chicago in the Seventies," *Western Architect* 10 (July 1907): 72–75. Jenney taught at the University of Michigan from 1876 until 1880.

53. John Bancroft was the assistant who instructed Adler in the office of H. Willard Smith. See Adler, "Autobiographical Essay," n.d., Archives of American Art, Smithsonian Institution, New York, 1–2. For the reference to graduating from the drawing board, see Adler, "Proposed Technological School from the Standpoint of the Architect," *Inland Architect* 19 (August 1892): 36–37.

54. Magonigle, "A Half Century of Architecture—1," 477.

55. Van Brunt, "Richard Morris Hunt," 72.

56. Charles Babcock, "The Ways and Means of Accomplishing the Elevation of the Architect's Profession," *The Crayon* 4 (December 1857): 372. Babcock gave this speech at an October 1857 AIA meeting.

57. Ibid., 372; and William Robert Ware, *An Outline of Architectural Education* (Boston, 1866), 20.

58. Thomas Davidson (1888), quoted in Samuel Haber, *The Quest for Honor and Authority in the Professions* (Chicago: University of Chicago Press, 1991), 201; Glenn Brown, *1860–1930, Memories* (Washington, D.C.: Press of W. F. Roberts Company, 1931), 24–25; and William Robert Ware, "Professional Draughtsmen as Special Students," *School of Mines Quarterly, Columbia University* 17 (July 1897): 7.

59. William Robert Ware, "On the Condition of Architecture and Architectural Education in the United States," *Sessional Papers of the Royal Institute of British Architects* (1866–67), 818–882. Ware delivered this address at the RIBA on 20 January 1867.

60. Robin Middleton, introduction to *The Beaux-Arts and Nineteenth-Century French Architecture* (Cambridge, Mass.: MIT Press, 1982), 6–7; and David Van Zanten, *Designing Paris* (Cambridge, Mass.: MIT Press, 1987), 3–4, 74, 124–130.

61. *Proceedings of the AIA* (1867), AIA Archives, 4, 13–16. The committee members who drew up the proposal were Leopold Eidlitz, William Robert Ware, R. G. Hatfield, Emlen Littell, and S. A. Warner.

62. Ibid. The school also included a two-year preparatory course in drawing, science, and modern languages. Graduation from this program was a prerequisite for admission into the technical and academic curricula.

63. *Proceedings of the AIA* (1869), AIA Archives, 143–144.

64. Architecture was part of the engineering schools at MIT, Cornell, and the University of Illinois. At Columbia it was a part of the School of Mines. Architecture at Tuskegee was taught within the industrial arts department.

65. Daniel Calhoun, *The American Civil Engineer: Origins and Conflict* (Cambridge, Mass.: MIT Press, 1960), 39–45; and Sinclair, *Philadelphia's Philosopher Mechanics,* 319–324.

66. Arthur Weatherhead, *Collegiate Education in Architecture in the United States* (Los Angeles: Hennessey and Ingalls, 1941), 235–236.

67. "Architectural Education in the United States, I: M.I.T.," *American Architect and Building News* 24 (4 August 1888): 47; and J. A. Chewing, "William Robert Ware at M.I.T. and Columbia," *Journal of Architectural Education* 33 (November 1979): 25–29.

Ware's influence persisted at MIT after his departure for Columbia. W. P. P. Longfellow and T. M. Clark, who knew Ware from their work at the *American Architect and Building News* and then at MIT, took over the program. Although Longfellow stayed only a year, Clark taught until 1888. Furthermore, Eugène Létang, whom Ware had hired, remained at MIT until the 1890s. See my "The *American Architect and Building News, 1876–1906*" (Ph.D. diss., Columbia University, 1983), 124–130; and Chewing, "Ware at MIT and Columbia," 25–29.

68. For Ware's remarks on his insecurity and European study and travels, see his Letter of 26 September 1891 to Frank Dempster Sherman, quoted in "Manuscript Biography of William Robert Ware," Ware Papers, MIT Archives, Cambridge, Massachusetts, 150–151.

69. Letter of 25 April 1865 from Ware to John Runkle, Ware Papers, MIT Archives. Donald Drew Egbert described the Ecole design method as beginning with the general or "the most ideal aspects of a design before turning to the particularities." See Donald Drew Egbert, *The Beaux-Arts Tradition in French Architecture* (Princeton, N.J.: Princeton University Press, 1980), 12.

70. "Architectural Education, MIT," 47, 251; and "Manuscript Biography of Ware," MIT Archives.

71. While Ware's MIT students tended to be older and usually had some office experience, his Columbia students were just out of high school. See Ware, "Instruction in Archi-

tecture," *School of Mines Quarterly, Columbia University* (November 1888): 37–38; "Architectural Education, M.I.T.," 47; and "Architectural Education in the United States, IV: Columbia University," *American Architect and Building News* 24 (1 December 1888): 251.

Between 1902 and 1906, Ware published *The American Vignola,* a textbook for designing classical architecture. It contained measured drawings of ancient, Renaissance, and Baroque monuments, tables of classical orders, guides for drawing and establishing proportional relationships, and practical instruction on designing vaults, doors, and windows. It was an erudite and elaborate version of an early nineteenth-century builder's guide.

The classical orders were, however, more of a design discipline than a stylistic imperative. Henry Van Brunt, Ware's partner, wrote: "The classical orders may thus be considered the primer of design; if they are not mastered in the beginning by the student, he can hardly express his thought grammatically even in the medieval language." See his "Delicacy of Perception Dependent upon Study," *American Architect and Building News* 2 (11 August 1877): 254. This editorial ran unsigned, but the *American Architect* editor identified Van Brunt as the author in his annotated copy of the magazine, now in the Loeb Library collection at the Harvard Graduate School of Design. See my "*American Architect and Building News,*" 352, 382n 31.

72. Letter of 7 December 1909 from Ware to Wallace Sabine, MIT Archives. See also Ware, "Architectural Instruction in New York and Paris," *American Architect and Building News* 70 (6 October 1900): 4; and Letter of 12 April 1911 from Ware to Mr. Wheeler, Ware Papers, MIT Archives.

73. Letter of 10 June 1871 from Ware to A. D. White, White Papers, Cornell University Archives, Ithaca, New York. White, the first president of Cornell, sought advice from Ware on founding an architecture program. See also Ware, *Outline of Architectural Education,* 9, 20.

On Ecole training see Egbert, *Beaux-Arts Tradition,* 11–13, 25–26, 41–44; and Richard Chafee, "Teaching of Architecture at the Ecole des Beaux-Arts," in *The Architecture of the Ecole des Beaux-Arts,* ed. Arthur Drexler (Cambridge, Mass.: MIT Press, 1977), 82–83.

74. Letter of 29 August 1897 from Ware to Mr. Aldrich, Ware Papers, MIT Archives.

75. Letter of 7 December 1909 from Ware to Wallace Sabine, MIT Archives.

76. Babcock, "The Ways and Means of Accomplishing the Elevation of the Architect's Profession," 372; and Babcock, "A Course of Instruction," *Builder* (1887): 695.

77. Ethel Goodstein, "Charles Babcock, Architect, Educator and Churchman" (master's thesis, Cornell University, 1979), 117–118.

78. "Architectural Education in the United States, III: Cornell," *American Architect and Building News* 24 (6 October 1888): 155–156; and Babcock, "A Course of Instruction," 696.

79. Goodstein, "Charles Babcock," 117–118. See *American Architect* (October 1888), 155, for illustrations of student work.

80. "Architectural Education, Cornell," 155–156. For the Babcock quotation, see Babcock, "A Course of Instruction," 695. Yet Babcock did not require students to design a rolled I beam. They needed only enough information to choose the best beam from a manufacturer's catalog or table. See Babcock, "A Course of Instruction," 695.

81. "Architectural Education, Cornell," 156; and Babcock, "A Course of Architectural Instruction," 696.

82. Babcock, "A Course of Instruction," 696. See also Arthur Cates, "The Higher Education of the Architect, II: The College of Architecture at Cornell University," *Journal of the RIBA* 22 (24 November 1900): 39.

83. James Bellanger, a science graduate of the University of Michigan with experience in a Chicago office, taught the first courses at Illinois. Harold Hansen, who had studied architecture at the School of Architecture in Christiana, Sweden, and then the Bauakademie in Berlin, succeeded Bellanger in 1871. See the following: "Architectural Education in the United States, II: The University of Illinois," *American Architect and Building News* 24 (1 September 1888): 99; Turpin Bannister, "Pioneering in Architectural Education: Recalling the First Collegiate Graduate in Architecture in the United States, Nathan Clifford Ricker," *Journal of the AIA* 20 (July and August 1953): 5–7, 76–81.

84. Anthony Alofsin, "Tempering the Ecole: Nathan Ricker at the University of Illinois, Langford Warren at Harvard, and Their Followers," in *The History of History in American Schools of Architecture, 1865–1975,* ed. Gwendolyn Wright and Janet Parks (New York: Princeton Architectural Press, 1990), 73–74. See also Roula Geraniotis, "The University of Illinois and German Architectural Education," *Journal of Architectural Education* 38 (summer 1984): 15–21.

85. Bannister, "Pioneering in Architectural Education," 5–7; and Alofsin, "Tempering the Ecole," 74.

86. Alofsin, "Tempering the Ecole," 76. Alofsin notes that Ricker was the first to translate Wagner's text into English. He published an abridgement of his translation in *Brickbuilder* for 1901.

87. Ricker, Report to AIA Committee on Education, *Proceedings of the A.I.A.* (1881), 30–32; Richard Levy, *Professionalization of American Architects and Civil Engineers, 1865–1917* (Ann Arbor, Mich.: University Microfilms, 1983), 269–271; Edwin O. Sachs, "The Architectural School of the Berlin Technical College," *American Architect and Building News* 57 (10 July 1897): 17–19; and Herbert Baer, "The Course in Architecture at a German Technische Hochscule," *American Architect and Building News* 71 (16 March 1901): 83–85.

88. Ricker, Report to AIA Committee, 38; and Bannister, "Pioneering in Architectural Education," 78. Dankmar Adler supposedly encouraged Ricker to implement an architectural engineering program. On the Berlin institutions, see Sachs, "Architectural School of the Berlin Technical College," 17–19.

89. See Ricker, Report to AIA Committee, 35; "Architectural Education, University of Illinois," 95–96, 99; Levy, *Professionalization of American Architects,* 272–273; and Bennett, *History of Manual and Industrial Education,* 15–22. The Russian system was also exhibited at the Centennial Exposition in Philadelphia in 1876.

90. Ricker, Report to AIA Committee, 32–35; and "Architectural Education, University of Illinois," 95–96.

91. Ricker, Report to AIA Committee, 34.

92. On office internships, see *American Architect* 24 (1888): 48, 96. See Richard Dozier,

"Tuskegee: Booker T. Washington's Contributions to the Education of Black Architects" (Ph.D. diss., University of Michigan, 1990), 132–137; and Curtis Sartor, "Booker T. Washington's Legacy of Architecture: Tuskegee Institute," in *Diversity in Architecture,* comp. Diane Ghirardo, Barbara Allen, and Howard Smith (Washington, D.C.: American Collegiate Schools of Architecture Association, 1996), 41.

93. While Babcock drew on the High Victorian Gothic for his Cornell designs, Ricker used a different architectural style for each building. Drill Hall, which Ricker completed in 1890, had elaborate exposed woodwork and steel trusswork. See Kermit Carlyle Parsons, *The Cornell Campus* (Ithaca, N.Y.: Cornell University Press, 1968), 55–58, 81–84, 131–136, 138; Alofsin, "Tempering the Ecole," 75; and Janice Stein, "The Ricker Legacy," *Inland Architect* 30 (September/October 1986): 19–20, 55.

Richard Dozier refers to a work requirement for University of Illinois students. It was abandoned, however, because the students simply refused to work. See Dozier, "Tuskegee," 46.

94. Ibid., 1–7, 202–205.

95. Washington, *Up from Slavery* (1901), quoted in Sartor, "Booker T. Washington's Legacy of Architecture," 39.

96. Washington, *Working with the Hands* (1904: reprint, New York: Negro Universities Press, 1969), 78; Dozier, "Tuskegee," 209.

97. Alabama Polytechnical Institute offered an architectural degree in 1907. Tulane and the Georgia Institute of Technology established architectural programs in 1908. Like their predecessors in the North and Midwest, all three programs were situated within engineering schools. See Weatherhead, *Collegiate Education in Architecture,* 120–123.

There were always fewer architects in the South than elsewhere in the country. Dozier notes that while the 1870 census listed 2,017 architects in the United States, only 101 were in the South. Louisiana, with 55, had the greatest number and Virginia, with only 5, the fewest. By contrast, New York had 470 architects, Massachusetts 195, and Pennsylvania 101. See Dozier, "Tuskegee," 28.

98. Ibid., 42, 45, 205. On Russian training, see Bennett, *History of Manual and Industrial Education,* 13–20.

99. Ellen Weiss, "Robert Taylor of Tuskegee," *Arris: Journal of the Southeastern Chapter of the Society of Architectural Historians* 2 (1991): 1–3; and Dozier, "Tuskegee," 54–56, 64–65. The 1899–1900 catalog, with the description of the architecture program, is quoted in Dozier, "Tuskegee," 217.

100. Dozier, "Tuskegee," 110, 123, 173; and Weiss, "Robert Taylor of Tuskegee," 2–5.

101. For Pittman, Rayfield, Tandy, Bowman, and Lankford, see Dozier, "Tuskegee," 67–68, 73–74, 176–178. For Williston, see Kirk Muckle and Dreck Wilson, "David Augustus Williston," *Landscape Architecture* 72 (January 1982): 82–85; for Hazel, see Harrison Ethridge, "The Black Architects of Washington, D.C., 1900 to the Present" (Ph.D. diss., Catholic University of America, 1979), 41–42. For Williams quote, see Dozier, "Tuskegee," 191.

102. Tuskegee conferred a certificate in architecture. While architecture was a four-year program in 1899, it became a three-year course open only to juniors in 1901. Other histori-

cally black colleges and universities like Alabama State University in Montgomery, Alabama, and Claflin College in Orangeburg, South Carolina, offered courses in architectural drafting during the late nineteenth century, but they did not, Dozier observes, develop a complete architectural curriculum like Tuskegee. See Dozier, "Tuskegee," 49–50, 217.

Howard University in Washington, D.C., was the first historically black university to offer a bachelor's degree in architecture from its School of Manual Arts and Applied Sciences in 1911. William Hazel, architectural instructor at Howard since 1910, organized a separate department of architecture there in 1919. The Howard program, unlike Tuskegee's, emphasized architecture as a fine art. See Vinson McKenzie, comp., "Chronology of African American Architects," in Jack Travis, ed., *African-American Architects in Current Practice* (New York: Princeton Architectural Press, 1991), 92; Walter Dyson, *Howard University: The Capstone of Negro Education* (Washington, D.C.: Graduate School of Howard University, 1941), 140–141; and Ethridge, "Black Architects of Washington, D.C.," 41–42.

103. Weiss, "Robert Taylor of Tuskegee," 3; and Michael Adams, "A Legacy of Shadows," *Progressive Architecture* 72 (February 1991): 85.

Southern states got around the color-blind provisions of the second land-grant act by funding existing black institutions like Tuskegee and founding new segregated schools for agriculture, mechanical arts, and home economics. See "Land Grant Colleges," *Britannica Online,* 1996 edition.

104. Quoted in Parsons, *The Cornell Campus,* 57–58. In spite of White's remark, the first woman was not admitted to Cornell until 1870. He believed the university must be well established before he introduced coeducation.

105. See "Architectural Education: Cornell," 157; and "Architecture Open to Women," *American Architect and Building News* 19 (15 June 1886): 266, for information on the Cornell and Illinois women graduates. On Hayden, see Judith Paine, "Sophia Hayden and the Women's Building Competition," in *Women in American Architecture,* ed. Susanna Torre (New York: Whitney Library of Art, 1977), 70–73. For Bethune's statistics, see Louise Bethune, "Women in Architecture," *Inland Architect* 17 (March 1891): 20–21. See Adriana Barbasch, "Louise Blanchard Bethune," in *Architecture: A Place for Women,* ed. Ellen Perry Berkeley and Matilda McQuaid (Washington, D.C.: Smithsonian Institution Press, 1989), 15–25, for information on Bethune. See Sara Holmes Boutelle, *Julia Morgan, Architect* (New York: Abbeville Press, 1988), 30, for Morgan. See *Special Reports, Occupations: The Twelfth Census,* l, for census statistics.

Norma Merrick Sklarek, who graduated from Columbia's architecture program in 1950, is probably the first African American woman to become a registered architect (in New York and California), and the first admitted to the AIA. See "Norma Merrick Sklarek," and Vinson McKenzie, comp., "Chronology of African American Architects," in Travis, *African-American Architects in Current Practice,* 66, 92.

106. Adams, "A Legacy of Shadows," 85–86; and Elizabeth Grossman and Lisa B. Reitzes, "Caught in the Crossfire: Women and Architectural Education, 1880–1910," in Berkeley and McQuaid, *Architecture: A Place for Women,* 27–28, 38, 87–89, 94.

107. Another disheartening statistic was that only 120 out of the 650 architectural graduates even went on to practice architecture between 1867 and 1898. See Education Committee Report, *Proceedings of the AIA* (1898), 71–82, for all the information. See "Architectural Education, University of Illinois," 97, and "Architectural Education, Columbia," 252, for the costs of university training and "Architectural Education, MIT," 47, for the writer's remark.

108. "Architectural Education, MIT," 47; "Architectural Education, University of Illinois," 95; "Architectural Education, Cornell," 157; and "Architectural Education, Columbia," 251.

109. "Architectural Education, University of Illinois," 95; and "Architectural Education, Cornell," 155.

110. "Architectural Education, MIT," 48; "Architectural Education, University of Illinois," 97; and "Architectural Education, Cornell," 157. Comparable figures for Columbia are not available because it did not distinguish between degree candidates and special students in its enrollment statistics.

111. Letter of 13 July 1893 from McKim to Prescott Butler and Letter of 4 July 1896 from McKim to Mrs. John Oakley, Charles F. McKim Papers, Manuscript Division, Library of Congress, Washington, D.C. On Americans at the Ecole, see Richard Chafee, "Hunt in Paris," in *The Architecture of Richard Morris Hunt,* ed. Susan Stein (Chicago: University of Chicago Press, 1986), 16.

Foreigners were not eligible for study at the French Academy. For McKim and the American Academy, see my "Charles McKim and the Foundation of the American Academy in Rome," in *Light on the Eternal City: Papers in Art History from the Pennsylvania State University,* ed. Hellmut Hager and Susan Munshower (University Park, Pa.: Penn State Press, 1987), vol. 2, 307–327; and Fikret Yegül, *Gentlemen of Instinct and Breeding* (New York: Oxford University Press, 1991), 7–15.

112. "Formation of the Beaux-Arts Society in New York," and "The Society of Beaux-Arts Architects," *American Architect and Building News,* 43 and 92 (3 February 1894 and 7 December 1907): 49 and 185–186; and "A Too Vaulting Ambition," and "Some Phases of Architectural Education in This Country," *American Architect and Building News,* 87 and 88 (13 May and 30 December 1905): 150 and 210.

113. A. L. Brockway, "Influence of the French School of Design upon Architecture in America," *Proceedings of the AIA* (1899), 306; and Ware, "Architectural Instruction in New York and Paris," 4.

114. *American Architect and Building News* 24 (20 October 1888): 178; and Education Committee Reports, *Proceedings of the AIA* (1904 and 1909), 62 and 28–29.

115. "Cornell's Architectural Curriculum," *American Architect and Building News* 42 (4 April 1896): 1; and Cates, "The Higher Education of an Architect," 39.

116. W. T. Partridge, "Reminiscences of William Robert Ware," typescript in William Robert Ware Papers, Avery Fine Arts and Architecture Library, 1–2; and Steven Bedford and Susan Strauss, "History II, 1881–1912," in *The Making of an Architect, 1881–1981,* ed. Richard Oliver (New York: Rizzoli, 1981), 36–39.

117. Partridge, "Reminiscences of William Robert Ware"; and Bedford and Strauss, "History II," 36–39.

CHAPTER 4

1. William Dunlap, *A History of the Rise and Progress of the Arts of Design in the United States* (1834; reprint, Boston: C. E. Goodspeed, 1918), vol. 1, 5–6, 10–11.

2. Paul Staiti, *Samuel F. B. Morse* (New York: Cambridge University Press, 1989), 152–153, 235–236, 239.

3. Alexander Jackson Davis, "Vitruvius and Soane on Architectural Patronage with Some Remarks on the Profession of Architecture and the Acceptance of the Arts of Design," 15 March 1841 address to the Apollo Association, Davis Collection, Avery Library.

As a result of his design work for New York University in the 1830s, Davis surely knew about plans to provide education for merchants, mechanics, farmers, engineers, and architects at that institution. This proposed practical course of study ultimately failed, and a classical curriculum was in place when New York University opened in 1832. See Thomas Bender, *New York Intellect* (Baltimore: Johns Hopkins University Press, 1987), 94–98, 101–104.

4. On the New York Mechanics Institute, see Owen Warren to Davis, 1 August [1835], Davis Collection, Avery Library; references to the institute fairs and exhibits are found in *Mechanics' Magazine* 6 (July 1835): 249, 260; and in Letterbook for 18–23 October 1843, Davis Collection, New York Public Library. Undated newspaper advertisements for his practice are located in the Davis Collection, Avery Library. Jane B. Davies, Davis scholar, dates the conversazione announcement from around 1836. These new marketing efforts all begin after Davis and Town dissolved their partnership in May of 1835.

5. Five hundred copies of *Rural Residences* were printed, colored editions for $2.00, and uncolored for $1.50. The entire venture cost $750, more than Davis recorded as his entire income from architecture in some years. See Jane B. Davies, introduction to Alexander Jackson Davis, *Rural Residences* (1838; reprint New York: Da Capo Press, 1980).

6. Davis, "An Economical Farmer's House of Wood," Plate II, *Rural Residences,* n.p. Davis wrote that English publications like J. C. Loudon's *Encyclopedia of Cottage, Farm, and Villa Architecture* (1833) were not suitable for the American market. They showed buildings that were either too vast or too humble for the American Republic.

7. See, for example, Andrew Jackson Downing, *Cottage Residences* (New York: John Wiley, 1842), 185; and George B. Tatum, *Andrew Jackson Downing, Arbiter of American Taste, 1815–1852* (Ann Arbor, Mich.: University Microfilms, 1975), 148.

Downing's publications were the first truly popular architectural books printed in the United States. His first book, *Treatise on the Theory and Practice of Landscape Gardening Adapted to North America* (1841), went through sixteen printings, *Cottage Residences* thirteen, and *The Architecture of Country Houses* nine, by the 1880s. See Vincent Scully, *The Shingle and Stick Styles* (New Haven, Conn.: Yale University Press, 1971), xxviii n. 19. Downing's success must have pained Davis. His client Robert Donaldson consoled him with these words:

"Downing Stole Your Thunder . . . but I always, on suitable occasions, claimed for you the seminal ideas which have been so fruitful." Quoted in Davies's introduction.

8. Davis had published a design for a country church and school in *Rural Residences*. Specialized books for such designs included Richard Upjohn's *Rural Architecture* (New York: Putnam, 1852); and G. P. Randall, *Book of Designs for School Houses* (Chicago: Knight and Leonard, 1884).

Upjohn may have been one of the few architects who published a pattern book to keep clients at bay. After his success with Trinity Church, he was inundated with requests from small congregations to donate designs. He referred them to his book after 1852. See preface to *Rural Architecture,* n.p. See also William Ranlett, *The Architect* (1847; reprint, New York: Da Capo Press, 1976); Samuel Sloan, *The Model Architect,* 2 vols. (Philadelphia: E. G. Jones, 1852); and J. H. Kirby, introduction to *Modern Cottages* (Syracuse, N.Y., 1886), 9.

9. "Everyman His Own Architect," *AMJ* 1 (7 January 1860): 91.

10. George Woodward, introduction to *Woodward's National Architect* (New York: George E. Woodward, ca. 1869), n.p.; and Scully, *Shingle and Stick Styles,* 167. Ranlett's and Sloan's books from the 1840s and 1850s also contained complete documentation for each design.

11. *Shoppell's Modern Homes* 1–4 (January 1886): 1–2.

12. Roger Moss and Sandra Tatman, *Biographical Dictionary of Philadelphia Architects* (Boston: G. K. Hall, 1985), s.v. "Price"; and Benjamin D. Price and Max Charles Price, *Church Plans* (Philadelphia: Philadelphia Board of Church Extension, 1901).

13. Michael Tomlan, "Toward the Growth of an Artistic Taste," in *The Cottage Souvenir,* no. 2 (Watkins Glen, N.Y.: American Life Foundation, 1982), 5–16.

14. "Letter to an Architectural Student—2" *AMJ* 3 (5 January 1861): 132. I attribute the article to Eidlitz because it is signed "T-Square," the pseudonym he used for the series of the same name published in the *AMJ.*

15. Ingham advertisement, 25 March 1894, *Elmira, New York Telegram;* and Letter of 19 June 1895 from Alfred Stone to Ingham, AIA Secretary's Letterbooks, AIA Archives. An unidentified correspondent complained and sent the newspaper clipping to Stone. Ingham practiced for twenty-three years in Elmira.

16. "Building," *Puck* 29 (10 June 1891): n.p. I am very grateful to Michael Radow for calling my attention to the *Puck* poem and giving me a copy.

17. "Morality in Architecture," *American Builder* 8 (October 1873): 223.

18. "New York Letter," *American Builder* 1 (July 1869): 138; and Letter of Joseph W. Murphy to John H. Hopkins Jr., 2 August 1859, quoted in Catherine Bishir, "A Spirit of Improvement," in Catherine Bishir, Carl Lounsbury, Charlotte Brown, and Ernest Wood, *Architects and Builders in North Carolina* (Chapel Hill: University of North Carolina Press, 1990), 163.

19. Elliott Krause, *Death of the Guilds: Professions, States, and the Advance of Capitalism, 1930 to the Present* (New Haven, Conn.: Yale University Press, 1996), 54.

20. Letter of 28 July 1811 to Constantin Volney, in John Van Horne, ed., *The Correspondence and Miscellaneous Papers of Benjamin Henry Latrobe* (New Haven, Conn.: Yale

University Press, 1986), vol. 2, 121. Walter's heirs claimed that the government owed the architect over one hundred thousand dollars in back fees for the Capitol and other federal projects. See Minutes of 1 February 1888, Trustees Meeting, AIA Archives.

21. Bates Lowry, *Building a National Image* (Washington, D.C.: National Building Museum, 1985), 48–58; and Daniel Bluestone, "Civic and Aesthetic Reserve," *Winterthur Portfolio* 25 (autumn 1990): 131–133. See "Government Architecture," *American Architect and Building News* 1 (18 March 1876): 92, for Peter B. Wight's remarks on the monotony of government architecture.

22. See Letter of 25 April 1885 from John Smithmeyer to Henry Lord Gay, WAA Papers, American Architectural Archives, for alleged corruption and an undated letter of Root's, possibly 1878 or 1879, quoted in Harriet Monroe, *John Wellborn Root* (1896; reprint, Park Forest, Ill.: Prairie School Press, 1966), 36–37.

23. Catharine Hunt, "Biography of Richard M. Hunt," Hunt Collection, Prints and Drawings Collection, American Architectural Foundation, 329–330; on Carrère, see Minutes of 1 April 1895, Board of Trustees, AIA Archives; and for Adler, see Report of Committee on Building Laws, WAA Convention (1885), WAA Papers, AIA Archives.

24. Mariana Van Rensselaer, *H. H. Richardson and His Works* (1888; reprint, New York: Dover, 1969), 135.

25. James Gallier, *The Autobiography of James Gallier* (1864; reprint, New York: Da Capo Press, 1973), 18–20. Gallier knew the problem well, since he and Lafever, as partners, had drafted for builders. See Dell Upton, "The Traditional House and Its Enemies," *Traditional Dwellings and Settlements Review* 1 (1990): 80–81, for the information on Walter.

26. "Death of Chicago's First Architect," *Inland Architect* 18 (January 1892): 69; John Van Osdel, "History of Chicago Architecture," *Inland Architect* 1 (August 1883): 89; and William W. Boyington, "Differences between the Methods of Architectural Practice Prevalent Now and Those of Fifty Years Ago," *Proceedings of the AIA* (1887), 103–104

27. *A History of Real Estate, Building, and Architecture in New York* (New York: Real Estate Record and Guide, 1898), 287–290.

28. "Important Trial," *AMJ* 3 (9, 16, and 23 March 1861): 222, 232, 243.

29. Town to T. L. Donaldson, 21 November 1836, quoted in Rhodri Liscombe, "A New Era in My Life," *JSAH* 50 (March 1991): 15; Adolf K. Placzek, ed., *Macmillan Encyclopedia of Architects* (New York: Free Press, 1982), s.v. "Town"; and Gallier, *Autobiography,* 26–32. See Upton, "Traditional House and Its Enemies," 81, for the risks of contracting and real estate development.

30. Letter of 2 March 1841 from Stirewalt to Davis, Davis Collection, New York Public Library.

31. "The Architect of Other Days," *Proceedings of the AIA* (1893), 172.

32. Catherine Bishir, "A Workmanlike Manner," and "A Spirit of Improvement," both in Bishir et al., *Architects and Builders in North Carolina*, 126, 166–168. See also Charlotte Brown, "Building with New Technology," in Bishir et al., *Architects and Builders in North Carolina,* 277.

33.   Strickland's recollections a.re from an undated autobiographical sketch in J. K. Kane Papers, American Philosophical Society Library.

34.   Agnes Gilchrist, *William Strickland, Architect and Engineer, 1788–1854* (Philadelphia: University of Pennsylvania Press, 1950); and Moss and Tatman, *Biographical Dictionary of Philadelphia Architects,* s.v. "Strickland."

35.   Gallier, *Autobiography;* and Arthur Scully, *James Dakin, Architect* (Baton Rouge: Louisiana State University Press, 1973).

36.   "George R. Mann," *The City of St. Louis and Its Resources* (St. Louis: Continental Printing Company, 1893), 141–142; William Coles, "Life and Career," in *Architecture and Society: Selected Essays of Henry Van Brunt,* ed. William Coles (Cambridge, Mass.: Belknap Press of Harvard University, 1969), 20–21; and Richard Longstreth, *On the Edge of the World: Four Architects in San Francisco at the Turn of the Century* (New York: Architectural History Foundation, 1983), 5–6, 40, 51–58.

37.   Randall, *Book of Designs for School Houses,* 6–7; and Henry Ericsson, *Sixty Years a Builder* (Chicago: A. Kroch, 1942), 128.

38.   "John B. Legg," in *The City of St. Louis and Its Resources* (St. Louis: Continental Printing Company, 1893), 141; and Henry Withey and Elise Withey, *Biographical Dictionary of American Architects* (Los Angeles: New Age Press, 1956), s.v. "Jerome [*sic?*] B. Legg."

39.   Robert Bruegmann, *The Architects and the City: Holabird and Roche of Chicago, 1880–1918* (Chicago: University of Chicago Press, 1997), 40–45.

40.   See my "First American Architectural Journals," *JSAH* 48 (June 1989): 135–138.

41.   Dennis Francis, *Architects in Practice, New York City, 1840–1900* (New York: Committee for the Preservation of Architectural Records, 1980); 7. *Special Reports, Occupations: The Twelfth Census* (Washington, D.C.: Government Printing Office, 1904), l, cxxv.

42.   Richard Dozier, "Tuskegee: Booker T. Washington's Contributions to the Education of Black Architects" (Ph.D. diss., University of Michigan, 1990), 29–30; and *Special Reports, Occupations: The Twelfth Census,* cxiv.

43.   In 1975 the first woman completed a union apprenticeship and received a journeyman's card in a building trade. Today women and minorities continue to face discrimination in the building trade unions. See Nancy F. Gabin, "Women and Work," *Encyclopedia of American Social History,* ed., Mary Cayton, Elliott Gorn, and Peter Williams (New York: Scribner's, 1993), vol. 2, 1542; Janice Goldfarb, ed., *Women Builders and Designers: Making Ourselves at Home* (Watsonville, Calif.: Papier Mache Press, 1995), 25; and "Non-Traditional Employment for Women," *New York Times,* 8 May 1993, sec. 2, 25.

For Bethune, see Adriana Barbasch, "Louise Blanchard Bethune," and Elizabeth Grossman and Lisa B. Reitzes, "Caught in the Crossfire," both in Ellen Perry Berkeley and Matilda McQuaid, eds., *Architecture: A Place for Women* (Washington, D.C.: Smithsonian Institution Press, 1989), 15–16 and 31. On the importance of husband-and-wife firms today, see *Architecture* 85 (June 1996): 89–91.

44.   Letter of 12 October 1894 from McKim to S. Van Rensselaer, McKim Papers, Library of Congress and Matilda McQuaid, "Educating for the Future," in Berkeley and McQuaid, *Architecture: A Place for Women,* 254–255. In the late 1880s and early 1890s McKim,

Mead and White hired its first women stenographers. See Charles Moore, *The Life and Times of Charles F. McKim* (Boston: Houghton Mifflin, 1929), 329–330.

Francis lists five women who practiced in New York before 1900: Mary N. Gannon and Alice J. Hands, 1897–1900; Caroline E. Ashley, 1897–1899; Kate Cotheal Budd, 1899; and Laura Charsley, 1899. See his *Architects in Practice,* 7, 12, 19, 21, 33.

45. Sarah Holmes Boutelle, *Julia Morgan* (New York: Abbeville Press, 1988), 44–47.

46. Doris Cole and Karen Cord Taylor, *The Lady Architects: Lois Lilley Howe, Eleanor Manning, and Mary Almy, 1893–1937* (New York: Midmarch Arts Press, 1990), 1–14; Boutelle, *Julia Morgan,* 1–23; and Withey and Withey, *Biographical Dictionary of American Architects,* s.v. "Schenck."

47. Dozier, "Tuskegee," 29–32; Robert Kapsch, "Building Liberty's Capitol," William C. Allen, "Capitol Construction," and Henry Chase, "Black Life in the Capital," all in Robert Kapsch, William C. Allen, and Henry Chase, "Liberty's Capitol," *American Visions* 10 (February/March 1995): 8–15, 10–11, 14–15. Bishir notes that white mechanics in North Carolina had a law passed forbidding free black artisans from taking on apprentices or owning slaves in 1860. See her "Spirit of Improvement," *Architects and Builders in North Carolina,* 186–188. Dozier notes that other southern states placed legal restrictions on African American craftsmen and architects after the Civil War. See his "Black Architectural Experience in America," *Journal of the AIA* 65 (July 1976): 166.

48. Dozier, "Tuskegee," 37–42, 54, 64–68, 173–179, 181–186, 207–209; and his "Black Architectural Experience in America," 162–164, 166, 168; Ellen Weiss, "Robert Taylor of Tuskegee," *Arris: Journal of the Southeastern Chapter of the Society of Architectural Historians* 2 (1991): 1–4; Michael Adams, "A Legacy of Shadows," *Progressive Architecture* 72 (February 1991): 85–87; and Harrison Ethridge, "The Black Architects of Washington, D.C., 1900 to the Present" (Ph.D. diss., Catholic University of America, 1979), 1–10, 29–30.

49. "Vertner W. Tandy," *New York Times,* 8 November 1949, 31; Dozier, "Tuskegee," 73; Adams, "Legacy of Shadows," 85; and Carson Anthony Anderson, "The Architectural Practice of Vertner Tandy" (master's thesis, University of Virginia, 1982).

50. Adams, "Legacy of Shadows," 87.

51. See Judith Blau, *Architects and Firms* (Cambridge, Mass.: MIT Press, 1984), chaps. 1, 5; Robert Gutman, *Architectural Practice* (New York: Princeton Architectural Press, 1988), 1–5; and Dana Cuff, *Architecture: The Story of Practice* (Cambridge, Mass.: MIT Press, 1991), 4–26, on the disjuncture between ideals of the atelier and realities of architectural practice.

52. Royal Cortissoz, *Art and Common Sense* (New York: Scribner's, 1903), 391; and Henry Van Brunt, "Richard Morris Hunt," *Proceedings of the AIA* (1895), 81. See Paul Baker, introduction to *The Architecture of Richard Morris Hunt,* ed. Susan Stein (Chicago: University of Chicago Press, 1986), 3, for the reference to the dean of architecture.

53. Paul Baker, *Richard Morris Hunt* (Cambridge, Mass.: MIT Press, 1980), 1–20.

54. Van Buren to Upjohn, 4 February 1854, Upjohn Collection, New York Public Library. Van Buren knew Hunt's father, and Upjohn had remodeled Lindenwald, Van Buren's home in Kinderhook, New York, in 1849.

55. "Important Trial," 244.

56. This description is from *Cecil Dreeme,* Winthrop's 1861 novel, in which the architect Harry Stillfleet was modeled after Hunt. One of the first appearances of an architect in American fiction, the novel is an indication of the profession's growing prominence. See Theodore Winthrop, *Cecil Dreeme* (Boston: Ticknor and Fields, 1861), 5–19; and William Coles, "Richard Morris Hunt and His Library," *Art Quarterly* 30 (fall–winter 1967): 224–238.

57. E. L. Marsh and Maurice Fornachon were the two longtime assistants. Richard Howland Hunt continued the practice after his father's death; his brother Joseph joined him in 1901. No office records survive; there are scattered references in reminiscences of his wife, pupils, and assistants. See Baker, *Richard Morris Hunt,* 163–164; "Important Trial," 232; Catharine Hunt, "Biography of Richard Morris Hunt," n.d. (Richard M. Hunt Collection, Prints and Drawings Collection, American Architectural Foundation, Washington, D.C.), 193–197, 223; Frank Wallis, "Master Architect and Man," *Architectural Review,* n.s., 5 (November 1917): 239; and Francis, *Architects in Practice,* 42.

58. "Studio Building," *The Crayon* 5 (January 1858): 55; and Annette Blaugrund, "The Tenth Street Studio Building," *Archives of American Art Journal* 114 (spring 1982): 64–71. Hunt left his Tribune office in 1892 because of a rent increase. By that time, his practice as a commercial architect had long since ceased. In 1893 he rented space in a high-profile building uptown, Napoleon LeBrun's Metropolitan Life Insurance Building on Madison Square, where he remained until his death in 1895. See Baker, *Richard Morris Hunt,* 163.

59. Wallis, "Master Architect and Man," 239; and Van Brunt, "Richard Morris Hunt," 81. Catharine Hunt noted her husband's profanity. See her "Biography of Richard Morris Hunt," 126b.

60. "Important Trial," *AMJ,* 3 and 4 (9 March 1861, 16 March 1861, 23 March 1861, 30 March 1861, and 6 April 1861): 222–224, 231–234, 242–245, 252–255, and 4–9; "The Paran Stevens Case," in *Arguments and Addresses of Joseph H. Choate,* ed. Frederick Hicks (St. Paul: West Publishing, 1926), 178–197; and Henry W. Sackett to Reid, 3 April 1889(?), Whitelaw Reid Papers, New York Public Library.

I am very grateful to Professor Lee Gray of the University of North Carolina at Charlotte for sharing his discoveries and sources on the Tribune Building imbroglio with me. Professor Gray believes that problems with the Tribune Building heating and ventilation system, budget overruns, and the disputed fees cost Hunt the commission for the Tribune Building addition. Reid turned instead to Edward Raht, Hunt's assistant. See Gray, "The Office Building in New York City, 1850–1880" (Ph.D. diss., Cornell University, 1993). For McKim's comment, see his letter to Thomas Kellogg, 21 May 1894, McKim Papers, Library of Congress.

61. Quoted in John Van Pelt, *A Monograph of the W. K. Vanderbilt House* (New York: Privately printed, 1925), 10; and Hunt, address, *Proceedings of the AIA* (1890), 11–12.

62. César Daly, "Les Trois Ecoles d'architecture contemporaine," *Revue générale de l'architecture* 21 (1863): 164.

63. Hunt, "Biography of Richard Morris Hunt," 128–129.

64. Henry Van Brunt, "H. H. Richardson" (1886), in Coles, *Architecture and Society,* 176–177. On the office as atelier, see Charles Coolidge, "H. H. Richardson, 1883–1886," in *Later*

Years of the Saturday Club, 1870–1920, ed. M. A. DeWolfe Howe (Boston: Houghton Mifflin, 1927), 193–194. After studying at MIT and working for Ware and Van Brunt, Coolidge joined Richardson's practice in 1884. He became a partner in the successor firm of Shepley, Rutan and Coolidge. See James O'Gorman, *H. H. Richardson and His Office* (Cambridge, Mass.: Harvard University Press, 1974), 8–10.

65. On his association with the builder, Richardson to Bell, 25 April 1866, Richardson Papers, Archives of American Art, New York, New York; Van Rensselaer, *H. H. Richardson and His Works,* 18; and O'Gorman, *H. H. Richardson and His Office,* 5–6.

66. Van Rensselaer, *H. H. Richardson and His Works,* 132–133. There were rumors that Gambrill and Richardson dissolved their partnership because of a dispute over the misappropriation of funds for Trinity Church. See Anon., "H. H. Richardson's Men," n.d., typescript, Richardson Papers, Archives of American Art.

67. Van Rensselaer, *H. H. Richardson and His Works,* 123–124; and "Studio and Office of Mr. H. H. Richardson," *American Architect and Building News* 16 (27 December 1884): 304.

68. Coolidge, "H. H. Richardson and His Work," n.d., typescript of talk for the Boston Society of Architects, 5, Archives of American Art.

69. Plates in *American Architect and Building News* 16 (27 December 1884): 304.

70. Coolidge, "H. H. Richardson," 195; O'Gorman, *H. H. Richardson and His Office,* 5–8; and William Welles Bosworth, "I Knew H. H. Richardson," *Journal of the AIA* 16 (September 1951): 116–118.

71. Bosworth, "I Knew H. H. Richardson," 123–125; and A. O. Elzner, "A Reminiscence of Richardson," *Inland Architect* 20 (September 1892): 15.

72. Elzner, "Reminiscence of Richardson," 15; Anon., "H. H. Richardson's Men," 1; and Coolidge, "H. H. Richardson," 193–195.

73. Elzner, "Reminiscence of Richardson."

74. See my "The Architectural Photograph as Tastemaker: *The American Architect* and H. H. Richardson," *History of Photography* 14 (April–June 1990): 155–163; and "Architectural Retrospect," *American Architect and Building News* 70 (29 December 1900): 98. McKim was the working editor of the *New York Sketchbook,* whose publisher, James Osgood, also produced the *American Architect and Building News.* See "McKim," *Architectural Record* 26 (November 1909): 381, for Richardson's role with the *New York Sketchbook.*

75. Jeffrey Ochsner, *H. H. Richardson: Complete Architectural Works* (Cambridge, Mass.: MIT Press, 1982), 9. For fees, see "H. H. Richardson Circular for Intending Clients: Used during Latter Part of His Life," appendix in Van Rensselaer, *H. H. Richardson and His Works,* 197.

76. James O'Gorman, "Documentation: An 1886 Inventory of H. H. Richardson's Library and Other Gleanings from Probate," *JSAH* 41 (May 1982): 151.

77. Elzner, "Reminiscence of Richardson," 15. Judith Blau discusses how success transformed small studios into offices during the 1980s in her *Architects and Firms.*

78. W. A. Langton, "On the Architect's Part in His Work as Exemplified in the Methods of H. H. Richardson," *Canadian Architect and Builder* 13 (February 1900): 28–30;

O'Gorman, *H. H. Richardson and His Office,* 18; and Bosworth, "I Knew H. H. Richardson," 117.

79. "Organization of an Architect's Office: Shepley, Rutan, and Coolidge," *Engineering and Building Record* 21 (15 February 1890): 165–166; and 1898 brochure, Wright Collection, Avery Library.

80. Roger Hale Newton, *Town and Davis, Architects* (New York: Columbia University Press, 1942), 19–20, 54, 95; and *Macmillan Encyclopedia of Architects,* s.v. "Town," by Jane B. Davies.

81. *Macmillan Encyclopedia of Architects,* s.v. "Town"; "Architecture," undated advertisement, Davis Letterbook, New York Public Library. Given that the office address is 34 Merchant's Exchange, this advertisement must be from the period between 1829 and 1831. See Francis, *Architects in Practice,* 76. On design collaboration and supervision, see *Macmillan Encyclopedia of Architects,* s.v. "Town and Davis" by Davies. Town personally supervised work on only two major commissions, the North Carolina and Indiana state capitols.

82. Gallier, *Autobiography,* 18–20; and *Macmillan Encyclopedia of Architects,* s.v. "Town and Davis."

83. "Journal of A. J. Davis," 517, New York Public Library; "Diary of Davis," 1:18–19, Davis Collection, Metropolitan Museum of Art, New York; and "Agreement of 1 May 1842," Joseph B. Davis Papers, Davis Collection, New York Public Library.

After the dissolution of the 1835 partnership, Davis formed brief associations with Isaac Thompson, a building surveyor and superintendent, and Russell Warren, an architect and bridge engineer. See advertisements for Thompson in Davis Collection, Avery Library, and for Warren as "Architecture and Bridge Engineering," Davis Letterbook, 517, New York Public Library.

84. Newton, *Town and Davis,* 60–61. There are drawings for the arrangement of Davis's 1827 office in the Merchant Exchange and his 1836 rooms in the University Building. See "Descriptive Catalogue of A. J. Davis's Library," Davis Collection, New York Public Library.

85. Adler and Sullivan were first listed as partners in 1883; Sullivan began working for Adler late in 1881 or early in 1882. See Robert Twombly, *Louis Sullivan* (Chicago: University of Chicago Press, 1987), 94.

86. Louis Sullivan, *The Autobiography of an Idea* (New York: AIA Press, 1924), 251.

87. Dankmar Adler, "An Autobiography," n.d., typescript, Archives of American Art, 7. See also Rochelle Elstein, "The Architecture of Dankmar Adler," *JSAH* 26 (December 1967): 247; and Twombly, *Louis Sullivan,* 182–183.

88. Adler, "Autobiography," 3; and "Engineering Supervision of Building Operations," *American Architect and Building News* 33 (4 July 1891): 12. Paul Sprague writes that Adler established the structure for Sullivan's design; see his "Adler and Sullivan's Schiller Building," *Prairie School Review* 2 (1965): 16.

89. Frank Lloyd Wright, *An Autobiography* (1943; reprint, New York: Horizon Press, 1977), 112, 129. Wright stated that Adler taught the young Sullivan much, and to honor the former was not to dishonor the latter. See his *Autobiography,* 129, and his *Saturday Review* comments of 12 June 1936 reprinted in *JSAH* 20 (October 1961): 141–142. George Elmslie,

Sullivan's assistant for fifteen years, angrily responded that Sullivan needed no schooling from anyone; see *JSAH* 20 (October 1961): 140–141.

90. "A Word to Subscribers," and "Tale of Hardship and Pluck," *American Architect and Building News* 46 and 73 (29 December 1894 and 31 August, 1901): 133 and 66, for financial difficulties of architects in 1893. On Adler and Sullivan, see Elstein, "Architecture of Dankmar Adler," 247, Twombly, *Louis Sullivan,* 324–325; Joan Salzstein, "Dankmar Adler," *Wisconsin Architect* 38 (July–August 1967): 19; and Arthur Woltersdorf, "Portrait Gallery of Chicago Architects: Adler," *Western Architect* 33 (July 1924): 78–79.

91. Richard Michell's three sons trained in the office and one, Hobart, practiced architecture. After studying architecture at Harvard, Everard Upjohn, Hobart's son, taught art history at Columbia University and wrote the first monograph on his great-grandfather's career. See Judith Hull, "The School of Upjohn," *JSAH* 52 (September 1993): 285–287.

92. Office records list Richard Michell as working in the office in 1846 and becoming a junior partner in 1851. Charles Babcock joined the firm around 1850 and was made a partner in 1853, three months after marrying Upjohn's daughter. The original partnership agreement stipulated that Upjohn receive eight-tenths of the profits, while his son and son-in-law got one-tenth each. See "Articles for Co-Partnership with Charles Babcock, Richard and Richard Michell Upjohn," 1 January 1853, Upjohn Papers, New York Public Library. See also Hull, "School of Upjohn," *JSAH,* 281–306; and Hobart Upjohn, "Architect and Client a Century Ago," *Architectural Record* 74 (November 1933): 377–378.

93. Hull, "School of Upjohn," 283, 287, 289, 293–294. A staff roster is published in Hull's article; see Appendix 1, 304–305.

94. Hull, "School of Upjohn," 292; and Everard Upjohn, *Richard Upjohn,* Appendix, 197–225.

95. Sullivan, *Autobiography of an Idea,* 285–286; and 9 July 1894 speech of Senator Francis Newlands, quoted in "The Tarsney Act," *American Architect and Building News* 101 (1912): 280.

96. John Carrère, "Making a Choice of a Profession, IX: Architecture," *Cosmopolitan* 35 (July 1903): 495.

97. "Organization of an Architect's Office: George B. Post," *Engineering and Building Record* 24 (7 November 1891): 326–363; and Diana Balmori, "George B. Post," *JSAH* 46 (December 1987): 352; "Organization of an Architect's Office: Burnham and Root," *Engineering and Building Record* 22 (11 January 1890): 83–84; Leland Roth, *The Works of McKim, Mead and White* (New York: Garland Press, 1978), xxxv; Robert Bruegmann, introduction to *Holabird and Roche/Holabird and Root: An Illustrated Catalog of Works, 1880–1940* (New York: Garland Press, 1991), vol. 1, xiii; and "Offices of Samuel Hannaford and Sons," *Engineering and Building Record* 22 (23 August 1890): 180.

98. Bruegmann, *The Architects and the City,* 37.

99. McKim to Bernard Green, 18 April 1904, McKim Papers, Library of Congress. For the large office today, see Gutman, *Architectural Practice,* 31–32. The Supervising Architect's Office was another early model for large practice, albeit in the public sector. In 1854 it included an engineer, architect, six draftsmen, a clerk, and a computer. See R. H. Thayer, *His-*

tory, Organization, and Functions of the Office of the Supervising Architect of the Treasury Department (Washington, D.C.: Government Printing Office, 1886), 15.

100. Bruegmann cites a few Detroit architectural practices that incorporated in the early twentieth century, but the corporate structure did not become common until liability issues arose in the 1970s. See Bruegmann, *The Architects and the City,* 116; and Douglas E. Gordon, "The Evolution of Architectural Practice," *Architecture* 76 (December 1987): 122–126.

101. "Organization of an Architect's Office: George B. Post," 326–363; see Harold van Buren Magonigle, "Some Suggestions as to the Making of Working Drawings," *Brickbuilder* 22 (July 1913): 99, for midcentury practice.

102. "City Architect's Office," *Inland Architect* 15 (July 1890): 85–86; and the thirty-nine-part series "Management of an Architect's Office," published in *American Architect and Building News,* volumes 33 (15 August 1891) to 39 (21 January 1893).

103. Everard Upjohn, *Richard Upjohn,* Appendix, 197–206; Balmori, "George B. Post," 353–355; Donald Hoffman, *The Architecture of John Root* (Baltimore: Johns Hopkins University Press, 1973), 248; Roth, *Works of McKim, Mead and White,* xv, xxiv; "Client Contracts," McKim, Mead and White Collection, Avery Library; and Bruegmann, *The Architects and the City,* 37.

104. Balmori, "George B. Post," 350 n. 33. See D. Everett Waid, "The Business Side of an Architect's Office: George B. Post and Sons," *Brickbuilder* 23 (February 1914): 47, for quotation. Post did practice with Charles Gambrill, his fellow student at Hunt's atelier, from 1860 until 1866 and then with a Mr. Mead from 1867 until 1868.

105. Balmori, "George B. Post," 342; Andrew Rebori, "Work of Burnham and Root," *Architectural Record* 38 (July 1915): 34; Theodore Starrett, "John W. Root," *Architecture and Building* 44 (July 1912): 282; Barr Ferree, "The Economic Conditions of American Architecture," *Proceedings of the AIA* (1893), 231; and "William Holabird," *The Economist* (28 July 1923), quoted in Bruegmann, *The Architects and the City,* 20.

106. Starrett, "John W. Root," 282, 429; Monroe, *John Wellborn Root,* 119; and Peter B. Wight, "An Appreciation of Daniel H. Burnham," *Architectural Record* 32 (August 1912): 181. See John Root, "Architects of Chicago" (1890), in *The Meaning of Architecture: Buildings and Writings of John Root,* ed. Donald Hoffman (New York: Horizon Press, 1967), 236, for Root's self-assessment; on Burnham as Root's critic, see Monroe, *John Wellborn Root,* 122–123; and Rebori, "Work of Burnham and Root," 41.

107. Leland Roth, *McKim, Mead and White, Architects* (New York: Harper and Row, 1983), chap. 1.

108. Lawrence Grant White, *Sketches and Designs of Stanford White* (New York: Architectural Book Publishing Company, 1920), 58.

109. William Boring to Charles Moore, 1927, McKim Papers, Library of Congress, for the remark on the partners' individual contributions; and Royal Cortissoz, review of Charles Moore's *Life and Times of Charles F. McKim, New York Daily-Herald,* 5 January 1930, for the importance of art.

110. D. Everett Waid, "The Business Side of an Architect's Office: McKim, Mead and White," *Brickbuilder* 22 (December 1913): 267; on McKim's indecisiveness, see Henry Bacon,

"McKim," *Brickbuilder* 19 (February 1910): 30–47; on Mead and the Boston library, see Mead to McKim, 19 December 1887, Moore Papers, Library of Congress. McKim wanted to return to the Ecole for additional study before completing the library design.

111. Lawrence Grant White wrote that his father's criticism made McKim melancholy. See his *Sketches and Designs of Stanford White,* 15; on the sculpture base, see White to McKim, 28 December 1892, Stanford White Papers, McKim, Mead and White Collection, Avery Library; and Roth, *McKim, Mead and White, Architects,* 243–244, for McKim's influence on White.

112. Bruegmann, *The Architects and the City,* 8–15, 24; and Bruegmann, *Holabird and Roche,* 1:x, xii–xiii. Edward Renwick wrote a recollection of the firm, now in the Holabird and Roche Collection of the Chicago Historical Society, in 1932.

113. Bruegmann, *Holabird and Roche,* ix; Franz Winkler, "The Work of Holabird and Roche," *Architectural Record* 31 (April 1912): 314; and Manierre Dawson Diary, March 1911 entry, Archives of American Art. Dawson began work as a Holabird and Roche draftsman in 1909.

114. "Organization of an Architect's Office: George B. Post," 362–363; Paul Starrett, *Changing the Skyline* (New York: McGraw-Hill, 1938), 37–38; "Organization of an Architect's Office: Burnham and Root," 83–84; Bruegmann, *The Architects and the City,* 39; and Bruegmann, *Holabird and Roche,* xii–xiii.

115. Harold van Buren Magonigle, "Half Century of Architecture—3," *Pencil Points* 15 (March 1934): 116; and Waid, "Business Side of an Architect's Office: McKim, Mead and White," 267–270; "Teunis Van der Bent," *Architecture* 76 (May 1936): 14.

116. "Organization of an Architect's Office: George B. Post," 362–363; "Organization of an Architect's Office: Burnham and Root," 83–84; and Waid, "Business Side of an Architect's Office: McKim, Mead and White," 267–270.

117. Magonigle, "Half Century of Architecture—7," *Pencil Points* 15 (November 1934): 563–564; and "Carrère and Hastings' Workshop," *Architectural Record* 10 (October 1900): 143–149.

118. Bruegmann, *Holabird and Roche/Holabird and Root,* xiv; and *Macmillan Encyclopedia of Architects,* s.v. "Daniel H. Burnham," by Thomas Hines.

119. McKim to Samuel Abbott, 29 January 1901, on library cost; McKim to Bernard Green, 18 April 1904, on office versus public building; McKim to Thomas Newbold, 27 June 1895, on two cents in bank. All letters in McKim Papers, Library of Congress.

Mead told McKim that the Boston library trustees would have to be persuaded to appropriate an additional $550,000 for the building or else the firm would be in financial trouble by 1887–1888. The building eventually cost $2 million. See Mead to McKim, 19 December 1887, Charles Moore Papers, Library of Congress.

120. Bacon, "McKim," 30–47.

121. White, *Sketches and Designs of Stanford White,* 15.

122. Magonigle, "Half Century of Architecture—3," 116.

123. See "Client List," McKim, Mead and White Papers, Avery Library, for Goelet com-

missions; on library profit, see McKim to Green, 18 April 1904, McKim Papers, Library of Congress.

124. Magonigle, "Half Century of Architecture—6," *Pencil Points* 15 (September 1934); 465.

125. McKim to Graphic Company of Chicago, 16 January 1892, and McKim to President Theodore Roosevelt, 11 July 1902; both letters in McKim Papers, Library of Congress. See McKim to Charles Rutan, 26 December (1886?) and 9 January 1887, Charles Rutan Papers, Archives of American Art, for his search for a practical man. On White's finances, see Paul Baker, *Stanny: The Gilded Life of Stanford White* (New York: Free Press, 1989), 339–348.

126. Balmori, "George B. Post," 352; Sally Chappell, *The Architecture and Planning of Graham, Anderson, Probst, and White* (Chicago: University of Chicago Press, 1992), 260–264; Bruegmann, *Holabird and Roche/Holabird and Root*, 1:xiii; and Roth, *McKim, Mead and White, Architects,* 48.

127. Peabody, *Proceedings of the AIA* (1901), 6. For New York and Chicago architects' views on the importance of art, science, and business to professional practice, see Charles McKim's "An Architect's Services and Remuneration," reprinted in Roth, *McKim, Mead and White, Architects,* 363; and Dankmar Adler's remarks, *Proceedings of the AIA* (1896), 61.

CHAPTER 5

1. Robert Andrews, "Conditions of Architectural Practice Thirty Years Ago," *Architectural Review* 5 (November 1917); 237–238; and William Haber, *Industrial Relations in the Building Industry* (Cambridge, Mass.: Harvard University Press, 1930), 15–34.

2. Leopold Eidlitz, "The Master Builder," *Real Estate Record and Guide* 7 (21 February 1891): 267.

3. "Architect and Builder," *Brickbuilder* 11 (December 1902): 257.

4. Beginning in the late nineteenth century, many women interested in architecture were shunted into allied fields like interior design. See Robert Gutman, *Architectural Practice* (New York: Princeton Architectural Press, 1988), 64–65. Today architects who work in government, contracting, development, and colleges receive higher pay and better benefits than their colleagues who work in private practice. See *Association of Collegiate Schools of Architecture Newsletter* 23 (October 1993): 16.

5. Michael Tomlan, "Toward the Growth of an Artistic Taste," in *Cottage Souvenir, no. 2* (Watkins Glen, N.Y.: American Life Foundation, 1982), 10, for Barber. See William Boring to Charles Moore, Letter of 1927, McKim Papers, Library of Congress, on the privilege of working for McKim, Mead and White. In 1893 McKim wrote that the unpaid proving period was usually "a matter of six months to a year for the brightest men." See McKim to Prescott Butler, 13 July 1893, McKim Papers, Library of Congress.

6. William Strickland, Autobiographical fragment, ca. 1825, J. K. Kane Papers, American Philosophical Library, Philadelphia, Pa.; "Organization of an Architect's Office: Burnham

and Root," *Engineering and Building Record* 21 (11 January 1890): 83–84; Burt Fenner to William Prendergast, 8 May 1912, McKim, Mead and White Collection, New-York Historical Society; and entry for 3 June 1909, Manierre Dawson Diary, Archives of American Art.

7. Andrews, "Conditions of Architectural Practice Thirty Years Ago," 237–238; Paul Starrett, *Changing the Skyline* (New York: McGraw-Hill, 1938), 30–31; Hobart Upjohn, "Architect and Client a Century Ago," *Architectural Record* 74 (November 1933): 377–378; and James O'Gorman, prolegomenon to *On the Boards* (Philadelphia: University of Pennsylvania Press, 1989), 13–14.

Donald Albrecht, an architect and curator, recalls that he used translucent linen to copy drawings in the large New York offices where he worked until Mylar was introduced in the early 1970s. Private conversation with author, June 1996.

8. W. T. Partridge, "McKim, Mead and White," typescript, 1948(?), 1, William Robert Ware Papers, Avery Library.

9. Bates Lowry, *Building a National Image* (Washington, D.C.: National Building Museum, 1985), 53, on photolithography; See also O'Gorman, *On the Boards,* 13, 18 n. 66; Christopher Gray, *Blueprints* (New York: Simon and Schuster, 1981), 8–9; "Organization of an Architect's Office: Burnham and Root," *Engineering and Building Record* 21 (11 January 1890), 83–85; and "Organization of an Architect's Office: George B. Post," *Engineering and Building Record* 24 (7 November 1891): 362–363.

10. "Organization of an Architect's Office: Burnham and Root," 83–84.

11. W. A. Langton, "On the Architect's Part in His Work as Exemplified in the Methods of H. H. Richardson," *Canadian Architect and Builder* 13 (February 1900): 28–29; D. Everett Waid, "The Business Side of an Architect's Office: McKim, Mead and White," *Brickbuilder* 22 (December 1913); 269; and Burt Fenner to Rudolph Miller, 12 December 1913, McKim, Mead and White Collection, New-York Historical Society; for Post and Burnham and Root, see "Organization of an Architect's Office: George B. Post," 362–363; and Robert Bruegmann, *Holabird and Roche/Holabird and Root: An Illustrated Catalog of Works, 1880–1940* (New York: Garland Press, 1941), vol. 1, xii.

12. W. A. Langton, "Methods of H. H. Richardson," 28; Mariana Van Rensselaer, *H. H. Richardson and His Works* (1888; reprint, New York: Dover, 1969), 118, for Richardson; Harold van Buren Magonigle, "Half Century of Architecture—3," *Pencil Points* 14 (March 1934): 116; and Boring to Moore, Letter of 1927, McKim Papers, Library of Congress.

13. Magonigle, "Half Century of Architecture—3," 117.

14. Harriet Monroe, *John Wellborn Root* (1896; reprint, Park Forest, Ill.: Prairie School Press, 1966), 198, on Root's drawings; Paul Starrett, *Changing the Skyline,* 37–38, on Root's morning rounds; and Theodore Starrett, "John W. Root," *Architecture and Building* 44 (November 1912): 430, on the private swear. For the "knuckle down" comment, see Monroe, *John Wellborn Root,* 112.

15. McKim to Carrère, 27 February 1904, McKim Papers, Library of Congress; Magonigle, "Half Century of Architecture—3," 116; Paul Starrett, *Changing the Skyline,* 32–33; and entry for 3 June 1909, Manierre Dawson Diary, Archives of American Art.

16. Latrobe to Henry Ormond, 20 November 1808, in John Van Horne, ed., *The Cor-*

respondence and Miscellaneous Papers of Benjamin Henry Latrobe (New Haven, Conn.: Yale University Press, 1986), vol. 2, 680–681; James Gallier, *The Autobiography of James Gallier* (1864; reprint, New York: Da Capo Press, 1973), 19; John Barry to Upjohn, 1 July 1851, and Morse to Upjohn, 27 May 1840?, Upjohn Collection, New York Public Library; and Judith Hull, "The School of Upjohn," *JSAH* 52 (September 1993): 304–305.

17. Charles Coolidge, "H. H. Richardson, 1883–1886" in *Later Years of the Saturday Club, 1870–1920,* ed. M. A. DeWolfe Howe (Boston: Houghton Mifflin, 1927), 196.

18. Brite to Philip Sawyer, 9 June 1938, Mildred Sawyer Papers, New-York Historical Society; McKim to Daniel Bell, 29 January 1901, McKim Papers, Library of Congress. The most detailed account of staff salaries at McKim, Mead and White is the following, from 1912:

tracer, five to fifteen dollars; junior draftsman, eighteen to thirty dollars; senior draftsman, thirty-five dollars; clerks-of-the-works, twenty to thirty; superintendents, thirty-five to seventy-five; specification writer, fifty to seventy-five; clerks, ten to thirty.

There is no indication if these are weekly or monthly rates. The former seems more likely given the salaries quoted in 1901. See Burt Fenner to William Prendergast, 8 May 1912, McKim, Mead and White Collection, New-York Historical Society.

19. Paul Starrett, *Changing the Skyline,* 41–42.

20. Peter B. Wight, "An Appreciation of Daniel H. Burnham," *Architectural Record* 32 (August 1912): 181, for Burnham's finances. See Mead to McKim, n.d., McKim Papers, Library of Congress, and balance sheet for 31 July 1905 to 30 November 1905, Office Ledgers, McKim, Mead and White Collection, New-York Historical Society.

21. "Organization of an Architect's Office: Burnham and Root," 83–84; "Office Rules, Carrère and Hastings," 30 January 1900, McKim, Mead and White Collection, New-York Historical Society. In 1907 Carrère wrote that he and Hastings "cribbed" their office rules from those of McKim, Mead and White. Carrère to Fenner, 14 March 1907, McKim, Mead and White Collection, New-York Historical Society.

22. "Organization of an Architect's Office: Burnham and Root," 84; and Paul Starrett, *Changing the Skyline,* 33.

23. William T. Partridge, "McKim, Mead and White," typescript, 1948(?), 3, William Robert Ware Papers, Avery Library, Columbia University.

24. On the Rhode Island celebration and other dinners, see ibid., 3–4; and undated typescript, Philip Sawyer Papers, Avery Library, Columbia University.

25. Swartout to McKim, Mead and White, 13 August 1941, McKim, Mead and White Collection, New-York Historical Society. Swartout wrote an account of the office, entitled "An Architectural Decade," around 1930. I have not read it, but Professor Leland Roth, University of Oregon, plans to publish it.

26. Magonigle, "Half Century of Architecture—3," 117.

27. McKim loaned money to John Galen Howard, Thomas Kellogg, and others for European trips. See McKim to Howard, 5 June 1893, McKim Papers, Library of Congress;

see Waid, "The Business Side of an Architect's Office: McKim, Mead and White," 269, on supervisory experience; for McKim's praise of his assistants, see his letter to Professor Ira Hollis of Harvard, 17 November 1903, McKim Papers, Library of Congress, commending George De Gerdsdorff for his contributions to the Harvard Stadium. James Brite recalled that Mead offered him help with job leads when he went into business for himself. See Brite to Philip Sawyer, 9 June 1938, Mildred Sawyer Papers, New-York Historical Society. See also William T. Partridge, "Memoirs of an Architect," typescript, 3b–4b, Ware Papers, Avery Library.

28. Leland Roth, *McKim, Mead and White, Architects* (New York: Harper and Row, 1983), 6; and C. H. Blackall, "Architectural Education: The Office," *American Architect and Building News* 121 (15 March 1922): 213–214, 217. See also Lionel Moses, "McKim, Mead and White: A History," *American Architect and Building News* 121 (24 May 1922): 424–425, for a list of architects who "graduated" from the McKim, Mead and White office.

29. William Welles Bosworth, "I Knew H. H. Richardson," *Journal of the AIA* 16 (September 1951): 116–118; and Monroe, *John Wellborn Root*, 198.

30. Magonigle, "Half Century of Architecture—3," 116. For salaries, see Burt Fenner to William Prendergast, 8 May 1912, McKim, Mead and White Collection, New-York Historical Society.

31. Letter to McKim, Mead and White, n.d., McKim, Mead and White Collection, Avery Library. Given that the petition includes names like Swartout's and lists the office address as 160 Fifth Avenue, the protest must be from between 1894 and 1900.

32. Glenn Brown, *1860–1930, Memories* (Washington, D.C.: Press of W. F. Roberts and Company, 1931), 25–27. See Magonigle, "Some Suggestions as to the Making of Working Drawings," *Brickbuilder* 22 (May 1913 and July 1913): 99 and 147, for information on the Municipal Building.

33. See Davis Letterbook, entries for 24 November 1825 and 20 March 1826, New York Public Library, for references to drafting Davis did for architects like Ithiel Town and Martin Thompson and builders like Josiah Brady; James O'Gorman, "H. and J. E. Billings of Boston," *JSAH* 42 (March 1983): 55–65; for Palmer and Upjohn, see Hull, "School of Upjohn," 293.

34. See O'Gorman, *On the Boards,* 11, for Langerfeldt and Deane; for Hawley, see William T. Partridge, "McKim, Mead and White," 1–2, Ware Papers; and for Ellis, scc William Purcell, "Forgotten Builders," *Northwest Architect* 8 (November–December 1944): 5–6; "Harvey Ellis," *American Architect and Building News* 83 (23 January 1904): 25–26; and Eileen Manning Michaels, "A Developmental Study of the Drawings Published in the *American Architect* and *Inland Architect*" (Ph.D. diss., University of Minnesota, 1971), 103–104.

35. See O'Gorman, "H. and J. E. Billings," 63–67; and Purcell, "Forgotten Builders," 5–6, respectively, for Billings's and Ellis's contributions as designers. Dawson was the Holabird and Roche draftsman turned renderer; see his diary entry for 7 May 1911. He studied painting in Paris and sold his first work to Gertrude Stein. Dawson, who had an engineering degree, finally left architecture and rendering for painting and farming. See also Abra-

ham Davidson, "Two from the Second Decade: Manierre Dawson and John Covert," *Art in America* 63 (September 1975): 51.

36. James Gallier, *The Autobiography of James Gallier* (1864; reprint, New York: Da Capo Press, 1973), 22–23, 26.

37. Roger Moss and Sandra Tatman, *Biographical Dictionary of Philadelphia Architects* (Boston: G. K. Hall, 1985), s.v. "Haviland," "Notman," "Sloan," "Walter"; Gallier, *Autobiography;* Adolf K. Placzek, ed., *Macmillan Encyclopedia of Architects* (New York: Free Press, 1982), s.v. "Town," "Thompson"; Edward Zimmer, *The Architectural Career of Alexander Parris* (Ann Arbor, Mich.: University Microfilms, 1986), 248–253; Constance Grieff, *John Notman, Architect* (Philadelphia: Athenaeum, 1979), 16, 42–43; and Harold Cooledge, *Samuel Sloan, Architect* (Philadelphia: University of Pennsylvania Press, 1986), 21–23. I am grateful to Professor Michael Lewis, Williams College, for reminding me of the number of prominent Philadelphia architects involved in contracting.

38. Gary Kornblith, "From Artisan to Businessman: Master Mechanics in New England, 1789–1850" (Ph.D. diss., Princeton University, 1983), v–ix. For Greene, see Frank D. Hurdis Jr., "Architecture of John Holden Greene" (master's thesis, Cornell University, 1973), 19, 35. For Hill's comment, see "Incidents in the Life of Hiram Hill," entries of 2 December 1824 and 31 July 1826, reproduced as an appendix in Hurdis, "Architecture of John Holden Greene."

39. Henry Ericsson, *Sixty Years a Builder* (Chicago: A. Kroch, 1942), 52–53. See also Dell Upton, "The Traditional House and Its Enemies," *Traditional Dwellings and Settlements Review* 1 (1990): 73–74.

40. William Haber, *Industrial Relations in the Building Industry,* 24–25; Walter Galenson, *United Brotherhood of Carpenters* (Cambridge, Mass.: Harvard University Press, 1983), 18, 76–77; see Herbert Gottfried, "Building the Picture: Trading on the Image of Production and Design," *Winterthur Portfolio* 27 (winter 1992): 235–253, for trade catalogs.

41. *Shoppell's Modern Homes* 1 (January 1886): 2, for speculators' profits.

42. "The T-Squares," *The Crayon* 5 (February 1858): 48–50; and Arthur Gilman, "On the Relation of the Architectural Profession to the Public," *Proceedings of the AIA* (1867), 26–27.

43. "One Cause of the Fall of Buildings," *Architects' and Mechanics' Journal* 1 (10 March 1861): 188; and "Death, the Builder," *Architects' and Mechanics' Journal* 1 (February 1860): 131.

44. "Concealed Defects in Blocks of Buildings," *American Architect and Building News* 26 (21 December 1889): 285–286.

45. See Henry Withey and Elsie Withey, *Biographical Dictionary of American Architects* (Los Angeles: New Age Press, 1956), s.v. "Edward Shaw." See also Upton, "The Traditional House and Its Enemies," 78, 82, for class solidarity between the authors of antebellum architectural literature and their prospective clients. My interpretation of the Shaw frontispiece is at odds with the traditional view that it portrays the cleavage between the professional architect and the building mechanic. See, for example, O'Gorman, *On the Boards,* 2.

46. For the statistics on immigrants in the New York building trades, see Robert Auchmuty, address, *National Association of Builders Convention Proceedings* (1889), 143–144.

47. See "The T-Squares," *The Crayon* 5 (February–December 1858): 48–50, 346–351. For Leopold Eidlitz's poem on Philologus Brown, see *Architects' and Mechanics' Journal* 1 (3 March 1860): 171.

48. The image and caption contain a reference to an article that appeared in the *Quarterly Review*. On the far left a man's top hat bears the inscription "Quarterly Review" on the inside band. The title of the *Quarterly Review* article praising the craftsman, which enraged Tilden and Preston, was "The Hope of English Architecture." See my "First American Architectural Journals," *JSAH* 48 (June 1989): 132–133, on the *Architectural Sketchbook*.

49. See also Upton, "The Traditional House and Its Enemies," 82, for architects' stereotypes of builders.

50. *A History of Real Estate, Building, and Architecture in New York* (New York: Real Estate Record and Guide, 1898), 304–305; and *National Cyclopaedia of American Biography* (New York: J. T. White, 1891), s.v. "John Crimmins."

51. Montgomery Schuyler, "Recent Building in New York," *Harper's Monthly* 67 (September 1883): 561. See also M. Christine Boyer, *Manhattan Manners: Architecture and Style, 1850–1900* (New York: Rizzoli, 1985), 27–30.

52. Boyer, *Manhattan Manners,* 213–214. For the quote, see *History of Real Estate, Building, and Architecture in New York,* 233. Since this publication was a promotional directory for architecture and building, True may have written this description himself.

53. See *History of Real Estate, Building, and Architecture in New York,* 321; and O. P. Hatfield, *National Association of Builders Proceedings* (1898), 126–127, for information on builders. See William Haber, *Industrial Relations in the Building Industry,* 52–59; Mark Erlich, *Working with Our Hands: The Story of Carpenters in Massachusetts* (Philadelphia: Temple University Press, 1986), 40–43; Arne Delhi, "General Contractors versus Individual Contractors," *Architectural Record* 24 (September 1908): 231–232; and Robert Bruegmann, *The Architects and the City: Holabird and Roche of Chicago, 1880–1918* (Chicago: University of Chicago Press, 1997), 81–82, for general contractors.

Thomas Cubbitt, a London master carpenter, was one of the first general contractors. Cubbitt erected buildings without subcontracting the work to other artisans. During the first half of the nineteenth century, his workshops provided the skilled labor for carpentry, bricklaying, ironwork, and glazing. Cubbitt's brother created the architectural designs. To keep his large workforce occupied, Cubbitt developed real estate throughout London. See *Macmillan Encyclopaedia of Architects,* s.v. "Thomas Cubbitt."

54. Paul Starrett, *Changing the Skyline,* 65. See R. W. Gibson, "Superintendence in America," and Cass Gilbert, "Relations of Architects to the Contracting System," *Proceedings of the AIA* (1893 and 1906), 89–90 and 361, for general contractors' fees.

55. William Haber, *Industrial Relations in the Building Industry,* 52–59; Erlich, *Working with Our Hands,* 40–43; and Delhi, "General Contractors," 231–232.

56. Ericsson, *Sixty Years a Builder,* 238–239; Bruegmann, *The Architects and the City,* 82; Paul Starrett, *Changing the Skyline,* 130–136; and *History of Real Estate, Building, and Architecture in New York,* 321–324, 415–416.

57. "Organization of an Architect's Office: George B. Post," 362; "Organization of an Architect's Office: Burnham and Root," 84; and Waid, "The Business Side of an Architect's Office: McKim, Mead and White," 269.

58. Delhi, "General Contractors," 231; and William Haber, *Industrial Relations in the Building Industry,* 59.

59. Erlich, *Working with Our Hands,* 52–54; Delhi, "General Contractors," 235; O. W. Norcross, *National Association of Builders Proceedings,* (1891), 102; and John R. Commons, "The New York Building Trades," *Quarterly Journal of Economics* 18 (1903–4): 414, for rumors of Fuller's bribes.

60. J. A. Schweinfurth, "Great Builders I Have Known," *American Architect and Building News* 140 (November 1930): 92–96; *Dictionary of American Biography,* s.v. "Orlando Norcross," by Robert K. Shaw; James O'Gorman, "O. W. Norcross, Richardson's Master Builder," *JSAH* 32 (May 1973): 104–113; and Diana Prideaux-Brune, "The Builder as Technical Innovator: Orlando Norcross and the Beamless Flat Slab" (master's thesis, Cornell University, 1989).

61. O'Gorman, "O. W. Norcross," 110 n. 20; *Dictionary of American Biography* and *National Cyclopaedia of American Biography,* s.v. "O. W. Norcross." See *National Association of Builders Proceedings* (1890), 88, for remark on carpentry and brick contractors.

62. McKim to Meredith, Letter of 21 April 1894, on Norcross, McKim Papers, Library of Congress; and Brown, *1860–1930 Memories,* 25–26, and 31–32.

63. "Marc Eidlitz," *American Architect and Building News* 36 (7 May 1892): 77; *Marc Eidlitz and Sons, 1854–1904* (New York: Privately printed, 1904), n.p.; *Marc Eidlitz and Sons* (New York: Privately printed, 1914), n.p. Alfred and Otto Eidlitz studied engineering at Cornell, and Robert Eidlitz studied architecture there as well as in Berlin. Alfred, the eldest son, died young; his two brothers joined the family firm and succeeded their father when he became president of the Germania Bank in 1888.

64. *Marc Eidlitz and Sons.*

65. "George Fuller," *American Architect and Building News* 70 (22 December 1900): 90.

66. Ericsson, *Sixty Years a Builder,* 220; Paul Starrett, *Changing the Skyline,* 21–22; *Prominent Buildings Erected by the George A. Fuller Company* (1893?), n.p., Avery Library; David Carlson, "Building's Number 1 Contractor," *Architectural Forum* 114 (April 1961): 112–113; and Bruegmann, *The Architects and the City,* 82.

67. William Haber, *Industrial Relations in the Building Industry,* 58–59; Carlson, "Building's Number 1 Contractor," 112–113; and Commons, "New York Building Trades," 414.

68. Gilbert, "Relations of Architects to the Contracting System," 90, 94; Reginald Bolton, "The Engineer, Architect, and General Construction Company," *Brickbuilder* 13 (October 1904): 214–215. On profits, see Letter of 18 April 1904 from Charles McKim to Bernard Green, McKim Papers, Library of Congress. Today many architects claim that a project budget is turned into a profit or loss during working drawings rather than the supervisory phase. See Dana Cuff, "Divisive Tactics: Design-Production Practices in Architecture," *Journal of Architectural Education* 45 (July 1992): 209.

69. Daniel Calhoun, *The American Civil Engineer: Origins and Conflict* (Cambridge, Mass.: MIT Press, 1960), viii, 8, 16, 93, 199. B. H. Latrobe Jr., for example, worked for the Baltimore and Ohio Railroad.

70. Richard Levy, *Professionalization of American Architects and Civil Engineers, 1865–1917* (Ann Arbor, Mich.: University Microfilms, 1983), 23–24, 187, 341 nn. 126, 127, and Tables A-6 and A-32, 372 and 402.

71. Ibid., 341, nn. 126, 127; C. T. Purdy, "Relation of Engineering to Architecture," *Proceedings of the AIA* (1904), 122–123; see Paul Starrett, *Changing the Skyline,* 37; and *Proceedings of the AIA* (1906), 84–85, for discussions of architects' use of manufacturers' plans and specifications.

72. "Organization of an Architect's Office: Burnham and Root," 83. See Monroe, *John Wellborn Root,* 117–118, for the quotation from Root's brother, who also wrote that Root intuitively understood enough about structure to "suggest to a specialist an idea which would . . . enable him to work out a solution of a hard problem."

73. Paul Starrett, *Changing the Skyline,* 37, 43.

74. Bolton, "The Engineer, Architect, and General Construction Company," 215.

75. Dankmar Adler, "Engineering Supervision of Building Operations," *American Architect and Building News* 33 (4 July 1891): 12.

76. Levy, *Professionalization of American Architects and Civil Engineers,* Table A-16, 383.

77. *A Catalogue of Work Executed, Accompanied by Illustrations, by Wilson Brothers and Company* (Philadelphia: Lippincott, 1885), 3, 5–6; "Organization of an Architect's Office: Wilson Brothers," *Engineering and Building Record* 21 (22 February 1890): 181; Moss and Tatman, *Biographical Dictionary of Philadelphia Architects,* s.v. "John A. Wilson," "Joseph M. Wilson"; see John Maas, *The Glorious Enterprise* (Watkins Glen, N.Y.: American Life Foundation, 1973), 32–38, on the 1876 fair building. Calvert Vaux and George Radford were the architects forced to withdraw.

78. *Catalogue of Work by Wilson Brothers and Company,* 3–6.

79. Purdy, "Relation of Engineer to Architect," 122–123; and Bolton, "Engineer, Architect, and General Construction Company," 215.

80. "Organization of an Architect's Office: George B. Post," 83; and Diana Balmori, "George B. Post," *JSAH* (December 1987): 342, 350–352.

81. McKim to Bernard Green, Letter of 18 April 1904, McKim Papers, Library of Congress; "An Architect's Services and Remuneration," in Leland Roth, *McKim, Mead and White, Architects,* 363; Edgar V. Seeler, "The Relations of Specialists to Architects," *Proceedings of the AIA* (1904), 133–135; and Bolton, "Engineer, Architect, and General Construction Company," 214–215.

82. Henry Glassie, "Architects, Vernacular Traditions, and Society," *Traditional Dwellings and Settlements Review* 1 (1990): 9–21.

83. Latrobe to Lenthall, Letter of 3 May 1805, in Edward Carter II, *The Papers of Benjamin Henry Latrobe* (Clifton, N.J.: James T. White, 1976).

84. Upjohn to Hunt, Letter of 30 October 1849, Upjohn Collection, New York Public Library. Hunt's original letter to Upjohn does not seem to have survived.

85. Upjohn to Hunt, Letters of 16(?) November 1849 and 7 January 1850, and Hunt to Upjohn, Letters of 20 December 1849 and 21 January 1850, Upjohn Collection, New York Public Library.

86. Upjohn to Hunt, Letter of 1 February 1850, Upjohn Collection, New York Public Library.

87. Hunt to Upjohn, Letter of 14 February 1850, Upjohn Collection, New York Public Library.

88. "Client Questionnaire," Upjohn Collection, New York Public Library. The client's handwriting seems to be L. N. Walthall's when compared with his signed letters in the Upjohn Collection. Walthall commissioned a house in Marion, Alabama, from Upjohn in 1854. See Everard Upjohn, *Richard Upjohn: Architect and Churchman* (1938; reprint, New York: Columbia University Press, 1968), 212.

89. Alva Smith Vanderbilt Belmont, "Autobiography," undated typescript, 92, Matilda Young Papers, Rare Books and Manuscripts Collection, Duke University Library, Durham, North Carolina. Alva divorced Vanderbilt in 1895 and married financier Oliver Hazard Perry Belmont in 1896. Young was a companion to her during her final years.

90. Belmont, "Autobiography," 111.

91. See Monroe, *John Wellborn Root,* 176, for Madame anecdote; John W. Root, "The City House in the West" (1890), in *The Meaning of Architecture,* ed. Donald Hoffmann (New York: Horizon Press, 1967), 232–233, for the intelligent layman.

92. Bruegmann, *Holabird and Roche/Holabird and Root,* xii.

93. Pope to Mead, Letter of 17 September 1898, McKim, Mead and White Collection, Avery Library.

94. Ibid. See also Judith Paine, *Theodate Pope Riddle* (New York: National Park Service, 1979), n.p.

95. Paine, *Theodate Pope Riddle.*

96. William Dean Howells, *The Rise of Silas Lapham* (1885; reprint, New York: Collier Books, 1962), 45–47. McKim was the partner whom Howells and his wife, Elinor, dealt with in the design of their home, Redtop. See Ginette B. Merrill, "Redtop and the Belmont Years of William Dean Howells and His Family," *Harvard Library Bulletin* 28 (January 1980): 33–57. Roth, however, believes that Howells's fictional architect was based on White rather than McKim. See his *McKim, Mead and White, Architects,* 60–61.

97. "Important Trial," *Architects' and Mechanics' Journal* 3 (16 and 23 March 1861): 233, 243.

98. Ibid.

99. Ericsson, *Sixty Years a Builder,* 135–136.

100. Louis Sullivan, "The Tall Building Artistically Considered" (1896), in Leland Roth, ed., *America Builds* (New York: Harper and Row, 1983), 340–346.

101. Paul Starrett, *Changing the Skyline,* 109–110.

1. Alan Trachtenberg makes a similar argument for the artist's and photographer's acceptance in American society in his *Reading American Photographs: Images as History, Mathew Brady to Walker Evans* (New York: Hill and Wang, 1989), 9–10.

2. The state was traditionally the focus of professional life in France. This was also true in Germany and Italy. Although Italian architects occasionally moonlighted in the private sector, they still coveted state positions. See Elliott Krause, *Death of the Guilds: Professions, States, and the Advance of Capitalism, 1930 to the Present* (New Haven, Conn.: Yale University Press, 1996), 280–286.

3. Ruskin quoted in Martin J. Wiener, *English Culture and the Decline of the Industrial Spirit, 1850–1980* (New York: Cambridge University Press, 1981), 38. For English architects' opposition to professionalization, see Richard Norman Shaw and T. G. Jackson, comps., *Architecture: A Profession or an Art?* (London, John Murray, 1892).

Andrew Saint recognized, somewhat disdainfully, that business was an important part of nineteenth-century American architects' identity. While he titled his chapter on American architects "The Architect as Businessman," his chapter on the English architect was called "The Architect as Gentleman." See his *The Image of the Architect* (New Haven, Conn.: Yale University Press, 1983), 72, 94–95, 96.

4. Robert Bruegmann, *The Architects and the City: Holabird and Roche of Chicago, 1880–1918* (Chicago: University of Chicago Press, 1997), 116–117.

5. Many clients still assume that architecture is a male pursuit. Architect Jane Goody believes that corporate clients feel more comfortable with male architects. Businessmen "would allow themselves to be beguiled by men, although this was somehow a female role which represented the artistic 'other-world'. . . . When I come to the ten percent leap of faith and I say 'Trust me, this is the way it will look better, I have done many buildings of this size,' . . . they can't quite do it." Quoted in Magali Larson, *Behind the Postmodern Facade* (Berkeley and Los Angeles: University of California Press, 1993), 119–120. See Denise Scott Brown's similar comments in her "Room at the Top: Sexism and the Star System in Architecture," in *Architecture: A Place for Women,* ed. Ellen Perry Berkeley and Matilda McQuaid (Washington, D.C.: Smithsonian Institution Press, 1989), 237–246.

6. Krause, *Death of the Guilds,* 54–55.

7. Bruegmann, *The Architects and the City,* 163.

8. Although the first canal, turnpike, and railroad companies were quasi-state agencies, they were financed with private capital, public stock offerings, and government bonds. By the early 1820s and 1830s, however, they were organized as private corporations. See Will Roy, *Socializing Capital: The Rise of the Large Industrial Corporation in America* (Princeton, N.J.: Princeton University Press, 1997), 261–264.

9. Olivier Zunz, *Making America Corporate, 1870–1920* (Chicago: University of Chicago Press, 1990), 1.

10. Griselda Pollock, "Vision, Voice, and Power: Feminist Art Historians and Marxism," in *Vision and Difference: Femininity, Feminism, and the Histories of Art* (London: Rout-

ledge, 1980), 18–49; and Jack Blicksilver, *Defenders and Defense of Big Business, 1880–1900* (New York: Garland Press, 1985), 4–7.

11. Mark Crinson and Jules Lubbock, *Architecture: Art or Profession? Three Hundred Years of Architectural Education in Britain* (Manchester, England: Manchester University Press, 1994), 3–5.

12. See my "From City Beautiful to Workers' Paradise: The Architecture of American Political Reform, 1900–1940," in *Architecture and Politics: 1910–1940,* ed. Roberto Behar (Miami Beach, Fla: Wolfsonian Foundation, 1995), 72–73.

13. Larson, *Behind the Postmodern Facade,* 169.

14. Ibid., 169, 246; see Dell Upton, *Architecture in the United States* (New York: Oxford University Press, 1998), 254, for information on the SOM offices.

15. Quoted in Larson, *Behind the Postmodern Facade,* 171. Tigerman overlooked the contributions of Denise Scott Brown and Steven Izenour, Venturi's partners and collaborators, to this sea change in architectural thought.

16. Ibid., 61, 199–200.

17. Douglas E. Gordon, "The Evolution of Architectural Practice," *Architecture* 76 (December 1987): 122–126. In the 1990s the AIA encourages its members to build and own as ways to control their work. See Brad Buchanan, "You Can Design It. You Can Build It. So, Why Not Own It?" *AIArchitect* 4 (May 1997): 15.

18. Robert Gutman, "Redesigning Architectural Schools," *Architecture* 85 (August 1996): 87.

19. Burton J. Bledstein, *The Culture of Professionalism: The Middle Class and the Development of Higher Education in America* (New York: Norton, 1976).

20. Ernest Boyer and Lee Mitgang, *Building Community: A New Future for Architectural Education and Practice* (Princeton, N.J.: Carnegie Foundation for the Advancement of Teaching, 1996), 5, 15–16.

21. Robert Gutman, "Two Discourses on Architectural Education," *Practices* 3/4 (spring 1995): 11–19; and his "Redesigning Architectural Schools," 88.

22. Dana Cuff, *Architecture: The Story of Practice* (Cambridge, Mass.: MIT Press, 1991), 44–45.

23. Cuff, *Architecture,* 63–66, 107–108, 250–257, 259–260; Boyer and Mitgang, *Building Community,* xvii, 15–25, 111–116.

24. Gutman, "Redesigning Architectural Schools," 88.

25. I am grateful to Professor Jonathan Ochshorn, my Cornell colleague, for his knowledge of university consulting policies and the implications for architectural practice.

26. Gutman, "Redesigning Architectural Schools," 88; Michael Crosbie, "The Schools: How They Are Failing the Profession," *Progressive Architecture* 76 (September 1995): 47–53, 94, 96; and Richard Sennett, "Architectural Theory: Its Uses and Abuses," *GSD News,* summer 1995, 5.

27. Larson, *Behind the Postmodern Facade,* 11–12; and Gutman, "Two Discourses on Architectural Education," 11–19 and "Redesigning Architectural Schools," 88.

28. Pradeep Dalal, "Graduate Salaries Inch Up," *AIArchitect* 5 (Summer 1998): 1. Dana Cuff, "The Architecture Profession," in *The Architect's Handbook of Professional Practice,* ed. David Haviland (Washington, D.C.: AIA Press, 1994), vol. 1, sec. 1.1, 4; Gutman, "Redesigning Architectural Schools," 88; and Diane Favro, "Ad-Architects: Women Professionals in Magazine Ads," in *Architecture: A Place for Women,* ed. Ellen Perry Berkeley and Matilda McQuaid (Washington, D.C.: Smithsonian Institution Press, 1989), 187–200.

29. Robert Gutman, "Emerging Problems of Practice," *Journal of Architectural Education* 45 (July 1992): 198–202; and David Haviland, "Practice Roles and Settings," in *The Architect's Handbook of Professional Practice,* ed. David Haviland (Washington, D.C.: AIA Press, 1994), vol. 1, sec. 1.31, 68–70.

30. Roger Montgomery, "Commentary on Center for the Study of Professional Practice of Architecture Symposium," *Journal of Architectural Education* 45 (July 1992): 230–231.

31. See especially Peter Rowe, introduction, and Rem Koolhaas, "Architecture and Globalization," in *Reflections on Architectural Practices in the Nineties,* ed. William Saunders (New York: Princeton Architecture Press, 1996), 2–5, 232–239.

32. Gutman, "Redesigning Architectural Schools," 88.

33. Lee Mitgang, "Making the Connections," preface to Boyer and Mitgang, *Building Community,* xvi, xvii.

34. Gutman, "Redesigning Architectural Schools," 88–89.

35. See Alexander Stille, "Invisible Cities," *Lingua Franca* 8 (July–August 1998): 40, for the cyberarchitects; for disenchantment with computer-aided design, see Garry Stevens, "Reflections of an Apostate CAD Teacher," *Journal of Architectural Education* 51 (September 1997): 78–80.

36. Private conversation with Kim and Paul Saporito, Boulder, Colorado, March 1996; for Gehry, see Stille, "Invisible Cities," 42–43.

37. Stille, "Invisible Cities," 47.

38. Larson, *Behind the Postmodern Facade,* 253–255; Cuff, *Architecture,* 247–263; Gutman, "Redesigning Architectural Schools," 87–89; Anthony T. Jackson, *Reconstructing Architecture for the Twenty-First Century* (Toronto: University of Toronto Press, 1995), 3–9, 188–195; and Donald A. Schön, *The Reflective Practitioner: How Professionals Think in Action* (New York: Basic Books, 1983), 49–56, 68–69.

39. Krause, *Death of the Guilds,* ix, 264–265.

40. Ibid., 36–42; and Paul Starr, *The Social Transformation of American Medicine* (New York: Basic Books, 1982).

41. Krause, *Death of the Guilds,* 46; and Thomas Haskell, "The New Aristocracy," *New York Review of Books* 54 (7 December 1997): 47.

42. Krause, *Death of the Guilds,* 44–49.

43. Colin Clipson, "Contradictions and Challenges in Managing Design," *Journal of Architectural Education* 45 (July 1992): 221.

44. Haskell, "The New Aristocracy," 47.

45. Michael Pollan, "Town Building Is No Mickey Mouse Operation," *New York Times*

Magazine, 14 December 1997, 62; and "Downtown Celebration: Architectural Walking Tour" (n.p.: Walt Disney Company, 1996), 2. I am grateful to Kristin Larsen, Cornell doctoral student in city and regional planning, for sharing her Celebration materials with me.

46. Krause, *Death of the Guilds,* 60–67.

47. Barr Ferree, "The Economic Conditions of American Architecture," *Proceedings of the AIA* (1893), 231.

SELECTED BIBLIOGRAPHY

ARCHIVES

The American Institute of Architects Archives, American Institute of Architects, Washington, D.C.
    AIA Board of Trustees Meeting Minutes
    AIA Scrapbooks
    AIA Secretary's Incoming and Outgoing Correspondence
    Proceedings of the American Institute of Architects, (1857–1871)
    Western Association of Architects Papers
American Architectural Foundation, Washington, D.C., Prints and Drawings Collection
    Richard Morris Hunt Collection
American Philosophical Society Library, Philadelphia, Pennsylvania
    William Strickland, Autobiographical fragment, ca. 1825, J. K. Kane Papers
Archives of American Art, Smithsonian Institution, New York, New York
    Charles Rutan Papers
    Dankmar Adler, "Autobiographical Essay"
    Henry Hobson Richardson Papers
    Manierre Dawson Diaries
Art Institute of Chicago, Archives, Ryerson and Burnham Libraries, Chicago, Illinois
    Daniel H. Burnham Papers
Columbia University, The Avery Fine Arts and Architectural Library, New York, New York
    Alexander Jackson Davis Papers and Drawings
    McKim, Mead and White Collection
    Philip Sawyer Papers
    Richard Upjohn Drawings and Papers
    Stanford White Papers
    William Robert Ware Papers
Duke University Library, Rare Books and Manuscripts Collection, Durham, North Carolina
    Alva Smith Vanderbilt Belmont, "Autobiography," in Matilda Young Papers

Library of Congress, Manuscript Division, Washington, D.C.
    Charles Follen McKim Papers
    Charles Moore Papers
Massachusetts Institute of Technology Archives, Massachusetts Institute of Technology,
    Cambridge, Massachusetts
    William Robert Ware Papers
Metropolitan Museum of Art, Prints and Drawings Collection, New York, New York
    Alexander Jackson Davis Collection
New-York Historical Society, New York, New York
    A. J. Bloor Papers
    McKim, Mead and White Collection
    Mildred Sawyer Papers
    Stanford White Papers
New York Public Library, Astor, Tilden, and Lenox Foundation, Manuscripts Room, New
    York, New York
    Alexander Jackson Davis Papers and Letterbooks
    Richard and Richard Michell Upjohn Collections
Philadelphia Athenaeum, Philadelphia, Pennsylvania
    Thomas U. Walter Papers

PUBLISHED WORKS

Adams, Michael. "A Legacy of Shadows." *Progressive Architecture* 72 (February 1991): 85–87.

Adler, Dankmar. "Engineering Supervision of Building Operations." *American Architect and Building News* 33 (4 July 1891): 11–12.

———. "Influence of Steel and Plate Glass upon Style." *American Architect and Building News* 54 (31 October 1896): 37–39.

———. "Proposed Technological School from the Standpoint of the Architect." *Inland Architect* 19 (April 1892): 36–37.

"The Advertising Fake." *Real Estate Record and Guide* 57 (25 April 1896): 696.

"The Advertising Fake Scandal Again." *American Architect and Building News* 53 (1 August 1896): 39–40.

Alexander, Robert. *The Architecture of Maximilian Godefroy.* Baltimore: Johns Hopkins University Press, 1974.

Alofsin, Anthony. "Tempering the Ecole: Nathan Ricker at the University of Illinois, Langford Warren at Harvard, and Their Followers." In *The History of History in American Schools of Architecture, 1865–1975.* Edited by Gwendolyn Wright and Janet Parks, 73–88. New York: Princeton Architectural Press, 1990.

Anderson, Carson Anthony. "The Architectural Practice of Vertner Tandy," Master's thesis, University of Virginia, 1982.

Andrews, Robert. "Conditions of Architectural Practice Thirty Years Ago." *Architectural Review* 5 (November 1917): 237–238.

Andrews, Wayne. *Architecture, Ambition, and Americans.* New York: Free Press, 1964.

Annals of the Massachusetts Charitable Mechanics Association, 1795–1892. Boston, 1892.

"Architect and Builder." *Brickbuilder* 11 (December 1902): 257–258.

"Architectural Education in the United States, I: MIT" *American Architect and Building News* 24 (4 August 1888): 47–49.

"Architectural Education in the United States, II: The University of Illinois." *American Architect and Building News* 24 (1 September 1888): 95–97.

"Architectural Education in the United States, III: Cornell." *American Architect and Building News* 24 (6 October 1888): 155–157.

"Architectural Education in the United States, IV: Columbia University." *American Architect and Building News* 24 (1 December 1888): 251–252.

"Architectural Retrospect." *American Architect and Building News* 70 (29 December 1900): 98.

Architecture. Vol. 1. Scranton, Pa.: International Correspondence School, 1899.

"Architecture Open to Women." *American Architect and Building News* 19 (15 June 1886): 266.

Babcock, Charles. "The Ways and Means of Accomplishing the Elevation of the Architect's Profession." *The Crayon* 4 (December 1857): 371–372.

Bacon, Henry. "McKim." *Brickbuilder* 19 (February 1910): 30–47.

Baer, Herbert. "The Course in Architecture at a German Technische Hochschule." *American Architect and Building News* 71 (16 March 1901): 83–85.

Baker, Paul. *Richard Morris Hunt.* Cambridge, Mass.: MIT Press, 1980.

———. *Stanny: The Gilded Life of Stanford White.* New York: Free Press, 1989.

Balmori, Diana. "George B. Post," *Journal of the Society of Architectural Historians* 46 (December 1987): 342–355.

Bannister, Turpin. *The Architect at Midcentury.* 2 vols. New York: Reinhold Corp., 1954.

———. "Pioneering in Architectural Education: Recalling the First Collegiate Graduate in Architecture in the United States, Nathan Clifford Ricker." *Journal of the American Institute of Architects* 20 (July and August 1953): 5–7, 76–81.

Beirne, Rosamund, and John Scarff. *William Buckland 1734–1774: Architect of Virginia and Maryland.* Baltimore: Maryland Historical Society, 1958.

Bender, Thomas. *New York Intellect.* Baltimore: Johns Hopkins University Press, 1987.

Benjamin, Asher. *The Elements of Architecture.* 1843. Reprint, New York: Da Capo Press, 1974.

———. *The Practice of Architecture.* 1833. Reprint, New York: Da Capo Press, 1972.

———. *The Rudiments of Architecture.* 1814. Reprint, New York: Da Capo Press, 1972.

Bennett, Charles A. *A History of Manual and Industrial Education, 1870 to 1917.* Peoria, Ill.: Manual Arts Press, 1937.

Berkeley, Ellen Perry, and Matilda McQuaid, eds. *Architecture: A Place for Women.* Washington, D.C.: Smithsonian Institution Press, 1989.

Bethune, Louise. "Women in Architecture." *Inland Architect* 17 (March 1891): 20–21.

Biographical Dictionary of Architects in Maine. 7 vols. Augusta, Maine: Maine Historic Preservation Commission, 1984–1995.

Bishir, Catherine, Carl Lounsbury, Charlotte Brown, and Ernest Wood. *Architects and Builders in North Carolina.* Chapel Hill: University of North Carolina Press, 1990.

Blackall, C. H. "Architectural Education: The Office." *American Architect and Building News* 121 (15 March 1922): 213–214, 217.

Blau, Judith. *Architects and Firms.* Cambridge, Mass.: MIT Press, 1984.

Blaugrund, Annette. "The Tenth Street Studio Building." *Archives of American Art Journal* 114 (spring 1982): 64–71.

Bledstein, Burton J. *The Culture of Professionalism: The Middle Class and the Development of Higher Education in America.* New York: Norton, 1976.

Blicksilver, Jack. *Defenders and Defense of Big Business, 1880–1900.* New York: Garland Press, 1985.

Bloor, A. J. "Sketch of the History and Status of the A.I.A." *Proceedings of the American Institute of Architects* (1890), 98–105.

Bluestone, Daniel. "Civic and Aesthetic Reserve." *Winterthur Portfolio* 25 (autumn 1990): 131–156.

Bolton, Reginald. "The Engineer, Architect, and General Construction Company." *Brickbuilder* 13 (October 1904): 213–220.

Bosworth, William Welles. "I Knew H. H. Richardson." *Journal of the American Institute of Architects* 16 (September 1951): 116–118.

Boutelle, Sarah Holmes. *Julia Morgan, Architect.* New York: Abbeville Press, 1988.

Boyer, Ernest, and Lee Mitgang. *Building Community: A New Future for Architectural Education and Practice.* Princeton, N.J.: Carnegie Foundation for the Advancement of Teaching, 1996.

Boyer, M. Christine. *Manhattan Manners: Architecture and Style, 1850–1900.* New York: Rizzoli, 1985.

Boyington, William W. "Differences between the Methods of Architectural Practice Prevalent Now and Those of Fifty Years Ago." *Proceedings of the American Institute of Architects* (1887), 102–106.

Bridenbaugh, Carl. *Peter Harrison.* Chapel Hill: University of North Carolina Press, 1949.

Briggs, Martin. *The Architect in History.* Oxford: Clarendon Press, 1927.

Brown, Glenn. *1860–1930, Memories.* Washington, D.C.: Press of W. F. Roberts and Company, 1931.

———. "The Tarsney Act." *Brickbuilder* 15 (May 1906): 95–98.

———. "Washington Letter." *American Architect and Building News* 39 (21 January 1893): 44–45.

Bruegmann, Robert. *The Architects and the City: Holabird and Roche of Chicago, 1880–1918.* Chicago: University of Chicago Press, 1997.

———. *Holabird and Roche/Holabird and Root: An Illustrated Catalog of Works, 1880–1940.* 3 vols. New York: Garland Press, 1991.

Buckingham, Joseph T., comp. *Annals of the Massachusetts Charitable Mechanics Association.* Boston: Press of Crocker and Brewster, 1853.

Burnham, Daniel. "Suggestions toward the Best and Speediest Methods for Harmonizing and Utilizing All the Architectural Societies in the United States." *Proceedings of the American Institute of Architects* (1887), 114–119.

Caemmerer, H. Paul. *The Life of Pierre Charles L'Enfant.* Washington, D.C.: National Republic, 1950.

Calhoun, Daniel. *The American Civil Engineer: Origins and Conflict.* Cambridge, Mass.: MIT Press, 1960.

————. *Professional Lives in America.* Cambridge, Mass.: Harvard University Press, 1965.

Calvert, Monte. *The Mechanical Engineer in America, 1830–1910.* Baltimore: Johns Hopkins University Press, 1967.

Carlson, David. "Building's Number 1 Contractor." *Architectural Forum* 114 (April 1961): 112–113, 168, 172, 176.

Carr-Saunders, Alexander, and P. A. Wilson. *The Professions.* 1933. Reprint, London: Frank Cass, 1964.

"Carrère and Hastings' Workshop." *Architectural Record* 10 (October 1900): 143–149.

Carrère, John. "Making a Choice of a Profession, IX: Architecture." *Cosmopolitan* 35 (July 1903): 488–498.

Carter, Edward, II, ed. *Benjamin Henry Latrobe and Public Works.* Washington, D.C.: Public Works Historical Society, ca. 1976.

————. *The Papers of Benjamin Henry Latrobe.* Microfiche edition. Clifton, N.J.: James T. White, 1976.

————. *The Virginia Journals of Benjamin Henry Latrobe, 1795–1798.* 2 vols. New Haven, Conn.: Yale University Press, 1977.

A Catalogue of Work Executed, Accompanied by Illustrations, by Wilson Brothers and Company. Philadelphia: Lippincott, 1885.

Cates, Arthur. "The Higher Education of the Architect, II: The College of Architecture at Cornell University." *Journal of the Royal Institute of British Architects* 22 (24 November 1900): 39–44.

Centennial Celebration of the General Society of Mechanics and Tradesmen. New York, 1885.

Chappell, Sally. *The Architecture and Planning of Graham, Anderson, Probst, and White.* Chicago: University of Chicago Press, 1992.

Charter, Articles, Supplement and By-Laws of the Bricklayers' Company. Philadelphia, 1888.

Chewing, J. A. "William Robert Ware at M.I.T. and Columbia." *Journal of Architectural Education* 33 (November 1979): 25–29.

Choate, Joseph. "The Paran Stevens Case." In *Arguments and Addresses of Joseph H. Choate.* Edited by Frederick Hicks, 178–197. Saint Paul, Minn.: West Publishing, 1926.

"City Architect's Office." *Inland Architect* 15 (July 1890): 85–86.

Clark, Eliot. *History of the National Academy of Design, 1825–1953.* New York: Columbia University Press, 1954.

Clipson, Colin. "Contradictions and Challenges in Managing Design." *Journal of Architectural Education* 45 (July 1992): 218–224.

Cohen, Jeffrey. "Building a Discipline: Early Institutional Settings for Architectural Education in Philadelphia, 1804–1890." *Journal of the Society of Architectural Historians* 53 (June 1994): 139–183.

Cohen, Jeffrey, and Charles Brownell. *The Architectural Drawings of Benjamin Henry Latrobe.* 2 parts. New Haven, Conn.: Yale University Press, 1994.

Cole, Doris, and Karen Cord Taylor. *The Lady Architects: Lois Lilley Howe, Eleanor Manning, and Mary Almy, 1893–1937.* New York: Midmarch Arts Press, 1990.

Coles, William, ed. *Architecture and Society: Selected Essays of Henry Van Brunt.* Cambridge, Mass.: Belknap Press of Harvard University, 1969.

———. "Richard Morris Hunt and His Library." *Art Quarterly* 30 (fall–winter 1967): 224–238.

Collin, Richard H. *Roosevelt, Culture, Diplomacy, and Expansion.* Baton Rouge: Louisiana State University Press, 1985.

Commons, John R. "The New York Building Trades." *Quarterly Journal of Economics* 18 (1903–4): 409–436.

———, ed. *History of Labor in the United States.* 4 vols. New York: Macmillan, 1918–35.

"Concealed Defects in Blocks of Buildings." *American Architect and Building News* 26 (21 December 1889): 285–286.

Constitution and By-Laws of the American Institution of Architects. Philadelphia: Lydia Bailey, 1837.

Constitution of the American Institute of Architects. New York: John W. Amerman, 1858.

Cooledge, Harold. *Samuel Sloan, Architect.* Philadelphia: University of Pennsylvania Press, 1986.

Coolidge, Charles. "H. H. Richardson, 1883–1886." In *Later Years of the Saturday Club, 1870–1920.* Edited by M. A. DeWolfe Howe, 193–200. Boston: Houghton Mifflin, 1927.

Cortissoz, Royal. *Art and Common Sense.* New York: Scribner's, 1903.

Craig, Lois. *The Federal Presence.* Cambridge, Mass.: MIT Press, 1978.

Crosbie, Michael. "The Schools: How They Are Failing the Profession." *Progressive Architecture* 76 (September 1995): 47–53, 94, 96.

Cuff, Dana. *Architecture: The Story of Practice.* Cambridge, Mass.: MIT Press, 1991.

———. "Divisive Tactics: Design-Production Practices in Architecture." *Journal of Architectural Education* 45 (July 1992): 204–212.

Daly, César. "Les Trois Ecoles d'architecture contemporaine." *Revue générale de l'architecture* 21 (1863): 163–165.

Davies, Margaret Gay. *The Enforcement of English Apprenticeship, 1563–1642.* Cambridge, Mass.: Harvard University Press, 1956.

Davis, Alexander Jackson. *Rural Residences.* 1838. Reprint, New York: Da Capo Press, 1980.

"Death of Chicago's First Architect." *Inland Architect* 18 (January 1892): 69–70.

"Death, the Builder." *Architects' and Mechanics' Journal* 1 (4 February 1860): 131.

Delhi, Arne. "General Contractors versus Individual Contractors." *Architectural Record* 24 (September 1908): 231–232.

Detwiller, Frederic. "Thomas Dawes: Boston's Patriot Architect." *Old-Time New England* 68 (summer–fall 1977): 1–18.

Dostoglu, Sibel. "Toward Professional Legitimacy and Power." Ph.D. diss., University of Pennsylvania, 1982.

Downing, Andrew Jackson. *Cottage Residences.* New York: John Wiley, 1842.

Dozier, Richard. "The Black Architectural Experience in America." *Journal of the American Institute of Architects* 65 (July 1976): 162–163, 166, 168.

————. "Tuskegee: Booker T. Washington's Contributions to the Education of Black Architects." Ph.D. diss., University of Michigan, 1990.

Drexler, Arthur, ed. *The Architecture of the Ecole des Beaux-Arts.* Cambridge, Mass.: MIT Press, 1977.

Dunlap, William. *A History of the Rise and Progress of the Arts of Design in the United States.* 3 vols. 1834. Reprint, Boston: C. E. Goodspeed, 1918.

Dyson, Walter. *Howard University: The Capstone of Negro Education.* Washington, D.C.: Graduate School of Howard University, 1941.

Eastlake, Charles. "An Historical Sketch of the Institute." *Sessional Papers of the Royal Institute of British Architects* (1875–76): 258–272.

Egbert, Donald Drew. *The Beaux-Arts Tradition in French Architecture.* Princeton, N.J.: Princeton University Press, 1980.

Eidlitz, Leopold. "The Master Builder." *Real Estate Record and Guide* 7 (21 February 1891): 267.

———— (?). "The T-Squares." *The Crayon* 5 (February, March, April, June, July, September, October, November, December 1858): 48–50, 77–79, 107–108, 165–167, 196–199, 262–264, 287–289, 318–319, 346–351.

Elstein, Rochelle. "The Architecture of Dankmar Adler." *Journal of the Society of Architectural Historians* 26 (December 1967): 242–249.

Elzner, A. O. "A Reminiscence of Richardson." *Inland Architect* 20 (September 1892): 15.

Ericsson, Henry. *Sixty Years a Builder.* Chicago: A. Kroch, 1942.

Erlich, Mark. *Working with Our Hands: The Story of Carpenters in Massachusetts.* Philadelphia: Temple University Press, 1986.

Ethridge, Harrison. "The Black Architects of Washington, D.C., 1900 to the Present." Ph.D. diss., Catholic University of America, 1979.

Ferree, Barr. "The Economic Conditions of American Architecture." *Proceedings of the American Institute of Architects* (1893), 228–241.

Formwalt, Lee. *Benjamin Henry Latrobe and the Development of Internal Improvements in the New Republic, 1796–1820.* New York: Arno Press, 1982.

Francis, Dennis. *Architects in Practice, New York City, 1840–1900.* New York: Committee for the Preservation of Architectural Records, 1980.

Friedman, Alice. "Feminist Practice in History?" *Design Book Review* 25 (summer 1992): 16–18.

Gabin, Nancy F. "Women and Work." *Encyclopedia of American Social History*. 3 vols. Edited by Mary Cayton, Elliott Gorn, and Peter Williams, 2:1542. New York: Scribner's, 1993.

Galenson, Walter. *The United Brotherhood of Carpenters: The First Hundred Years*. Cambridge, Mass.: Harvard University Press, 1983.

Gallier, James. *The Autobiography of James Gallier*. 1864. Reprint, New York: Da Capo Press, 1973.

"George Fuller." *American Architect and Building News* 70 (22 December 1900): 90.

Geraniotis, Roula. "The University of Illinois and German Architectural Education." *Journal of Architectural Education* 38 (summer 1984): 15–21.

Gilchrist, Agnes. *William Strickland, Architect and Engineer, 1788–1854*. Philadelphia: University of Pennsylvania Press, 1950.

Gilman, Arthur. "On the Relation of the Architectural Profession to the Public." *Proceedings of the American Institute of Architects* (1867), 26–27.

Goldfarb, Janice. *Women Builders and Designers: Making Ourselves at Home*. Watsonville, Calif.: Papier Mache Press, 1995.

Goldthwaite, Richard. *The Building of Renaissance Florence*. Baltimore: Johns Hopkins University Press, 1980.

Goodstein, Ethel. "Charles Babcock, Architect, Educator, and Churchman." Master's thesis, Cornell University, 1979.

Gordon, Douglas E. "The Evolution of Architectural Practice." *Architecture* 76 (December 1987): 122–126.

Gotch, J. A., ed. *The Growth and Work of the Royal Institute of British Architects, 1834–1934*. London: Simson and Company, 1934.

Gottesman, Rita S. *Arts and Crafts in New York, 1726–1776*. New York: New-York Historical Society, 1938.

Gottfried, Herbert. "Building the Picture: Trading on the Image of Production and Design." *Winterthur Portfolio* 27 (winter 1992): 235–253.

Gray, Christopher. *Blueprints*. New York: Simon and Schuster, 1981.

Gray, Lee. "The Office Building in New York City, 1850–1880." Ph.D. diss., Cornell University, 1993.

Grieff, Constance. *John Notman, Architect*. Philadelphia: Philadelphia Athenaeum, 1979.

Gutman, Robert. *Architectural Practice*. New York: Princeton Architectural Press, 1988.

———. "Emerging Problems of Practice." *Journal of Architectural Education* 45 (July 1992): 198–202.

———. "Redesigning Architecture Schools." *Architecture* 85 (August 1996): 87–89.

———. "Two Discourses on Architectural Education." *Practices* 3/4 (spring 1995): 11–19.

Haber, Samuel. *The Quest for Honor and Authority in the Professions*. Chicago: University of Chicago Press, 1991.

Haber, William. *Industrial Relations in the Building Industry*. Cambridge, Mass.: Harvard University Press, 1930.

Hall, Louise. "Artificer to Architect in America." Typescript, American Institute of Architects Archives, Washington, D.C., 1954.

―――. "The First Architectural Schools? No But . . ." *Journal of the American Institute of Architects* 14 (August 1950): 79–82.

Hamlin, Talbot. *Benjamin Henry Latrobe.* New York: Oxford University Press, 1955.

"Harvey Ellis." *American Architect and Building News* 83 (23 January 1904): 25–26.

Haviland, David, ed. *The Architect's Handbook of Professional Practice.* 4 vols. Washington, D.C.: AIA Press, 1994.

Hines, Thomas. *Burnham of Chicago, Architect and Planner.* New York: Oxford University Press, 1974.

A History of Real Estate, Building, and Architecture in New York. New York: Real Estate Record and Guide, 1898.

Hoffman, Donald. *The Architecture of John Root.* Baltimore: Johns Hopkins University Press, 1973.

―――, ed. *The Meaning of Architecture: Buildings and Writings of John Root.* New York: Horizon Press, 1967.

Hofstadter, Richard. *Anti-Intellectualism in American Life.* New York: Vintage, 1963.

Howells, William Dean. *The Rise of Silas Lapham.* 1885. Reprint, New York: Collier Books, 1962.

Hull, Judith. "The School of Upjohn." *Journal of the Society of Architectural Historians* 52 (September 1993): 281–306.

Hurdis, Frank D., Jr. "Architecture of John Holden Greene." Master's thesis, Cornell University, 1973.

"Important Trial." *Architects' and Mechanics' Journal* 3 and 4 (9 March 1861, 16 March 1861, 23 March 1861, 30 March 1861, 6 April 1861), 222–224; 231–234; 242–245; 252–255; and 4–9.

Jackson, Anthony. *Reconstructing Architecture for the Twenty-First Century.* Toronto: University of Toronto Press, 1995.

Jenkins, Charles. "A Review of the Work of Holabird and Roche." *Architectural Reviewer* 3 (June 1897): 1–41.

Jenkins, Frank. *Architect and Patron.* London: Oxford University Press, 1961.

Jenney, William LeBaron. "Autobiography of William LeBaron Jenney." *Western Architect* 10 (June 1907): 59–66.

―――. "An Old Atelier in Chicago in the Seventies." *Western Architect* 10 (July 1907): 72–75.

Kapsch, Robert, William C. Allen, and Henry Chase. "Liberty's Capitol." *American Visions* 10 (February/March 1995): 8–15.

Kaye, Barrington. *The Development of the Architectural Profession in Britain.* London: George Allen and Unwin, 1960.

Kimball, Fiske. *Thomas Jefferson, Architect.* 1916. Reprint, New York: Da Capo Press, 1968.

Kimball, Leroy. "Old University Building and the Society Years on Washington Square." *New-York Historical Society Quarterly Bulletin* 32 (July 1948): 149–219.

Kirby, J. H. *Modern Cottages.* Syracuse, N.Y., 1886.

Kirker, Harold. *Architecture of Charles Bulfinch.* Cambridge, Mass.: Harvard University Press, 1969.

Kornblith, Gary. "From Artisan to Businessman: Master Mechanics in New England, 1789–1850." Ph.D. diss., Princeton University, 1983.

Kostof, Spiro, ed. *The Architect.* New York: Oxford University Press, 1977.

Kramer, Stella. *English Craft Guilds and the Government.* New York: AMS, 1968.

Krause, Elliott. *Death of the Guilds: Professions, States, and the Advance of Capitalism, 1930 to the Present.* New Haven, Conn.: Yale University Press, 1996.

Langton, W. A. "On the Architect's Part in His Work as Exemplified in the Methods of H. H. Richardson." *Canadian Architect and Builder* 13 (February 1900): 28–30.

Larson, Magali. *Behind the Postmodern Facade.* Berkeley and Los Angeles: University of California Press, 1993.

———. *The Rise of Professionalism.* Berkeley and Los Angeles: University of California Press, 1977.

Levy, Richard. *Professionalization of American Architects and Civil Engineers, 1865–1917.* Ann Arbor, Mich.: University Microfilms, 1983.

Longstreth, Richard. *On the Edge of the World: Four Architects in San Francisco at the Turn of the Century.* New York: Architectural History Foundation, 1983.

Lounsbury, Carl. *An Illustrated Glossary of Early Southern Architecture.* New York: Oxford University Press, 1994.

Lowry, Bates. *Building a National Image.* Washington, D.C.: National Building Museum, 1985.

Lynn, Kenneth, ed. *The Professions in America.* Boston: Houghton Mifflin, 1965.

Maas, John. *The Glorious Enterprise.* Watkins Glen, N.Y.: American Life Foundation, 1973.

Magonigle, Harold van Buren. "Half Century of Architecture." *Pencil Points* 14 and 15 (November 1933, January 1934, March 1934, May 1934, July 1934, September 1934, November 1934), 477–480, 9–12, 115–118, 223–226, 357–359, 464–466, 563–565.

———. "Some Suggestions as to the Making of Working Drawings." *Brickbuilder* 22 (May 1913, July 1913, August 1913), 99–103, 147–153, 174–178.

"Management of an Architect's Office." *American Architect and Building News* 39 parts from 33 (15 August 1891) to 39 (21 January 1893): 97–99, 37–39.

Mann, George R. *Selections from an Architect's Portfolio: George R. Mann.* Saint Louis, Mo.: National Chemigraph Company, 1893.

Manning Michaels, Eileen. "A Developmental Study of the Drawings Published in the *American Architect* and *Inland Architect.*" Ph.D. diss., University of Minnesota, 1971.

"Marc Eidlitz." *American Architect and Building News* 36 (7 May 1892): 77.

Marc Eidlitz and Sons. New York: Privately printed, 1914.

Marc Eidlitz and Sons, 1854–1904. New York: Privately printed, 1904.

"McKim." *Architectural Record* 26 (November 1909): 381.

McLaughlin, Jack. *Jefferson and Monticello.* New York: Henry Holt, 1988.

Merrill, Ginette B. "Redtop and the Belmont Years of William Dean Howells and His Family." *Harvard Library Bulletin* 28 (January 1980): 33–57.

Middleton, Robin, ed. *The Beaux-Arts and Nineteenth-Century French Architecture.* Cambridge, Mass.: MIT Press, 1982.

Misner, Christopher. "Management: Architect-Developers." *Progressive Architecture* 69 (January 1988): 61–62.

Monroe, Harriet. *John Wellborn Root.* 1896. Reprint, Park Forest, Ill.: Prairie School Press, 1966.

Montgomery, Robert. "Commentary on the Center for the Study of the Practice of Architecture Symposium." *Journal of Architectural Education* 45 (July 1992): 230–231.

Moore, Charles. *The Life and Times of Charles F. McKim.* Boston: Houghton Mifflin, 1929.

Moses, Lionel. "McKim, Mead and White: A History." *American Architect and Building News* 121 (24 May 1922): 424–425.

Moss, Roger, and Sandra Tatman. *Biographical Dictionary of Philadelphia Architects.* Boston: G. K. Hall, 1985.

Muckle, Kirk, and Dreck Wilson. "David Augustus Williston." *Landscape Architecture* 72 (January 1982): 82–85.

Neil, J. Meredith. "Benjamin H. Latrobe's Precarious Professionalism." *Journal of the American Institute of Architects* 53 (May 1970): 67–71.

Newton, Roger Hale. *Town and Davis, Architects.* New York: Columbia University Press, 1942.

Norton, Paul. "Latrobe's Ceiling for the Hall of Representatives." *Journal of the Society of Architectural Historians* 10 (May 1951): 5–10.

Ochsner, Jeffrey. *H. H. Richardson: Complete Architectural Works.* Cambridge, Mass.: MIT Press, 1982.

O'Gorman, James. "Documentation: An 1886 Inventory of H. H. Richardson's Library and Other Gleanings from Probate." *Journal of the Society of Architectural Historians* 41 (May 1982): 151–155.

———. "H. and J. E. Billings of Boston." *Journal of the Society of Architectural Historians* 42 (March 1983): 54–73.

———. *H. H. Richardson and His Office.* Cambridge, Mass.: Harvard University Press, 1974.

———. *On the Boards.* Philadelphia: University of Pennsylvania Press, 1989.

———. "O. W. Norcross, Richardson's Master Builder." *Journal of the Society of Architectural Historians* 32 (May 1973): 104–113.

———, ed. *Drawing toward Building.* Philadelphia: University of Pennsylvania Press, 1986.

Oliver, Richard, ed. *The Making of an Architect, 1881–1981.* New York: Rizzoli, 1981.

"One Cause of the Fall of Buildings." *Architects' and Mechanics' Journal* 1 (10 March 1861): 188.

"Organization of an Architect's Office: Burnham and Root." *Engineering and Building Record* 21 (11 January 1890): 83–85.

"Organization of an Architect's Office: George B. Post." *Engineering and Building Record* 24 (7 November 1891): 362–363.

"Organization of an Architect's Office: Samuel Hannaford and Sons." *Engineering and Building Record* 22 (23 August 1890): 180.

"Organization of an Architect's Office: Shepley, Rutan, and Coolidge." *Engineering and Building Record* 21 (15 February 1890): 165–166.

"Organization of an Architect's Office: Wilson Brothers." *Engineering and Building Record* 21 (22 February 1890): 181.

Paine, Judith. "Sophia Hayden and the Women's Building Competition." In *Women in American Architecture.* Edited by Susanna Torre, 70–73. New York: Whitney Library of Art, 1977.

———. *Theodate Pope Riddle.* New York: National Park Service, 1979.

Park, Helen. *A List of Architectural Books Available in America before the Revolution.* Los Angeles: Hennessey and Ingalls, 1973.

Parsons, Kermit Carlyle. *The Cornell Campus.* Ithaca, N.Y.: Cornell University Press, 1968.

Peterson, Charles. "Carpenters' Hall." *Transactions of the American Philosophical Society* 43 (March 1953): 96–128.

———, ed. *Building Early America.* Radnor, Pa.: Chilton Book Company, 1976.

Placzek, Adolf K., ed. *Macmillan Encyclopedia of Architects.* 4 vols. New York: Free Press, 1982.

Pollock, Griselda. *Vision and Difference: Femininity, Feminism, and the Histories of Art.* London: Routledge, 1988.

Prestiano, Robert. *The Inland Architect.* Ann Arbor, Mich.: University Microfilms, 1985.

Price, Benjamin D., and Max Charles Price. *Church Plans.* Philadelphia: Philadelphia Board of Church Extension, 1901.

Prideaux-Brune, Diana. "The Builder as Technical Innovator: Orlando Norcross and the Beamless Flat Slab." Master's thesis, Cornell University, 1989.

Proceedings of the American Institute of Architects (1872–1910).

Proceedings of the Architectural League (1881–89).

Prominent Buildings Erected by the George A. Fuller Company. N.p.: 1893(?).

Purcell, William. "Forgotten Builders." *Northwestern Architect* 8 (November–December 1944): 3–7, 13.

Purdy, C. T. "Relation of Engineer to Architect." *Proceedings of the American Institute of Architects* (1904), 121–132.

Quill, Charles. *The American Mechanic.* Philadelphia: Henry Perkins, 1838.

Quimby, Ian. *Apprenticeship in Colonial Philadelphia.* New York: Garland Press, 1985.

Quinan, Jack. "Some Aspects of the Development of the Architectural Profession in Boston between 1800 and 1830." *Old-Time New England* 68 (summer–fall 1977): 32–37.

Randall, G. P. *Book of Designs for School Houses.* Chicago: Knight and Leonard, 1884.

———. *Descriptive and Illustrated Catalog of Plans in Perspective.* Chicago, 1865.

Ranlett, William. *The Architect.* 1847. Reprint, New York: Da Capo Press, 1976.

Reader, W. J. *Professional Men: The Rise of the Professional Classes in Nineteenth-Century England.* London: Weidenfeld and Nicolson, 1966.

Rebori, Andrew. "Work of Burnham and Root." *Architectural Record* 38 (July 1915): 32–168.

"Report of the Legislative Committee on Apprenticeship." *National Association of Builders Proceedings* (1888), 142–145.

Reps, John. *Monumental Washington.* Princeton, N.J.: Princeton University Press, 1967.

Richman, Michael. "George Hadfield." *Journal of the Society of Architectural Historians* 33 (October 1974): 234–235.

Ricker, N. Clifford. "Results of the Illinois Licensing Law." *Brickbuilder* 10 (February 1901): 28–31.

Roach, Hannah Benner. "Thomas Nevell." *Journal of the Society of Architectural Historians* 24 (May 1965): 153–164.

Rock, Howard. *Artisans of the New Republic.* New York: New York University Press, 1984.

Rorabaugh, W. J. *The Craft Apprentice.* New York: Oxford University Press, 1986.

Roth, Leland. *McKim, Mead and White, Architects.* New York: Harper and Row, 1983.

———. *The Works of McKim, Mead and White.* New York: Garland Press, 1978.

———, ed. *America Builds.* New York: Harper and Row, 1983.

Roy, Will. *Socializing Capital: The Rise of the Large Industrial Corporation in America.* Princeton, N.J.: Princeton University Press, 1997.

The Rules of Work of the Carpenters' Company of the City and County of Philadelphia. 1786. Reprint, Princeton, N.J.: Pyne Press, 1971.

Sachs, Edwin O. "The Architectural School of the Berlin Technical College." *American Architect and Building News* 57 (10 July 1897): 17–19.

Saint, Andrew. *The Image of the Architect.* New Haven, Conn.: Yale University Press, 1983.

Salzstein, Joan. "Dankmar Adler." *Wisconsin Architect* 38 (July–August, September, November 1967): 15–19, 10–14, 16–19.

Sartor, Curtis. "Booker T. Washington's Legacy of Architecture: Tuskegee Institute." In *Diversity in Architecture.* Compiled by Diana Ghirardo, Barbara Allen, and Howard Smith, 38–43. Washington, D.C.: American Collegiate Schools of Architecture Association, 1996.

Saunders, William S., ed. *Reflections on Architectural Practices in the Nineties.* New York: Princeton Architectural Press, 1995.

Saylor, Henry H. *The A.I.A.'s First Hundred Years.* Washington, D.C.: The Octagon, 1957.

"A Scandal to the Profession." *American Architect and Building News* 52 (2 May 1896): 47–48.

Schuyler, Montgomery. "Recent Building in New York." *Harper's Monthly,* 67 (September 1883): 557–578.

Schweinfurth, J. A. "Great Builders I Have Known." *American Architect and Building News* 140 (November 1930): 92–96.

Scott, Pamela. "Stephen Hallet's Designs for the United States Capitol." *Winterthur Portfolio* 27 (summer/autumn 1992): 145–170.

———, ed. *The Papers of Robert Mills.* Wilmington, Del.: Scholarly Film Resources, 1990.

Scott, Pamela, and Antoinette Lee. *The Buildings of the District of Columbia.* New York: Oxford University Press, 1993.

Scully, Vincent. *The Shingle and Stick Styles.* New Haven, Conn.: Yale University Press, 1971.

Seeler, Edgar V. "The Relations of Specialists to Architects." *Proceedings of the American Institute of Architects* (1904), 133–135.

Shaw, Edward. *The Modern Architect or Every Carpenter His Own Master.* Boston: Dayton and Wentworth, 1855.

Shaw, Richard Norman, and T. G. Jackson, comps. *Architecture: A Profession or an Art?* London: John Murray, 1892.

Sinclair, Bruce. *Philadelphia's Philosopher Mechanics: A History of the Franklin Institute.* Baltimore: Johns Hopkins University Press, 1974.

Sloan, Samuel. *The Model Architect.* 2 vols. Philadelphia: E. G. Jones, 1852.

Soane, John. *Plans, Elevations, and Sections of Buildings.* London: I. Taylor, 1788.

Sprague, Paul. "Adler and Sullivan's Schiller Building." *Prairie School Review* 2 (1965): 1–2, 5–20.

Staiti, Paul. *Samuel F. B. Morse.* New York: Cambridge University Press, 1989.

Stanton, Phoebe. *The Gothic Revival in America.* Baltimore: Johns Hopkins University Press, 1968.

Stapleton, Darwin. *The Engineering Drawings of Benjamin Henry Latrobe.* New Haven, Conn.: Yale University Press, 1988.

Starrett, Paul. *Changing the Skyline.* New York: McGraw-Hill, 1938.

Starrett, Theodore. "Daniel H. Burnham." *Architecture and Building* 44 (July 1912): 281–283.
———. "John W. Root." *Architecture and Building* 44 (November 1912): 429–431.

Stearns, Elinor, and David N. Yerkes. *William Thornton: A Renaissance Man in the Federal City.* Washington, D.C.: American Institute of Architects Foundation, 1976.

Stein, Janice. "The Ricker Legacy." *Inland Architect* 30 (September/October 1986): 19–20, 55.

Stein, Susan, ed. *The Architecture of Richard Morris Hunt.* Chicago: University of Chicago Press, 1986.

"Studio and Office of Mr. H. H. Richardson." *American Architect and Building News* 16 (27 December 1884): 304.

"Studio Building." *The Crayon* 5 (January 1858): 55.

Sullivan, Louis. *The Autobiography of an Idea.* New York: AIA Press, 1924.

Tatum, George. *Andrew Jackson Downing, Arbiter of American Taste, 1815–1852.* Ann Arbor, Mich.: University Microfilms, 1974.

Thayer, R. H. *History, Organization, and Functions of the Office of the Supervising Architect of the Treasury Department.* Washington, D.C.: Government Printing Office, 1886.

Tomlan, Michael. "Toward the Growth of an Artistic Taste." In *The Cottage Souvenir,* no. 2. Watkins Glen, N.Y.: American Life Foundation, 1982.

Travis, Jack, ed. *African-American Architects in Current Practice.* New York: Princeton Architectural Press, 1991.

Turak, Theodore. *William LeBaron Jenney.* Ann Arbor, Mich.: University Microfilms, 1986.

Tuthill, Louisa. *A History of Architecture from the Earliest Times.* 1848. Reprint, New York: Garland Press, 1988.

Twombly, Robert. *Louis Sullivan.* Chicago: University of Chicago Press, 1987.

Upjohn, Everard. *Richard Upjohn: Architect and Churchman.* 1938. Reprint, New York: Columbia University Press, 1968.

Upjohn, Hobart. "Architect and Client a Century Ago." *Architectural Record* 74 (November 1933): 377–382.

———. "The Early Years of the A.I.A." Typescript. Avery Fine Arts and Architectural Library, Columbia University, New York. 1940(?).

Upjohn, Richard. *Rural Architecture.* New York: Putnam, 1852.

Upton, Dell. *Architecture in the United States.* New York: Oxford University Press, 1998.

———. *Holy Things and Profane.* New York: Architectural History Foundation, 1986.

———. "Pattern Books and Professionalism." *Winterthur Portfolio* 19 (Autumn 1984): 107–150.

———. "The Traditional House and Its Enemies." *Traditional Dwellings and Settlements Review* 1 (1990): 71–84.

Van Brunt, Henry. "Delicacy of Perception Dependent upon Study." *American Architect and Building News* 2 (11 August 1877): 254.

———. "Richard Morris Hunt." *Proceedings of the American Institute of Architects* (1895), 71–84.

Van Horne, John, ed. *Correspondence and Miscellaneous Papers of Benjamin Henry Latrobe.* Vols. 2 and 3. New Haven, Conn.: Yale University Press, 1986, 1988.

Van Horne, John, and Lee Formwalt, eds. *Correspondence and Miscellaneous Papers of Benjamin Henry Latrobe.* Vol. 1. New Haven, Conn.: Yale University Press, 1984.

Van Osdel, John. "History of Chicago Architecture." *Inland Architect* 1 (August 1883): 88–91.

Van Pelt, John. *A Monograph of the W. K. Vanderbilt House.* New York: Privately printed, 1925.

Van Rensselaer, Mariana. *H. H. Richardson and His Works.* 1888. Reprint, New York: Dover, 1969.

Van Zanten, David. *Designing Paris.* Cambridge, Mass.: MIT Press, 1987.

"Vertner W. Tandy." *New York Times,* 8 November 1949, 31.

Vitruvius, Pollio Marcus. *The Ten Books of Architecture.* Translated by Morris Hickey Morgan. New York: Dover, 1960.

Waid, D. Everett. "The Business Side of an Architect's Office: George B. Post and Sons." *Brickbuilder* 23 (February 1914): 47–49.

———. "The Business Side of an Architect's Office: McKim, Mead and White." *Brickbuilder* 22 (December 1913): 267–270.

Wallis, Frank. "Master Architect and Man." *Architectural Review,* n.s., 5 (November 1917): 239–240.

Ware, William Robert. "Architectural Instruction in New York and Paris." *American Architect and Building News* 70 (6 October 1900): 3–4.

———. "On the Condition of Architecture and Architectural Education in the United States." *Sessional Papers of the Royal Institute of British Architects* (1866–67), 81–90.

———. *An Outline of Architectural Education.* Boston, 1866.

———. "Professional Draughtsmen as Special Students." *School of Mines Quarterly, Columbia University* 17 (July 1897): 3–9.

Ware, William Rotch (?). "Manuscript Biography of William Robert Ware." William Robert Ware Papers, MIT Archives, Cambridge, Massachusetts.

Washington, Booker T. *Working with the Hands.* 1904. Reprint, New York: Negro Universities Press, 1969.

Weatherhead, Arthur. *Collegiate Education in Architecture in the United States.* Los Angeles: Hennessey and Ingalls, 1941.

Weiss, Ellen. "Robert Taylor of Tuskegee." *Arris: Journal of the Southeastern Chapter of the Society of Architectural Historians* 2 (1991): 1–19.

White, Lawrence Grant. *Sketches and Designs of Stanford White.* New York: Architectural Book Publishing Company, 1920.

Wight, Peter B. "An Appreciation of Daniel H. Burnham." *Architectural Record* 32 (August 1912): 176–184.

———. "Daniel H. Burnham and His Associates." *Architectural Record* 35 (July 1915): 1–12.

Willis, Carol. *Form Follows Finance.* New York: Princeton Architectural Press, 1995.

Winkler, Franz (pseud. Montgomery Schuyler). "The Work of Holabird and Roche." *Architectural Record* 31 (April 1912): 313–387.

Winthrop, Theodore. *Cecil Dreeme.* Boston: Ticknor and Fields, 1861.

Wisely, William. *The American Civil Engineer.* New York: American Society of Civil Engineers, 1974.

Withey, Henry, and Elsie Withey. *Biographical Dictionary of American Architects.* Los Angeles: New Age Press, 1956.

Wittkower, Rudolf. "English Literature on Architecture." In *Palladio and Palladianism,* 95–112. New York: George Braziller, 1974.

Woltersdorf, Arthur. "Portrait Gallery of Chicago Architects: Adler." *Western Architect* 33 (July 1924): 75–79.

Wood, Charles B., III. "A Survey and Bibliography of Writings on English and American Architectural Books Published before 1895." *Winterthur Portfolio* 2 (1965): 127–137.

Woods, Mary N. "The *American Architect and Building News,* 1876–1906," Ph.D. diss., Columbia University, 1983.

———. "Charles McKim and the Foundation of the American Academy in Rome." In *Light on the Eternal City: Papers in Art History from the Pennsylvania State University.* Edited by Hellmut Hager and Susan Munshower, vol. 2, 307–327. University Park, Pa.: Penn State Press, 1987.

———. "The First American Architectural Journals." *Journal of the Society of Architectural Historians* 48 (June 1989): 117–138.

———. "The Photograph as Tastemaker: *The American Architect* and H. H. Richardson." *History of Photography* 14 (April–June 1990): 155–163.

Woodward, George. *Woodward's National Architect.* New York: George E. Woodward, 1869.

Wright, Frank Lloyd. *An Autobiography.* 1943. Reprint, New York: Horizon Press, 1977.

Wright, Gwendolyn. "Architectural Practice and Social Vision in Wright's Early Designs." In *The Nature of Frank Lloyd Wright.* Edited by Carol Bolon, Robert S. Nelson, and Linda Seidel, 98–124. Chicago: University of Chicago Press, 1988.

———. *Moralism and the Model Home.* Chicago: University of Chicago Press, 1980.

Yegül, Fikret. *Gentlemen of Instinct and Breeding.* New York: Oxford University Press, 1991.

Zimmer, Edward. *The Architectural Career of Alexander Parris.* Ann Arbor, Mich.: University Microfilms, 1986.

Zunz, Olivier. *Making America Corporate, 1870–1920.* Chicago: University of Chicago Press, 1990.

INDEX

Page numbers in italics refer to illustrations. Where known, both location and architect's name appear with main headings for buildings and other structures. Where buildings are known by the owner's name, they are listed by last name, for example, "Gardiner House" rather than "Edward Gardiner House."

Abele, Julian, 77; Duke houses, 101; Duke University, 101

Académie des Beaux-Arts, 67

ACSA (Association of Collegiate Schools of Architecture), 173

Adam, Robert, 56, 198n.10

Adler, Dankmar, 4; in American Institute of Architects, 42; Auditorium Building, 194n.56; Chicago World's Fair, 42; education / training of, 65, 80–81, 202n.53; engineers hired by, 160; on fees, 51–52; on licensing, 40, 41, 44–45, 194n.56; offices of, 116, *117;* prominence of, 72; and Ricker, 205n.88; and Sullivan, 111, 114–16, 127, 129, 216n.85, 216–17nn.88–89; on supervising architect, 93; in WAA, 39

advertising, *46–50,* 47, 49–50, 196n.81, 197n.85

African Americans: as architects, 74–75, 77, 99–101, 167, 207n.105; as artisans, 11, 54, 100; in South vs. North, 100, 101, 213n.47; Tuskegee Institute built by, 73–74

AIA. *See* American Institute of Architects; American Institution of Architects

Alabama Polytechnic Institute, 206n.97

Alabama State University (Montgomery), 75, 207–8n.102

Alberti, Leon Battista, 6

Albrecht, Donald, 221n.7

Almy, Mary, 99–100

Alofsin, Anthony, 205n.86

American Academy (Rome), 79, 208n.111

American Architect and Building News, 57, 109, 121, 150, 194n.58, 215n.74

American Art Union, 83

American Bar Association, 51

American Builder's Companion (Benjamin), 57

American Institute of Architects (AIA; 1857–), 36–38; after 1889, 42–47, 49–52; ceremony in, 34, 192n.33; on corporations, 230n.17; elitism of, 34, 36; engineering background of members, 160; ethics codes of, 46–47, 49–52, 196n.78, 197n.85; on fees / competitions, 36–38, 51–52, 161, 172, 192–93n.40, 197n.87; founding of, 33–34, 191n.27, 191–92n.31; on large offices, 136–37; on licensing / registration, 41, 44–45, 194n.58; on mail-order catalogs, 88–89; membership in, 34, 36, 40, 192n.32, 194n.54, 194–95n.61; and public architecture, 42–44, 52; school proposed by, 67–68, 203nn.61–62; and Tarsney Act, 42–43, 195n.63; training for members of, 36; and WAA, 39, 41, 42, 194–95n.61

American Institution of Architects (AIA; 1837),

28–33; admission to / educational requirements for, 31–32, 191nn.21–22; and architectural science, 30–32; demise of, 32, 38; founding of, 28–29, 188–89nn.6–7

The American Vignola (Ware), 57–58, 203–4n.71

Anderson, Peirce, 135

Apollo Association, 83

Appleton, Julia, 135

apprenticeship, 32, 36, 53–55, 198n.5

"architect," use / definition of, 5–6, 39–40

architects: in ancient Greece, 5; as artists, 1–3, 5–6, 34; as builders, 94–95; competition among, 33; as entrepreneurs, 82–86, 88–89, 91–92, 167–69, 229n.3; European, 168, 229n.2, 229n.3; European immigrants as, 14–15; in fiction, 1, 164, 214n.56, 228n.96; gentlemen-architects, 14, 16; geographic distribution of, 206n.97; liability of, 172; male, and their female clients, 163–64; and master builders, 29; in Middle Ages, 5; as peripatetic, 95–96; wages for, 174 (*see also* fees). *See also* architectural profession

Architects' and Mechanics' Journal, 150, 151

Architects' Club (England), 16

architectural books. *See* house pattern books

Architectural Catalogue Company (New York City), 196n.81

architectural engineering, 72–73

Architectural League of America, 197n.86

Architectural League of New York, 80, 197n.86

Architectural League of Pittsburgh, 80, 197n.86

architectural profession: as male pursuit, 169, 175, 229n.5; nineteenth-century emergence of, 4–5, 7. *See also* architects

architectural schools. *See* university programs in architecture

architectural science, 30–32, 34

Architectural Sketchbook, 152–53, 153, 225n.48

Architectural Sketches (Zucker), 46

Arkansas state capitol (Mann), 96

artisans, building. *See* master builders

artists: acceptance of, 229n.1; money management by, 21, 186n.47

Ashley, Caroline E., 213–14n.44

assistants: for building skyscrapers, 138; drafting by, 139–42, 144; fraternity / loyalty among, 144–47; vs. independent practice, 138–39;

recreation for, 142, *144;* wages of, 141–42, 146, 222n.18; working conditions for, 142, *143,* 146, 222n.21. *See also specific firms and architects*

Associated Housewrights Society, 28–29

Associated Mechanics of Boston, 11

Association of Collegiate Schools of Architecture (ACSA), 173

Astor Library (New York City), 157

ateliers / offices, 102–4, 106–10, 121. *See also specific firms and architects*

Atwood, Charles, 135

Auditorium Building (Chicago; Adler), 194n.56

Babcock, Charles, 33–34; Cornell University buildings, 73, 206n.93; as educator, 66–67, 70–71, 72, 73, 79, 204n.80; retires from Cornell University, 80; and R. Upjohn, 116, 118, 217n.92

Bacon, Henry, 146, 192n.33

Badger, Daniel, 159

Baker, Paul, 202n.46

balloon frames, 149

Balmori, Diana, 125

Baltimore Cathedral (Latrobe), 18–19, 22

Bancroft, John, 202n.53

Bank of Pennsylvania (Philadelphia; Latrobe), 19–20, 21, 23, 25

Barber, George F., 86, 92, 166

Barber, John, 23, 200n.32

Barry, Robert, 201–2n.45

Bauhaus, 172

Baumann, Frederick, 46–47, 72

Bayliss, Henry, 201–2n.45

beautification, 43, 170

Bellanger, James, 205n.83

Belmont, Oliver Hazard Perry, 228n.89

Benjamin, Asher, 4–5, 189n.8, 198–99n.15; *The American Builder's Companion,* 57; in American Institution of Architects, 188–89n.6; as architect, 29, 30; and architectural science, 31; in Bricklayers' Company, 28, 189–90n.9; *The Country Builder's Assistant,* 57; as educator, 55, 56; *The Elements of Architecture,* 57; *The Rudiments of Architecture,* 57

Bethune, Louise Blanchard, 39, 75–76, 99, 193–94n.50

Bilbao Museum (Spain; Gehry), 176

France: architects in, 168, 229n.2; licensing in, 40, 194n.56
Francis, Dennis, 98, 212–13n.44
Franklin, Benjamin, 12
Franklin Institute (Philadelphia; Haviland), 31, 58–59
fraternal organizations, 32
freelance draftsmen, 147–48
French immigrants, 150–51
Freret, James, 74
Fuller, George, 147, 154, 155, 156, 157, 158
Fulton, Robert, 22
Furness, Frank, 63, 64

Gage, Lyman, 42
Gallier, James, 4–5, 94, 95, 96, 141, 148–49, 211n.25
Gambrill, Charles, 63, 106, 215n.66, 218n.104
Gannon, Mary N., 212–13n.44
Gardiner, Edward, 191–92n.31
Gardiner House (R. Upjohn), 193n.43
Gehry, Frank, 174; Bilbao Museum, 176
general contractors, 154–61, 166; vs. architects, 157–58; Thomas Cubbitt, 225n.53; Marc Eidlitz, 154, 156–57, 158; fees for, 155; George Fuller, 147, 154, 155, 156, 157, 158; influence of, 155; Norcross Brothers, 110, 146, 147, 154, 156, 158; services / materials supplied by, 155; skyscraper work by, 155–56; Paul Starrett, 46, 141, 142, 154–55, 159; and trade unions, 156. *See also* engineers
General Society of Mechanics and Tradesmen (New York City), 11
Georgia Institute of Technology, 206n.97
Germanic influences, 71, 72
German immigrants, 150–51
Germany, architects in, 168, 229n.2
Getty Center (Los Angeles; Meier), 177
Gilbert, Cass, 43, 146, 158; New York Custom House, 42
Gilchrist, Agnes, 200n.32
Godefroy, Maximilian, 15, 22, 24, 25, 82
Godkin, E. L., 194n.58
Goelet, Ogden, 135, 157
Goelet, Robert, 135
Goelet house, 157
Goodhue, Bertram G., 66
Goody, Jane, 229n.5

Gothic style, 20, 70
Graff, Frederick, 23, 200n.32
Graham, Anderson, Probst and White, 135
Graham, Ernest, 46, 135
Graves, Michael, 172, 179
Gray, Lee, 214n.60
Great Britain: architects in, 168, 171, 229nn.2–3; licensing in, 40–41
Greene, John Holden, 56, 149
Greenwood (Alabama), 73–74
Gropius, Walter, 172
guilds, 11
Gutman, Robert, 3, 173, 174–75, 176
Guttenberg, Sidney A.: *Recent Buildings by Sidney A. Guttenberg, Architect,* 47

Hadfield, George, 14–15, 25, 82
Hadrian, Emperor, 5
halftone process, 96
Hall, Louise, 56
Hallet, Stephen, 14–15, 24, 25, 56, 82
Hamilton, Alexander, 30
Hamilton, Governor James, 12
Hamlin, Talbot, 24, 200n.32
Hammond-Harwood house (Annapolis, Maryland), 13
Hampton Institute (Virginia; R. M. Hunt), 73, 74–75
handbooks, 198–99n.15. *See also* builders' guides
Hands, Alice J., 212–13n.44
Hannaford (Samuel) and Sons (Cincinnati), 119, *122,* 140
Hansen, Harold, 205n.83
Harper Brothers Building (New York City), 157
Harrison, Peter, 14
Harvard Graduate School of Design, 3, 175, 182n.6
Harvard University, 77, 81
Hastings, Thomas, 80, 129, *132–33,* 141, 142, 146, 157, 222n.21
Hatfield, R. G., 203n.61
Haviland, John, 189n.8; in American Institution of Architects, 188–89n.6, 190n.17, 191n.21; and architectural science, 31; as builder, 148–49; as educator, 56, 59; Franklin Institute, 58; in National Academy of Design, 30
Hawks, John, 12–13
Hawley, Hughson, 148

Hayden, Sophia: Women's Building, 75
Hazel, William, 206–7n.102
Hearst, Phoebe, 100
Hill, Hiram, 56–57, 149
Hillen, John, 18
Hoban, James, 201n.36
Holabird, William, 65, 160, 169. *See also*
  Holabird (William) and Roche
Holabird (William) and Roche, 223–24n.35;
  assistants to, 139, 140, 141, 145, 170; and
  clients, 164; and Lathrop, 98; offices of, 129;
  ornamental detail by, 127; partnership of,
  126–27; prominence of, 119, 125; Tacoma
  Building, 155, 157; unethical practices of, 47
Holabird (John) and Root, 135
Holden, Arthur, 171
house pattern books, 84–85, 92, 94, 166, 169,
  176–77, 209–10nn.6–8, 210n.10. *See also*
  builders' guides
housing, low-income, 170
Howard, John Galen, 146, 222–23n.27
Howard University (Washington, D.C.), 75,
  206–7n.102
Howe, Lois Lilley, 99–100
Howells, Elinor, 228n.96
Howells, William Dean: *The Rise of Silas
  Lapham,* 164, 228n.96
Howland, Catharine. *See* Hunt, Catharine
  Howland
Hull, Judith, 118
Hunt, Catharine, 102, 106, 202n.46, 202n.48,
  214n.59
Hunt, F. K., 162–63
Hunt, Joseph, 214n.57
Hunt, Richard Howland, 214n.57
Hunt, Richard M., 4, 34, 36, 42, 94, 193n.40;
  business practices of, 104, 106, 168–69;
  Delaware and Hudson Canal Company, 104;
  education / background of, 102–3; as educa-
  tor, 63–65, *64,* 201–2nn.45–46; Hampton
  Institute buildings, 73; litigiousness of, 104,
  106, 165, 169; Marble House, 163; profanity
  used by, 104, 106, 214n.59; refuses supervising
  architect appointment, 93; Rossiter House,
  103, 104, 165; Schmid mansion designs, 104,
  105; Stevens Apartments, 104; Studio Building, 104; studios / offices of, 103–4, 214nn.57–
  58; stylistic flexibility of, 104, 106; Tribune

Building, 104, 214n.60; Vanderbilt château,
  163; and Ware, 63–64, 65, 68–69
Hyde, E. L., 202n.46

Illinois, licensing in, 44–45
Illsley, Charles, 39
immigrants, 14–15, 150–53
independent practice, 93–101, 158–59, 166, 179;
  building, 94–95; during depression of 1930s,
  171; drafting, 93–94, 121; of peripatetic architects, 95–96; regional, 96–98, 169; of women
  and minorities, 98–101
industrialization, 54, 149, 166
Ingham, J. Q., 88–89, *89,* 92, 210n.15
Institute of British Architects (RIBA; London),
  191nn.20–21
International Correspondence School Company
  (Scranton, Pennsylvania), 57–58, 199n.20
Irish immigrants, 150, 153
iron, 159
Italian immigrants, 150
Italy, architects in, 168, 229n.2
Izenour, Steven, 230n.15

Jackson, Andrew, 27
Jefferson, Thomas, 11, 14, 54; and Latrobe, 17,
  21, 22–23, 24–25, 162, 185n.27
Jemison, Robert, 54
Jenney, William LeBaron, 39, 40, 65–66, 126,
  160, 202n.52
Jepson, Bill, 177
job superintendents, 155
Johnson, Philip, 179
Johnston, Frances Benjamin, 75
journeymen, 29–30, 54, 148. *See also*
  apprenticeship
Justice Department, 172, 197n.87

Kahn, Louis, 172
Kellogg, Thomas, 222–23n.27
Kendall, William, 135
King, Horace, 54
Kirby, J. H., 85
Koolhaas, Rem, 174

labor movement, 29–30, 156, 212n.43
labor unions vs. mechanics' institutes, 59
Lafever, Minard, 29, 189n.8; in American Insti-

Pope house (Farmington, Connecticut; McKim, Mead and White), 164

populism, 59, 82

Post, George B.: assistants to, 140, 146; Chicago World's Fair, 42; education of, 63; engineering background of, 160; engineers used by, 159, 161; on fees, 51–52; general contractors used by, 157; on gentlemen-scholars, 80; job superintendents used by, 155; offices / practice of, 119, 121, 129, *131*, 135, 218n.104; on profits / supervision, 158; on public commissions, 43; Western Union Building, 125

postmodernism, 171–72

Powell, Samuel, 184n.18

practice, 175–76. *See also* entrepreneurship; independent practice; practice, settings for

practice, settings for, 101; ateliers, 102–4, 106–10; and legacy of studios, 110–11; New York and Chicago offices, 116–37, *117, 119–20, 123–24, 128, 130–33;* partnerships, 111–16, 169, 216–17nn.88–89, 216n.81, 216n.83, 216n.85 (*see also* Burnham and Root; Holabird [William] and Roche; McKim, Mead and White)

preservation movement, 172

Preston, William, 152–53, *153,* 225n.48

Price, Benjamin D., 86, *87–88,* 92, 166

Price, Max Charles, 86, *87–88,* 92

prices. *See* fees

Priest, J. W., 191–92n.31

private practice. *See* independent practice

private sector vs. state, 170, 229n.8

privatization, 179

Prix de Paris, 79

"profession," use of, 6

professions: gentlemen in, 6 7; populist opposition to, 28, 33; stratification in, 168; urban rise of, 7. *See also* organizations, professional

profits, 158, 226n.68

Progressive movement, 43, 51

Protestantism, 27

Pruitt-Igoe housing project (Saint Louis), 172

Prussia, licensing in, 41

public housing projects, 172

Public Works Administration (PWA), 171

Puck, 89, *90–91,* 91

Purdy, C. T., 161

PWA (Public Works Administration), 171

Quarterly Review, 153, 225n.48

Quill, Charles, 58, 59

Quincy, Edward, 202n.46

Radford, George, 227n.77

Raht, Edward, 214n.60

railroads, 27, 29, 96, 158, 159, 227n.69, 229n.8

Rand, Ayn: *The Fountainhead,* 1

Randall, G. P., 96, 98, 210n.8; Northwestern University, 97

Ranlett, William, 85, 210n.10

Raphael, 5

Rashid, Hani, 172

rates. *See* fees

Rayfield, Wallace, 74–75, 100–101

Recent Buildings by Sidney A. Guttenberg, Architect (Guttenberg), 47

Redtenacher, Rudolf, 71

Redtop (Belmont, Massachusetts; McKim, Mead and White), 228n.96

regional practice, 96–98, 169

registration, 45, 196n.77. *See also* licensing

Reichardt, Karl F., 32, 188–89n.6, 189n.8, 189–90n.9

Reid, Whitelaw, 104, 214n.60

renderers, itinerant, 148

Rensselaer Polytechnic Institute (New York State), 68

Renwick, Edward, 126–27

republicanism, 59

Rhoads, Samuel, 184n.18

Richardson, Henry Hobson, 4; assistants to, 140, 142, 145, 146; celebrity / entrepreneurship of, 82, 108–10, 168–69; Cincinnati chamber of commerce, 98; at Ecole des Beaux-Arts, 74, 80–81; on general contractors, 158; on government posts, 93; health of, 110; and McKim, 106, 125–26, 142; and O. W. Norcross, 156; offices of, 106–9, *107, 109,* 110, 214–15n.64; Trinity Church, 106, 107, 156, 215n.66; and Stanford White, 106, 126

Richmond penitentiary (Latrobe), 20, 186n.39

Ricker, N. Clifford, 44–45; as educator, 71–73, 74, 78–79, 81, 205n.86, 205n.88; University of Illinois buildings, 73, 206n.93

The Rise of Silas Lapham (Howells), 164, 228n.96

Roberts, J. W., 71

Starrett, Paul, 46, 141, 142, 154–55, 159
steam technology, 27, 149
steel, 159
Stein, Gertrude, 223–24n.35
Steinway Hall (New York City), 157
Stern, Robert A. M., 172, 179
Stevens, Garry, 176
Stevens, John Calvin, 51, *51*
Stevens, Mrs. Paran, 104
Stevens Apartments (New York City; R. M. Hunt), 104
Stirewalt, John, 62, 74, 95
Strickland, William, 4–5, 17, 23; in American Institution of Architects, 28, 32, 189n.6; and architectural science, 31; career of, 95–96; as educator, 58–59; and Latrobe, 60–62, 139, 200n.32, 200–201n.34; in National Academy of Design, 30; Second Bank of the United States, 95, 96, 200–201n.34; southern / midwestern commissions of, 95; Tennessee state capitol, 96
Studio Building (New York City; R. M. Hunt), 104
studios. *See* ateliers / offices
suffrage, 27
Sullivan, Louis, 39, 41, 81, 165, 196n.78; and Adler, 111, 114–16, 127, 129, 216–17nn.88–89, 216n.85
superintendents, job, 155
Supervising Architect's Office, 42, 43, 92–93, 140, 195n.63, 217–18n.99
supervisory phase of building, 158, 226n.68
Swan, Abraham: *British Architect,* 61, 201n.38
Swartout, Egerton, 144

Tacoma Building (Holabird and Roche), 155, 157
Tandy, Vertner, 75, 101
Tarsney Act (1893), 42–43, 195n.63
Taylor, Dr. Brooke, 62
Taylor, Robert, 74–75, 81, 100; Thrasher Hall, 74; Washington house, 74
technologies: blueprints, 140; computers, 176–77; Mylar, 221n.7; photolithography, 96, 140; steam, 27, 149; telegraph, 96
telegraph, 96
Tennessee state capitol (Strickland), 96
Theodoros of Samos, 5
Thomas, Thomas, 188–89n.6, 189n.8

Thomas, Thomas, Jr., 188–89n.6, 189n.8
Thomas, William, 165
Thompson, Isaac, 216n.83
Thompson, Martin E., 112, 148–49, 165, 188–89n.6, 190n.14
Thornton, Dr. William, 14, 15, 18, 185n.30
Thrasher Hall (Tuskegee Institute; Taylor), 74
Tigerman, Stanley, 172, 230n.15
Tilden, George, 152–53, *153,* 225n.48
Tilton, Edward, 146; Ellis Island Immigration Center, 43
timber frames, 149
Tontine Crescent residence (Boston; Bulfinch), 14
Town, Ithiel, 4–5, 29, 189n.8; in American Institution of Architects, 188–89n.6; as builder, 148–49; and Davis, 111–14, 209n.4; as educator, 62–63, 201n.42; as engineer / inventor, 62–63, 201n.44; entrepreneurship of, 82, 95; in National Academy of Design, 30; New York University Building, 83–84, 103, *103;* southern / midwestern commissions of, 95; and Martin Thompson, 112
Trachtenberg, Alan, 229n.1
tracing, 139, 140, 221n.7
trade unions, 29–30, 156, 212n.43
training. *See* education
transportation: canals, 27, 29, 158, 229n.8; and economy, 27, 29; railroads, 27, 29, 96, 158, 159, 227n.69, 229n.8; turnpikes, 229n.8
Traquair, Adam, 23, 200n.32
Traquair, James, 21, 200n.32
Trautwine, John, 28, 188–89n.6
Tribune Building (New York City; R. M. Hunt), 104, 214n.60
Trinity Building (New York City; R. Upjohn), 118, *120*
Trinity Church (Boston; Richardson), 106, 107, 156, 215n.66
Trinity Church (New York City; R. Upjohn), 34, 118, *119,* 193n.43, 210n.8
Trowbridge, Alexander, 80
True, Clarence, 154, 166, 225n.52
Trumbauer, Horace, 101
Trumbull, John, 15
Tschumi, Bernard, 172, 174
T-Square Club (Philadelphia), 80
"The T-Squares," 192n.35

Tulane University (New Orleans), 74, 206n.97
turnpikes, 229n.8
Tuskegee Institute: architecture program at, 67, 68, 73–76, *76–77,* 81, 203n.64, 206–7nn.102–3; design of buildings on campus of, 73–74; women admitted to, 76
Tuthill, Louisa, 8

undertakers (carpenter-builders), 12
unions, 29–30, 156, 212n.43
United States government commissions, 38; architects' disdain for, 92–93; vs. private sector, 170, 229n.8; and stylistic uniformity, 92–93; Supervising Architect's Office, 42, 43, 92–93, 140, 195n.63, 217–18n.99; and Tarsney Act, 42–43, 195n.63
University of Illinois: architecture program at, 67, 68, 71–73, 75, 81, 203n.64, 205n.83, 206n.93; cost of attending, 78; design of buildings on campus of, 73, 206n.93; special students' programs at, 78–79, 81; women admitted to, 75
University of Pennsylvania, 77, 81
university programs in architecture, 53, 66–81; and academic credentials, 67; African Americans in, 75, 77, 206–7nn.102–3 (*see also* Tuskegee Institute *below);* Beaux-Arts curricula of, 80, 81, 173; at Columbia University, 67, 68, 69, 70, *78,* 81, 203n.64, 203n.67, 203–4n.71; at Cornell University, 66–67, 68, 70–71, 81, 203n.64, 204n.80; and cost / completion of degrees, 77–78; and graduates who went on to practice architecture, 208n.107; growth of, 172–73, 174; Hampton Institute, 73, 74–75; influence of, 80–81; Jews and Catholics in, 77; at MIT, 66–67, 68–69, 70, 81, 203n.64, 203n.67, 203–4n.71; and postmodernism, 172; and private practice, 173–74, 175, 177–78; southern, 74, 206n.97, 207n.103; and special students, 78–79, 208n.110; and stylistic uniformity, 67; at Tuskegee Institute, 67, 68, 73–76, *76–77,* 81, 203n.64, 207nn.102–3; at University of Illinois, 67, 68, 71–73, 75, 81, 203n.64, 205n.83, 206n.93; women in, 75–76, 77, 207n.104
Upjohn, Everard, 217n.91
Upjohn, Hobart, 217n.91
Upjohn, Richard, 4–5, 191n.31; in American

Institute of Architects, 36; assistants to, 141; and Babcock, 116, 118, 217n.92; and clients, 162–63; entrepreneurship of, 82; on ethics, 46; on fees, 37, 192–93n.40, 193n.43; founds American Institute of Architects, 33–34; freelance draftsmen used by, 148; Gardiner House, 193n.43; and F. K. Hunt, 162–63; Lindenwald remodeling, 213n.54; New York practice of, 116, 118, 121, 139, 217n.91; offices of, 118, 128–29, *131;* on ownership of drawings, 37; *Rural Architecture,* 210n.8; southern / midwestern commissions of, 95; training of, 36; Trinity Building, 118, *120;* Trinity Church, 34, 118, *119,* 193n.43, 210n.8; Walthall house, 228n.88
Upjohn, Richard Michell, 33–34, 116, 118, 217nn.91–92
urbanization, 166
Urban Simulation Laboratory (UCLA), 177

Van Brunt, Henry, 33, 42; on classical orders, 203–4n.71; on drawings, 66; as educator, 68; Electricity Building, 195n.63; and Hunt, 63, 64–65, *65,* 102, 104; Union Pacific Railroad commissions, 96
Van Buren, Martin, 102–3, 213n.54
Van der Bent, Teunis, 127
Vanderbilt, Alva Smith, 163, 165, 228n.89
Vanderbilt, W. K., 163, 228n.89
Vanderbilt château (New York City; R. M. Hunt), 163
Van Osdel, John, 94, 165
Van Rensselaer, Mariana, 106, 107, 110
Van Winkle, Cornelius S., 57
Vasari, Giorgio, 5–6
vaulted structures, 20, 186n.41
Vaux, Calvert, 227n.77
Vaux, Downing, 66
Venturi, Robert, 172, 179, 230n.15
Victoria, Queen, 191n.20
Vignola, Giacomo Barozzi da: *Rules of the Five Orders of Architecture,* 69
Viollet-le-Duc, Eugène Emmanuel, 70
Vitruvius, 5, 191n.21

WAA (Western Association of Architects), 38–42, 194n.51. *See also* American Institute of Architects
Wagner, Otto, 71, 205n.86

Designer:	Barbara Jellow
Compositor:	G&S Typesetters, Inc.
Text:	Adobe Garamond
Display:	Gill Sans
Printer and Binder:	Malloy Lithographing